The Best Christmas Decorations in Chicagoland

by Mary Edsey

TABAGIO PRESS

CHICAGO, ILLINOIS

Tabagio Press
P.O. Box 578913
Chicago, Illinois 60657-8913

All photographs are by the author unless otherwise indicated.
Typesetting by KSH Graphic Services, Morton Grove, IL.
Printed in Canada.

First printing 1995.

10 9 8 7 6 5 4 3 2 1

Publisher's Cataloging in Publication Data
Edsey, Mary M.
The Best Christmas Decorations in Chicagoland/Mary Edsey
Includes 192 pages, 181 photographs, 13 maps, appendix and index.
ISBN 0-9642799-2-4

1. Christmas Decorations.
2. Christmas—Pictorial works.
3. Christmas—Chicago (Ill.)—Pictorial works.
4. Chicago Region (Ill.)—Guidebooks.
5. Chicago Region (Ill.)—Description & Travel—Guidebooks.
6. Chicago (Ill.)—Guidebooks.
7. Chicago Region (Ill.)—History.
8. Christmas trees—Illinois—Chicago.

GT3925   94-090422
394.268282

Cover photo: The Wardzala home, pages 101-102

Individuals wishing to submit photos and/or information about current displays or past displays, including those featured, for possible future editions of this book may send them to Tabagio Press at the address above. All submissions will become the property of Tabagio Press for publication and reuse, unless they are accompanied by a request for return and a postpaid, self-addressed envelope.

To my dad,
who has been
my lifelong inspiration.

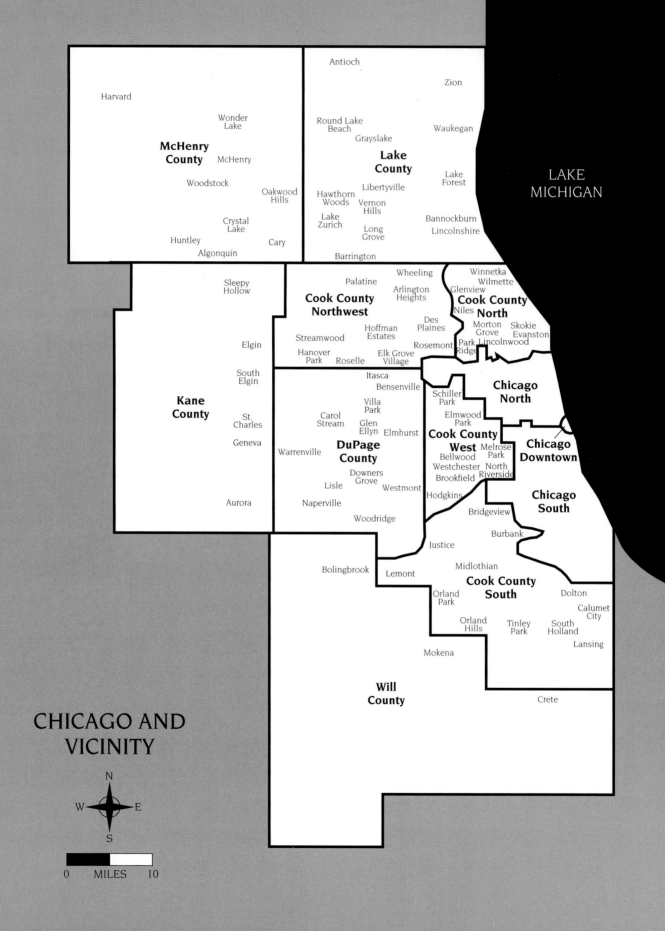

CHICAGO AND VICINITY

Contents

ACKNOWLEDGMENTS vi

INTRODUCTION vii

1 CHICAGO–DOWNTOWN 1

2 CHICAGO–NORTH 19

3 CHICAGO–SOUTH 35

4 COOK COUNTY–NORTH 43

5 COOK COUNTY–NORTHWEST 59

6 COOK COUNTY–SOUTH 81

7 COOK COUNTY–WEST 97

8 DUPAGE COUNTY 111

9 KANE COUNTY 133

10 LAKE COUNTY 141

11 McHENRY COUNTY 155

12 WILL COUNTY & OUTLYING AREAS 169

APPENDIX 181

INDEX 182

Acknowledgments

This book would certainly not have been possible without the encouragement and help of my family and friends to whom I am sincerely grateful. I would especially like to thank Lesley Martin for her editing, indexing, research, typing and friendship. To Kevin Hamilton of KSH Graphic Services for his excellent typesetting, long hours and patience. To Kristin Mount for her generous assistance and for completing the maps. To Jim McGreal for his kindness and help in starting the maps. To Jonathan Bloom for taking on the arduous task of "dot man" and for helping me through the last few months of production. To Pam Karlson for her skillful retouching and design help. To Diane Jaroch for lending her expertise in book design. To Tom O'Donnell of Color Image for his generous assistance and to his staff, especially Phil Davis and Don Gottlinger. To Steve Rokicki, Greg LaMont and the retouching staff at Steven James LaMont Company. To Petrice Dahl, Amy Martin, Tim Fast, Nancy Kingsley and Mike Marola for their printing advice and moral support. And especially to Cathy, Kevin and Tim Collins and John Stedronsky for their generous help and confidence in this project.

Special thanks to my mom for her constant support, love and willingness to help. To my brother Don for his faxing, stamping, organizational help and cheery phone calls that kept me going. To my sister Cathy for her editing, encouragement and cream soda. To my brother Dave for editing on his days off and my sister Chris for editing while on vacation. To my brothers Steve and Mike for their generous support. To my brother Tom and his family for helping to find houses. To Dave, Jeff, Dana and Mark Collins for their house-hunting and editing. And to my nephews Jace and Seth Armstrong for their Christmas drawings.

For the photography assistance of John Reed, John Stedronsky, Chris Cassidy, Linda Feicht, David Kordela, Dave Ireland, Mark Pastor, Lucas Bolchert and Eileen Flynn. For the additional graphic assistance of D. Bob Reiden-Bach, Dan Slomiany of 2nd Dimension, Walter Tabayoyong and Tommaso Bufano of Graphico.

For the additional editing assistance of Eileen Habash, Rick Michal, George Venetis and Barth Landor. To Nancy Gohla for her editing assistance and advice. To Larry Wardzala for decorating my ABA booth. To Roger Farrow for his lawn signs. To Linda Feicht for her calligraphy and moral support. To Margaret Annett and Jim Mazanek for their financial expertise. To the folks at Friesens, Imperial Color, Photofont and Copy Pro for their fine work. To Dave Ireland for getting me out of the house. And to librarians all over the Chicagoland area for their research assistance.

To Greg Wagner for leading me through the south side. To Laurie Goldberg, Denise Steurer, Pat Domanik, Dan Sheahan, Brian and Tracy Collins, Chris and Greg Grygiel, Linda and Al Honrath, Cathy and Kevin Collins, Don and Peggy Edsey, Lesley Martin, John Bolchert, Alain Dirninger, Laurent Huillet, André Motnyk and Alison Bullerman for helping me drive around on cold winter nights in search of decorated houses. To Chris Grygiel and Sandy McDonnell for their typing assistance. To Connie Matheu for her research assistance. To my neighbor Sharon Fitzsimmons for being there when I needed her and to her husband, Ken Rothschild, for mowing my lawn for the last two years.

To Jim Iovino, Mary Ann and John Ryan, Mildred Losey, Gus and Lena Guarino, Evelyn Hardell, Millie Munao, Fran Ogarzalek, Don Ferrone, Steve Schorsch and Louise Frawley for providing information about Candy Cane Lane. To Pat Domanik, Jean George, Stella LiPomi, Norma Bongiovanni, Sigrid Brynjolfsson, Dan Gigstad, Ema Guze and Ben Brady for their help with Lincolnwood history. To Jerry Ehernberger, Gene Teslovic, Kelly Blazek, Kyle Hall, Ann Paden and Don Featherstone for their help with the history of outdoor displays.

Additional thanks to Judy Krug, John McDonald, Margaret Hooper, Collette Sorenson, Anita and Jordan Miller, Pat Peterson, Sandy Popik, Ed Sacks, Keith Watson, Judith Cooper, Joann Kendzior, Kathleen Hook, Pam Dorband, Brian Clayton, Steve Starr, Jim Gustafson, Tom Tortorici, Liz McGreal, Mike Keating, Mia Tatic, Bill McGrath, Aaron Barlow, Corey Sapstein, Edith Vargas, Richard Derus, Dina Abbott, Sam Nuccio and Paul Gedwill.

And a special thank you to all the decorators in this book and everywhere, who put so much time and effort into trimming their homes and businesses to make other people happy.

Introduction

Homeowners have been decorating their houses for the holidays as far back as the days of the Roman Empire. Though today's plastic lighted figurines may differ from the greenery that trimmed homes for the ancient Roman new year's celebrations, both express the human desire to add merriment to a feast by dressing up our surroundings.

The Americanization of this tradition can be traced to the New York home of Edward Johnson, a colleague of Thomas Edison, who in 1882 became the proud owner of the first electrically-lighted Christmas tree. Trimmed in 80 hand-wired bulbs of red, white and blue, the glistening evergreen marked the beginning of our "love affair" with holiday lights.

By the late 1880s the General Electric Company was mass-producing the small bulbs. However, installation required the costly service of a "wireman," who would connect the lights to separate wires and then to an overhead light fixture. At thousands of today's dollars, it was a custom reserved for the wealthy. In 1903 the Ever-Ready Company manufactured the first ready-made Christmas light wiring. The strands were called "festoons" and came with 28 sockets and bulbs. Though less expensive than the previous methods, the cost was still equivalent to the weekly salary of the average man.

Holiday lights moved outdoors in 1909 when the first all-weather wiring prompted the city of Pasadena, California, to light a community tree atop Mt. Wilson. It was not until 1925, however, that General Electric began promoting the use of outdoor Christmas lights to the public. In a letter to GE employees, company executive J.K. Kewley wrote, "The use of incandescent lamps for the lighting of Christmas trees inside the home is now almost universal. Only in scattered instances, however, has there been any attempt to emphasize the application of lamps to outdoor Christmas time decorations…" To publicize the concept, the company exhibited a glowing display of Christmas trees, signs, stars, festoons and floodlighting outside its headquarters in Cleveland, Ohio, and has been displaying an outdoor lighted exhibit every year since.

Meanwhile, as early as 1899 Good Housekeeping magazine had suggested decorating outdoors with "a stiff round wreath hung in the center of the window sash." By the late thirties and early forties, gardening writers were promoting decorating the outside of the home for holiday fun. However, the trimmings were still a luxury in this era when a large number of homes had no running water, let alone electricity for decorations.

It was not until after World War II that outdoor Christmas displays finally became popular with the middle class. The end of the war brought a feeling of optimism and prosperity unknown to most who had lived through both the Depression and the war. "The late forties and early fifties were the heyday of outdoor illumination," says Gene Teslovic, a collector of Christmas lights and manufacturer's catalogs. "Mass-production brought down the cost, making lights more affordable for the average homeowner, and magazine advertisements featuring elaborately decorated homes brought the idea to the public's attention."

Homemade displays had been a popular addition to the trimmings until the early fifties when ready-made decorations made their appearance. Union Products, one of the oldest manufacturers of lawn ornaments, sold their first two-dimensional outdoor Christmas display of a sleigh and reindeer in 1952. Two years later they began selling three-dimensional foam-plastic outdoor figures. "They were very spongy and a favorite toy of dogs, who loved to eat them," said Don Featherstone, vice-president of the company. By 1956 styrene was found to be a plastic that could withstand the heat of a bulb, so the company began to use the material to mass-produce, through injection molding, plastic lighted figurines similar to those sold today. "At about the same time, aluminum Christmas trees became popular. Together with plastic figurines they created a more carefree attitude about house decorations that required less effort," said Gene Teslovic.

The energy crisis of 1973 brought an abrupt halt to the decorating craze, as Americans complied with President Nixon's request to refrain from holiday lighting. "We were a multi-million dollar business, whose sales dropped to $100,000 that year," Don Featherstone stated. "It took five or six years before people started buying decorations again as they had."

As the baby-boom generation is buying houses, the country is experiencing the second rise in the popularity of elaborate outdoor displays. Nostalgic for the past, decorators are re-creating their holiday childhood memories for their own children. New technology, low-cost miniature bulbs, blow-molded plastic figurines and mass-produced animated dolls have made decorating more affordable than ever. According to a recent survey 21% of Americans now trim the outside of their homes for Christmas.

Throughout the years Chicagoans have enjoyed this yuletide trend, now familiar throughout North America. The city's earnest displays have certainly been influenced by the local plant facilities of NOMA Christmas and Silvestri Corp., two of the world's largest light manufacturers. Polk Bros. appliance and furniture store also had a significant impact on local decorators by offering a 5-foot, 3-inch lighted plastic Santa with every major purchase. Over the course of the four-year promotion, which began in 1962, 250,000 "Jolly Polk Santas" began appearing on lawns all over Chicagoland.

Joint neighborhood efforts were first seen here in the thirties, when the affluent homes of Longwood Drive in the Beverly neighborhood were drawing crowds with their lighted homes and shrubbery. "At that time to see Christmas lights outlining a house was really something," recalls longtime Chicagoan John Ryan. In the late forties the northwest-side neighborhood of Sauganash was a holiday attraction with its numerous lights and homemade decorations. The themed streets of the Candy Cane Lane neighborhood and the well-lighted suburb of Lincolnwood were popular places to view decorations on the north side in the fifties and sixties. And in Evanston, manger scenes flourished as the Christian Family Christmas Committee sponsored its first "Put Christ Back into Christmas" drive in 1952, awarding an 8-inch bench saw for the best religious display. In downtown Chicago, the Merchandise Mart began to glow with the largest "Merry Christmas" sign in the world in 1941 and Marina Towers, built in 1964, lit up the Loop with its balconies of white lights.

Today downtown gleams with more decorated skyscrapers and lobbies than ever before, and neighborhoods twinkle from Tinley Park to Zion. The Best Christmas Decorations in Chicagoland takes you on a holiday tour of 243 of the most unique and outstanding displays that brighten the area, while also featuring notable exhibits of the past. Though unforeseen circumstances may arise, the author has made every effort to include only locations in which the decorators plan to continue their displays for many years. In fact, most of the exhibits grow more elaborate each season.

As the stories reveal, the decorators range in age from youngsters helping their parents to senior citizens still climbing out on the roof. They include families that work together and women who tackle the task alone. However, in most households interviewed, the men decorate the outside of the house and the women the inside. Decorating budgets vary from the frugal use of aluminum foil and the kid's stuffed animals to an annual splurge on commercial animation and megawatts of electricity. Tastes and styles may differ among those who practice this holiday craft, but to all it seems to be a source of creative expression. "It's interesting to take an idea and make it come alive," says decorator Larry Schneider of Bolingbrook. "It's also fun to watch other people enjoying the display."

To help you enjoy the displays, the book is divided alphabetically by county with the first three chapters devoted to the city of Chicago. Each chapter is subdivided alphabetically by town (or neighborhood within Chicago) and then by street address. If the town has a municipal display, it is listed first. Each location, except for references to past exhibits, is preceded by a number which can be found on the map at the beginning of each chapter. To locate a home, find the number on the map and then refer to the detailed directions at the end of the story. In the directions, mileage is estimated to the nearest 1/4 mile. Distances given in blocks (bl.) refer to the number of streets passed (whether cross streets or T's). Decorating hints and additional holiday stories are highlighted in grey boxes.

For an extra-pleasant tour pack a flashlight (so your navigator can read the directions), ice scrapers (so your passengers can keep the inside of the windows clear), and hot chocolate (just for the fun of it). To avoid possible crowds visit the displays early in the holiday season, after Christmas day or on weekdays before Christmas week. And whether you are loading the kids in the car with their pajamas under their snowsuits, taking Granny for a holiday ride, enjoying a romantic evening for two, or treating yourself to a yuletide drive—here's wishing you a fun-filled holiday adventure!

Chapter 1

CHICAGO – DOWNTOWN

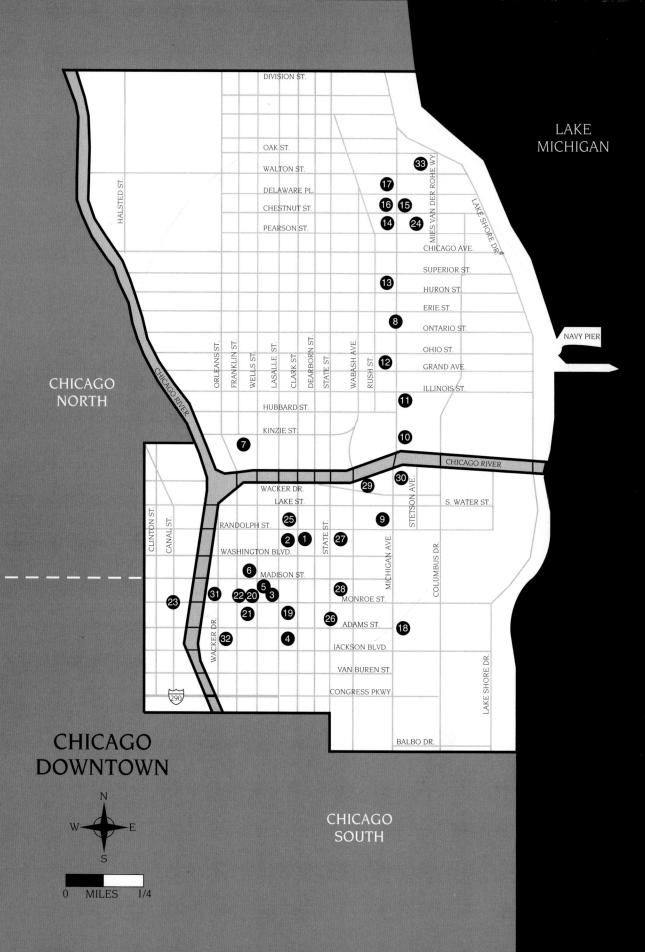

LAKE
MICHIGAN

DIVISION ST.

OAK ST.

WALTON ST.

DELAWARE PL.

CHESTNUT ST.

PEARSON ST.

CHICAGO AVE.

SUPERIOR ST.

HURON ST.

ERIE ST.

ONTARIO ST.

OHIO ST.

GRAND AVE.

ILLINOIS ST.

NAVY PIER

CHICAGO
NORTH

HALSTED ST.

CHICAGO RIVER

ORLEANS ST.

FRANKLIN ST.

WELLS ST.

LASALLE ST.

CLARK ST.

DEARBORN ST.

STATE ST.

WABASH AVE.

RUSH ST.

MIES VAN DER ROHE WY.

LAKE SHORE DR.

HUBBARD ST.

KINZIE ST.

CHICAGO RIVER

WACKER DR.

LAKE ST.

S. WATER ST.

STETSON AVE.

RANDOLPH ST.

WASHINGTON BLVD.

CLINTON ST.

CANAL ST.

STATE ST.

MICHIGAN AVE.

COLUMBUS DR.

Madison St.

Monroe St.

Adams St.

Jackson Blvd.

Van Buren St.

Congress Pkwy.

WACKER DR.

290

LAKE SHORE DR.

BALBO DR.

CHICAGO
DOWNTOWN

CHICAGO
SOUTH

N
W — E
S

0   MILES   1/4

Chicago's grand holiday tree has been a source of good cheer and civic pride since 1913.

❶ The Chicago Christmas Tree
Richard J. Daley Center

On the evening of December 24, 1913, twelve mounted trumpeters of the First Illinois cavalry escorted Mayor Carter H. Harrison from City Hall to Grant Park to light the town's first municipal Christmas tree.

The 85-foot Douglas spruce decorated with 600 colored lights was the main attraction of the evening. One hundred thousand onlookers were also treated to the songs of American opera singers, who projected into megaphones from the balcony of the Chicago Athletic Association, and the Paulist and Swedish choruses, who chanted from the portico of the Art Institute. As entertainment for the children

motion pictures were projected onto a large outdoor screen that could be seen from two blocks away.

Throughout the century the tradition of the city Christmas tree continued while changing with the times. Though the glorious evergreen maintained its stature, by 1956 it was constructed of one 45-foot crowning tree and 85 to 90 smaller trees that filled in the base. With over 2,000 ornaments and 4,400 lights, it was a spectacular sight at its Congress and Michigan location.

The tree was moved to its present site in 1966, where it has stood every year since (with the exception of 1982 when Mayor Jane Byrne had it moved to State and Wacker). At its grandest it measured 90 feet in height with a central system of platforms and ladders that made it possible to walk up the center of the tree. It also grew to a cost of nearly $150,000 and required a week's labor of workers from six city bureaus. In 1991 the height of the tree was shortened to 50 feet, which required only eight to 10 trees for the base and a third of the budget.

Though Chicago's Christmas tree is now nearly half its original size, and the opera singers have been replaced by Ronald McDonald and Donny Osmond, the magic feeling in the air when the tree is lit still remains the same.

Fri. after Thanksgiving–Jan.6, Day and night.
At Clark St. and Washington St.

❷ County Building/City Hall
118 North Clark Street
121 North LaSalle Street

Two trees and a wreath glisten from every windowsill of these stately twin buildings. County carpenters, electricians and laborers decorate their half on Clark Street, while city workers do the same on LaSalle.

Within the City Hall entrance, a magnificent 20-foot Christmas tree sets the stage for local school choirs, who perform throughout the holiday season in a series of lunchtime concerts. The city shares their joyous strains with the county as the children's voices echo through the marble corridor.

1st week of Dec.–Jan.1, (M–F) 8:30AM–4:30PM.
Call the Mayor's Office of Special Events for concert information (312)744–3315. *Between Randolph St. and Washington St.*

❸ Northern Trust Company
50 South LaSalle Street

The colorful tree decorating this downtown bank deserves more than a passing glance. In celebration of cultural diversity it is trimmed with handmade ornaments representing holiday customs throughout the world. These include woven decorations of pine boughs and bamboo from the New Year's festivities of Osaka, Japan; boy and girl dolls dressed in the traditional garb of Sweden's Santa Lucia Day; tasseled felt caps worn in Casablanca, Morocco in celebration of the birth of Mohammad; and ornaments of brightly-colored cloth and polished shells that decorate homes for "Buronya," the Christmas feast of Accra, Ghana.

Sixteen cities participate in decorating the tree. Each is a member of Chicago's Sister Cities Program, which promotes the exchange of international ideas in culture, education, politics and commerce.

2nd Fri. after Thanksgiving–Jan.1, (M–F) 8:30AM –5:00PM. *At Monroe St.*

COURTESY OF J. LYNN, INC.
Twin trees decorate the Light Court of the Rookery Building.

❹ The Rookery Building™
209 South LaSalle Street

Designed by the firm of Burnham and Root in 1885, with the interior court and lobbies updated by Frank Lloyd Wright in 1907, this historic landmark is a treasure to behold at any time of year. During the holiday season elegant decorations complement the building's unique architecture with festive charm.

The windows of the ornate masonry facade are trimmed with huge evergreen wreaths and satin bows. Within the Light Court on either side of the grand staircase, two 21-foot trees are fancifully adorned with full-size antique toys. Teddy bears, red ladders, snare drums, candy canes, brass horns, sleds and sailing ships rise to the domed skylight, where white carousel horses crown both trees. Lavish poinsettias fill the massive gold and marble planters on the staircase columns. Custom florist J. Lynn, Inc., who designed the display, continues the theme over the front desk with a lovely antique train vignette.

Fri. after Thanksgiving–Jan.1, (M–Sa) 8:00AM–8:00PM. *At Adams St.*

❺ 181 West Madison Building

Approaching the Loop on the Dan Ryan Expressway at Christmastime, building engineer José Chavarria proudly directs his children's attention to this glowing red and green skyscraper he helped to light. José and two other engineers, Jerry Palmere and Frank Hynes, spend several chilly hours manually covering 172 exterior lamps on five levels of balconies with sheets of heat-resistant colored film to create the delightful effect.

The 181 West Madison Building, managed by Miglin-Beitler, has been a beacon of holiday cheer since 1991 and a pioneer in the growing trend to paint the skyline in holiday hues. Company president and chief executive officer Paul Beitler explains, "I think all of us who manage the skyscrapers downtown are trying to spread the tradition across the Loop, so that it looks more festive during the holiday season."

The enthusiastic C.E.O. extends his philosophy to the interior of the buildings as well. Under his guidance, the lobbies of all the company's 37 properties are decorated with animated holiday displays

Children are welcome to ride the train in the playful lobby of the 181 West Madison Building.

The delightful decorations grow more elaborate each year as the building managers, who direct the creation of the displays, vie for Beitler's approval.

Santa Claus has arrived at the company's suburban office buildings in a red Ferrari and a helicopter. The 181 West Madison Building and Miglin-Beitler's other downtown properties, Madison Plaza, the 230 West Monroe Building and the Chicago Mercantile Exchange, provide some unexpected treats of their own and are open to the public. "We try to create a festival of lights and activities that allow the downtown urban resident to see things they might only expect in the suburbs," Beitler notes.

With the company president's love for the season it is no wonder that the home office at 181 Madison has had some of the most elaborate decorations. In past years viewers have enjoyed such themed displays as "The Polar Express," where visitors boarded on an old-fashioned locomotive to tour an animated scene of the North Pole in a re-creation of Chris Van Allsburg's popular children's Christmas story; "Circus Under the Bigtop," where a trio of raccoons balanced ornaments on their noses, bears sold cotton candy

and visiting children rode endlessly on a caterpillar train; "The Gingerbread House," where bakers twirled about in an edible bakeshop surrounded by gumdrop trees; and "Ice Fantasy," where snow princesses and Jack Frost wizards danced around a glittering castle.

In this building a visit to Mommy's or Daddy's office during the holidays is anything but dull. The kids may even get free candy and a train ride.

Dec.7–Jan.6, Lobby: (M–F) 7:00AM–6:00PM, (Sa) 8:00AM–3:00PM, Free train rides: (Sa–Su) 10:00AM– 2:00PM, Tower: 5:00PM–12:00AM nightly. *At Wells St.*

6 Madison Plaza
200 West Madison Street

Edible treats seem to be the yearly theme at this fanciful lobby. Though giant rag dolls, toy soldiers and teddy bears have brought smiles to visitors' faces, the free gumballs, peppermints and gum drops are what keep the visions of sugarplums dancing in their heads.

Dec.7–Jan.6, (M–F) 7:00AM–6:00PM, (Sa) 8:00AM–3:00PM. *At Wells St.*

❼ Merchandise Mart

When the second largest building in the United States is festooned for the holidays, it dusts the city with its joyful spirit like a fairy godmother spreading good cheer. The Merchandise Mart had been adorned since 1941 with up to 16,000 light bulbs that formed a display that changed annually and a giant "Merry Christmas" sign. With the energy crisis of the seventies all the building's outdoor lighting was discontinued, including the white incandescent flood lights that had illuminated the facade year-round.

The costly bulbs were eventually replaced with energy-efficient 150-watt high-pressure sodium flood lights. They not only reflect a golden glow around the massive building's two-block perimeter each evening, but since 1992 have allowed the Mart to dress for the holidays once again.

"We were able to develop a way to do it that was economical," explains Chuck Lorenz, electrical engineer and holiday lighting designer. Hinged metal frames were custom crafted for the 556 12" x 12" lights. When the colors are changed, theatrical gels are installed in the frames in an operation that four workers can complete in an afternoon. The lights, spaced 10 feet apart, rest on the balconies that surround the building, making them easily accessible.

The only difficult part of the operation is finding the proper gel to create the desired colors when using a gold sodium light source. Chuck proved he had mastered the problem when he was able to change the lights to red, white and blue for the 4th of July.

Thanksgiving–Jan.1, Dusk–12:00AM.
At the Chicago River between Wells St. and Orleans St.

The Merchandise Mart paints the city's skyline in holiday colors.

Electrician Howard Brody lights the trees on Michigan Avenue.

⑧ North Michigan Avenue

The exclusive shops of Chicago's famous "Magnificent Mile" dazzle even brighter during the holidays as trees sparkling with thousands of tiny white lights glisten along their path. The Greater North Michigan Avenue Association of local retailers promotes the display and recently added a "Festival of Lights" to officially begin the season. On the evening of the Saturday before Thanksgiving a procession of double-decker buses, cartoon characters, elves, carolers and strolling musicians travels south from Oak Street to Pioneer Court as the trees are illuminated block by block. Other festivities continue throughout the holiday season.

The lighting of the trees actually begins long before the ceremony when a crew of men from White Way Sign Co. hangs approximately 360,000 lights on 153 trees.

Howard Brody, a maintenance electrician who has been part of the crew since 1979, admits that hanging lights in the cold seven days a week for six weeks can be a bit repetitive, though an occasional bat or mistakenly turned on sprinkler system have been known to break the monotony. Compliments and thanks from passersby add cheer to the task. "My wife does the Christmas tree. I'm lighted out," Howard confides.

Bundles of 50 lights with long leaders are attached to circuits at the center of the tree and thrown to the outside limbs. Lights are wrapped once or twice around the branch and tied in a knot. At the end of the season they are cut and removed to prevent damage to the trees.

White Way Sign Co. has contracted with the individual store owners over the last 15 years to light the trees. They also do many of the trees and hedges throughout the north side including some on Lake Shore Drive that look like dandelions waiting to be blown away. "There's a knack to it," explains Ted Collyer, sales manager for the company. "We make sure that the old timers are out there running the newer crews. Instead of running a string of lights on a limb that's all by itself, they'll form it and drape it, so it's got some continuity to it."

The company also lights the Chicago Dock and Canal and North Pier terminal and may soon be decorating all the city bridges if festive town officials get their way. Howard may be out there a few more weeks than in years past, so if you see him, let him know how pretty it looks.

Sat. before Thanksgiving–Feb.1, Day and night. For an events schedule call The Greater North Michigan Avenue Association (312)642–3570. *From Oak St. to the Chicago River.*

"Lights and Sights" Bus Tour

The Chicago Motor Coach Company offers double-decker bus tours of Michigan Avenue, State Street, and other downtown holiday highlights in their "Lights and Sights" tour. The rides average 40 minutes.

Sat. before Thanksgiving–Jan.1, 5:00PM–8:00PM. For more information call (312)922–8919.

The diamond-shaped Stone Container Building is one of several downtown skyscrapers that dress for the holidays.

❾ Stone Container Building
150 North Michigan Avenue

A poinsettia paradise is abloom in the two-story glass-enclosed lobby of the Stone Container Building. Two hundred-eighty flaming red plants gloriously converge to form a stunning 14-foot holiday tree, while red and white blooms burst from planters throughout the lobby. While overhead…

If you think that hanging lights on the roof of your two-story home is a challenging task, consider the problem of chief engineer Dave Retterer and his crew. They decorate the 650-foot perimeter of the diamond-shaped glass roof of the Stone Container Building—52 stories high at a 57-degree angle.

The green and red lights that outline the structure's peak during the Christmas season were never in the plans of architect Sheldon Schlegman, nor were the red lights on Valentine's Day, the green lights on St.Patrick's Day, the red, white and blue lights on the 4th of July or the white lights on ordinary days.

Several years after the building's completion in 1982, the management company's chairman, Bob Wislow, suggested that the roof be lit for the Christmas season. In the initial attempt, the engineering crew trimmed the roofline with strings of colored 60-watt bulbs similar to those used at construction sights. The effect was delightful,

though numerous bulbs shorted out, so the company had the engineers install a permanent weather-resistant system.

The current design, though more reliable and efficient, still requires four engineers to spend three to four hours braving the wind to manually replace the 357 white bulbs with colored ones for each holiday. The engineers pair up at the bottom of the steep stairway that parallels the roofline. One engineer from each team unscrews the protective caps and the 75-watt white bulbs. The other replaces them with 60-watt colored bulbs and screws back the caps.

In the fall of 1988 the decorating idea expanded further. The rooftop beamed "GO BEARS" in huge 10-foot letters and began a tradition of rallying Chicago sports teams. This too is a manual operation created by the building's engineers, but is housed in the interior behind the glass diamond. A maze of conduit, sockets and wiring, which began as seven letters, has been added to and rewired for many other messages. Now it is capable of spelling any 14-letter phrase in the time it takes to screw and unscrew the bulbs.

When the work is complete, just like any home-decorator stepping back on his front lawn, Dave and his crew step back into Grant Park and look up with pride.

Outdoor Lighting: Dec.18–Jan.1, Dusk–Dawn.
Lobby: Dec.5–Jan.1, (M–F) 9:00AM–5:00PM.
At Randolph St.

The Christmas Flower

According to Mexican legend, the first poinsettia appeared in answer to the prayer of a small boy who had no birthday gift for the Christ Child. The brilliant red and green "Flower of the Holy Night" sprang from the ground at the boy's side and has since remained a part of Mexican holiday tradition.

Dr. Joel R. Poinsett, U.S. Minister to Mexico, first brought the flower to the United States in 1836, where it was named in his honor.

⑩ Pioneer Court
Equitable Building
401 North Michigan Avenue

The three flower beds of Pioneer Court, lush with the blooms during the summer months, are transformed into equally lovely displays during the yuletide season. Large white doves, glistening in lights, carry boughs of evergreens dotted with glowing red berries from the bushes below. Compass Management and Leasing, Inc., which manages the property and provides the display, added grazing reindeer to the scenes in 1994.

Within the lobby of the Equitable Building, an authentic sleigh makes a unique collection site for new toy donations for the U.S. Marine Corps' "Toys for Tots" program. The lobby is also host to carolers, opera singers and pianists, who entertain during lunch hours four times a week throughout the holidays.

Nov. 15 – Jan. 10, Dusk – 12:00AM. Holiday concerts: (Dates posted in lobby.) 12:00PM – 2:00PM.
Between Illinois St. and the Chicago River.

A grand 32-foot Christmas tree fills the historic Tribune lobby.

⑪ Tribune Tower
435 North Michigan Avenue

The Tribune Tower, built in 1925, is a fascinating landmark inside and out. When dressed in its holiday finest, it beckons visitors to share its rich history.

A double band of fresh evergreen boughs bathed in 15,000 twinkling white lights frames the three-story Gothic main entrance. A massive red-ribboned wreath hangs over the doorway where the stone carved figures of Aesop's fables can be seen peering through the branches.

Within the building, a stunning 32-foot Christmas tree reaches the oak-beamed ceiling in grand style. Surrounded by famous quotations inscribed in the marble walls, the tree bears its own message of the spirit of the season. The ornaments change yearly with the theme, from a world peace tree decked in white doves to one adorned with ornaments made by parents for their children.

The tree is assembled, lit and trimmed on scaffolding from the top down by a crew of six volunteers who work 16 hours a day three days straight. Al Gramzinski, building manager and a volunteer since 1968, speaks of the joy of being involved in the project, "In the evening, especially when it's quieted

The peaceful message of glistening doves decorates the flower beds at Pioneer Court.

In the air there's a feeling of Christmas as Chicago's sky-scrapers dress in holiday hues.

down, we start singing carols amongst ourselves. It's very emotional."

Along the south exterior wall are eighteen bronze plaques of historic Tribune front pages, among them Commander Perry's 1909 discovery of the North Pole. No mention of Santa Claus is made. Three evergreen trees glisten between the ornate vertical columns of the annex entryway in the Nathan Hale Court. In the north wall of the lobby is the most revered of all the stones set in the building from famous structures. It is from the Cave of the Nativity in Bethlehem, believed by many to be the birthplace of Christ.

Mon. after Thanksgiving–Jan. 1, Day and night.
Between Illinois St. and the Chicago River.

⑫ Chicago Marriott Downtown
540 North Michigan Avenue

Low occupancy in a normally bustling downtown hotel would usually be cause for alarm, but not during the slow holiday season. At the downtown Marriott, empty rooms in late December are not only expected but essential to transform the west side of the hotel into a colorful 25-story Christmas tree.

Guests paying luxury rates surely prefer tasteful lamps in their rooms to the open curtains and glaring flood lights used to form the tree, so management must wait until the required 106 "tree" rooms can be left vacant. In fact the hotel prefers to fill all reservations on the other side of the building, so the lights of occupied rooms won't spoil the silhouette.

When the rooms are finally available, often the week before Christmas, a volunteer task force that includes everyone from managers to bellhops makes a holiday party of creating the giant tree. With a computerized system, designed by assistant front office manager Ed Trott, printouts indicate which rooms require what color lights. Teams of volunteers equipped with red, green and amber bulbs and goose-neck adapters replace the lamp shades and bulbs in their assigned rooms and face the lamps out the windows. It often turns into a competition to see who can finish first.

Three hours later the task is nearly complete. Dave Nelson, Director of Services and Christmas tree coordinator, takes a look at the crew's handiwork from outside and relays necessary final adjustments via walkie-talkie.

Every year since the tradition began in 1991, a woman living in the apartments across from the hotel calls to say how happy the tree makes her—and she's not the only one.

Dec. 17–Dec. 25 (subject to occupancy), Dusk–Dawn. *At Ohio St.*

⑬ Saks Fifth Avenue
700 North Michigan Avenue

The six animated display windows of Saks Fifth Avenue present a new theme each year. Since the store moved to this location in 1990, the windows on Superior and Michigan have featured re-creations of children's stories and salutes to Chicago architecture and Broadway plays created by Spaeth Design of New York.

Wed. before Thanksgiving–Jan. 6, Dawn–12:00AM. *Between Huron St. and Superior St.*

⑭ FAO Schwarz
840 North Michigan Avenue

It's Christmas year-round in the magical toyland of FAO Schwarz where a 20-foot teddy bear waves from the second-floor window, a smiling bunny greets shoppers on the escalator and a talking tree chants, "Come along and play with me," among the many animated displays. The three-level store is a toy paradise with a floor sample of every item, which kids are invited to try.

For a schedule of holiday hours call (312)587–5000. *Between Pearson St. and Chestnut St.*

⑮ John Hancock Center
875 North Michigan Avenue

The towering John Hancock Building reigns over the holiday skyline with a crown of red, white and green lights and a glowing star 1,200 feet above the city. Managers of the building since 1992, U.S. Equities Realty, Inc. decided to decorate the tower as had been done in the seventies with a few innovations of their own.

The "Peace on Earth" sign, which had previously hung between the two giant antennas, was replaced with a 50-foot star trimmed with 750 7½ watt bulbs. In a half-day operation, a team of 10 to 15 iron workers and building engineers attach the 605-pound steel ornament to the antennas 100 feet above the roof with pulleys and heavy nylon rope. Though the task may appear frightening, project manager Mead Elliott says, "Being in our line of work, we're hard to scare."

For John Hancock's colorful crown, two-thirds of the 1,050 white fluorescent lights that circle the tower are individually covered with red and green gel tubes. The job requires eight man-hours and luckily can be performed from the interior of the building.

Sat. before Thanksgiving–Jan. 1 (weather permitting). *Between Chestnut St. and Delaware Pl.*

The Start of A Glowing Tradition

In 1959 Saks Fifth Avenue was located across the street from its present location, and Joe Kreis was the store's display artist. Having recently sold the ornate Christmas tree that traditionally decorated Saks' exterior, Mr. Kreis was looking for a new idea.

He approached local display manufacturer George Silvestri with whom he had worked in the past. Silvestri was enthused about some inexpensive strands of small white lights he had found while traveling in Italy. The tiny lights were quite a departure from the large multicolored bulbs being used at the time and seemed too fragile to withstand Chicago's winter winds. However, the two men had come up with an exciting idea that for merely three cents a light they were willing to try.

Kreis hired Arrow Sign Co. to outline every limb of the six bare elm trees in the front of the store with the unusual lights. After spending an entire day on one tree, the company increased their bill for the tedious task to Kreis' total holiday display budget. The end result was worth the price. It dazzled not only Joe Kreis, but other Michigan Avenue merchants as well.

The following year several other stores began to follow suit, and the Michigan Avenue Christmas tradition was born. It took a little over 10 years for the street to reach its present glow and become the "Avenue of White Lights."

Although the lighting ceremonies of the late fifties and early sixties never matched the current festivities, personalities on hand for the lighting included Betty Hutton, Carmen Miranda, Betty Grable, Geraldine Page and Jerry Lewis.

"Electric Sheep" by artist John David Mooney graze in the yard of the Fourth Presbyterian Church.

🄰 Fourth Presbyterian Church
North Michigan Avenue at Chestnut Street

The Fourth Presbyterian Church has always provided a tranquil oasis in the midst of the bustling shops of North Michigan Avenue. During the holiday season when the stores are at their busiest, this downtown sanctuary once again treats its visitors to a place of calm repose. For beneath its gothic arches trimmed with yuletide greenery, five grazing sheep with fleece of white lights twinkle in concert with the sparkling trees of the boulevard.

The "Electric Sheep" sculptures are the work of Chicago-based artist John David Mooney. Twelve sheep, each one unique, were originally commissioned by Prime Minister John Major for the European Community Summit held in Edinburgh, Scotland in 1992. Within view of the visiting 12 heads of state, the flock grazed on the highest hill in the city as an expression of the "new Europe."

Though Mr. Mooney's "Electric Sheep" were first seen at the Chicago International Art Exposition in May of 1993, many are familiar with the environmental artist's large-scale sculptures. They include "Lightscape 89," the transformation of Chicago's IBM Building into a 52-story light sculpture; "American's Sky Sculpture," a sculpture/performance barge which traversed the Chicago River; and a 1990 programmed searchlight piece for which Mooney wrote a 900-page score.

Sat. before Thanksgiving–Jan.6, 8:00AM–12:00AM. *Between Chestnut St. and Delaware Pl.*

🄱 900 North Michigan Avenue

It's certain that none of the architects from Perkins & Will or Kohn, Pedersen and Fox Associates, who collaborated on the design of this unique structure, ever imagined there would be a desire to change the colors of the four giant turrets that distinguish this building on the city's skyline. The blueprints would surely have included a system less arduous than that required of plant superintendent Dave Mullins and his crew.

Sixty-four 400-watt and 68 100-watt mercury vapor lights are manually covered with colored lens paper secured in sheet-metal frames. The crew uses a long hooked pole to reach the lights, some measuring as much as 40-feet above floor level. The system once required the assembly and reassembly of cumbersome scaffolding, but has been perfected over the years by Dave and his crew. They can now complete the task in eight man-hours.

Their engineering skill surely does the architects proud as the building adorns the skyline with its festive crown, which seems to resemble four candles on an advent wreath. The glowing turrets also change colors for the 4th of July and Bull's victories.

The interior lobby of the shopping area is bedecked for the season in as grand a style. A 45-foot tree adorned with 4,200 ornaments and 3,500 lights majestically greets shoppers through four levels of the atrium.

Thanksgiving–Jan.1, Lobby: (M–Sa) 10:00AM–8:00PM, (Su)–6:00PM. For holiday store hours call (312)915–3916. *Between Walton St. and Delaware Pl.*

Unique donation boxes decorate the AT&T and USG lobbies.

⓲ The Art Institute of Chicago
South Michigan Avenue at Adams Street

The Art Institute lions proudly attired in luxuriant balsam wreaths have come to symbolize the start of the holiday season in Chicago. Created by American sculptor Edward L. Kemeys in 1894, the bronze pair first donned their yuletide apparel in the fifties.

The city's affection for the stately felines prompted the Art Institute in 1992 to make the "Wreathing of the Lions" an annual public celebration. On the Friday morning after Thanksgiving, as large a crowd as will fill the museum's steps is treated to hot cider, cookies and the melodies of a brass trio while waiting for the festive moment. At 10:00AM the 200-pound wreaths are lifted over the lions' heads, and a lucky child waves a magic wand to light the four Christmas trees that flank their path.

Inside the museum the grand staircase is adorned with a radiant poinsettia tree, often the backdrop for school choirs that perform in the building throughout the holidays. Children's ornament-making workshops, holiday lectures on religious paintings and "Glad Tidings and Great Joy: Christmas at the Art Institute"—an exhibit of the Christmas story told with Renaissance and Baroque paintings are some of the museum's special events that make a holiday visit to this Chicago treasure a unique Christmas adventure.

Friday after Thanksgiving–Jan.1. For information on special events call (312)443–3600.

⓳ Harris Trust and Savings Bank
111 West Monroe Street

The tradition of elaborate Christmas displays at this downtown establishment seems to be as stalwart as the bank itself. Vice president Barbara Wystrach, who supervises the decorating, along with real estate leasing and development, recalls the displays dating back longer than the 30 years of her employment.

Though recent exhibits have been more modest in the smaller space of the redesigned building, they are just as delightful. Trees decorated with Wizard of Oz characters, a woodland scene with moving forest animals, and a village of 6-foot candy houses are among the memorable displays created by Phillip's Flowers & Gifts. Though the decorations change yearly, Hubert the Harris Lion is always a part of the scene whether riding a sleigh or posing as an elf.

The characters continue in Harris' other office window at 311 W. Monroe.

The entrance to the oldest part of the 111 West Monroe building is trimmed with lighted garland and a 10-foot wreath. Beyond the entryway is a lovely 25-foot tree, which for the past several years has been fancifully dressed in a stunning assortment of handmade miniature brass instruments.

2nd weekend after Thanksgiving–Weekend after New Year's. Lobby hours: (M–F) 8:30AM–5:00PM. *Between Clark St. and LaSalle St.*

⓴ 200 West Monroe Building

Property manager Rick Saulig takes credit for the fanciful holiday displays in his building's lobby. "I've got an active imagination," he explains.

Rick, his staff, and his wife, Pati, design and assemble the scenes from a storehouse of animated characters and accessories. They begin scheming for the next year as soon as the task is completed.

The playful crew's 1994 exhibit, one of their best, featured a band of elves in hard hats decorating the lobby tree from scaffolds and hydraulic lifts. As the Christmas season progressed, the elves gradually worked their way down the tree.

Thanksgiving weekend–Dec.30, 6:00AM–8:00PM. *At Wells St.*

㉑ AT&T Corporate Center/USG Building
227 West Monroe, 222 West Adams

The spirit of giving decorates the lobbies of these adjacent office buildings where a giant glittering ornament, a playful rocking horse and brightly-wrapped holiday presents are actually collection boxes.

Stein & Company, managing and leasing agent for the buildings, began the tradition in 1990 and has annually collected an average of 600 new toys, 600 articles of warm clothing and 725 pounds of non-perishable food. Items are donated to the U.S. Marines' "Toys for Tots" program, the Mental Health Association of Greater Chicago and the Greater Chicago Food Depository, respectively.

Though most donations are made by building tenants, the management invites visitors to make contributions and to enjoy the holiday display.

Dec.1–Dec.25, (M–F) 8:00AM–6:00PM. *Between Wells St. and Franklin St.*

㉒ 230 West Monroe Building

Animated characters are visible day and night in the glass-enclosed lobby of this festive office building. The management company of Miglin-Beitler combines its playful enthusiasm for the holidays with the creative artistry of The Meetinghouse Companies, Inc., of Elmhurst to design the imaginative displays. During Christmas week, musical entertainment adds to the holiday mood with lunchtime performances.

Dec.7–Jan.6, Day and night. *At Franklin St.*

㉓ 500 and 525 West Monroe Street

Although artificial Christmas trees in indoor public places have been the norm since the fire regulations of the early sixties, they have never quite replaced the vibrancy of real trees. Tishman Speyer Properties, the management company for these two downtown office buildings, retained Interior Garden Services, Inc. to design a creative alternative for their lobbies.

The Chicago-based florist ingeniously spiraled hundreds of potted Norfolk Island pines up metal frames to form dazzling live trees at each location. Complementing the rich marble and stained glass of the 500 West Monroe lobby, their tree is trimmed in Victorian dolls, gold lamé garlands and golden harps. Across the street in the 525 building, purple, cranberry and silver bulbs adorn the boughs along with iridescent crystal beads and packages. The ornaments are hung from custom-designed hooks that keep the fragile branches from bending. As an added treat, at season's end the plants are given to the tenants.

Sat. after Thanksgiving–Jan.6, (M–F) 7:00AM–6:30PM, (Sa) 7:00AM–1:00PM. *At Canal St.*

㉔ The Greenhouse at the Ritz-Carlton 160 East Pearson Street

For those who prefer classical fare, this luxury hotel hosts a "Holiday Tea" in the glow of a 25-foot Victorian Christmas tree trimmed in antique lace, velvet bows and handmade ornaments. Guests feast on a fine selection of teas and treats in this lovely skylit restaurant.

Wed. before Thanksgiving–Dec.31, Teatime: (Su–F) 3:00PM–5:00PM. (312)266–1000. *Between Michigan Ave. and Mies Van Der Rohe Wy.*

㉕ James R. Thompson Building 100 West Randolph Street
(formerly State of Illinois Center)

What better place for a grand 20-foot Christmas tree than the 17-story atrium of this architectural showplace. The work of famed designer Helmut Jahn shares the spotlight as the majestic tree, surrounded by animated figurines, becomes the focus of attention during the holidays. In addition the first of the balconies that rise along the perimeter of this massive glass structure is draped with wreaths and garlands that elegantly frame the festive decor.

The display is a joint effort of the State of Illinois and the retailers of the Atrium Mall. The theme changes yearly and once included ornaments made by children throughout the state.

A tree-lighting ceremony, usually performed by the governor, takes place at 12:00PM the Wednesday before Thanksgiving. Free refreshments are served, and local high school musicians entertain. Throughout the holiday season, student groups perform at noon in the food court of the lower concourse level.

Wed. before Thanksgiving–Jan.6, (M–F) 6:30AM–6:00PM. (Limited viewing from LaSalle St. entrance at other times.) *At Clark St.*

㉖ State Street

To many Chicagoans and out-of-towners alike, Christmas shopping on State Street is a holiday tradition that a mall could never replace. From Wacker Drive to Congress Parkway, stores along this famous thoroughfare are dressed in their yuletide finest, highlighted by the animated display windows of Marshall Field & Co. and Carson Pirie Scott department stores.

Parkway trees glisten with white lights. Bus terminals and subway entrances shimmer with garlands and bows. Outdoor food vendors sell hot chocolate and apple cider, and street carolers fill the air with songs of good cheer.

Those who prefer the warmth of their cars can drive down State Street, which is normally restricted to public transportation, from 7:00PM to 6:00AM Monday through Saturday and all day Sunday throughout the holidays.

Street decorations: 2nd week of Nov.–Jan.31. *From Wacker Dr. to Congress Pkwy.*

The tale of "Pinocchio" unfolds in Marshall Field's windows.

27 Marshall Field & Co.
111 North State Street
(pictured on page 1)

Forty-two golden trumpets herald the start of the holiday shopping season from this department store world-famous for its Christmas displays both inside and out.

The tradition began when Marshall Field's first visual merchandiser, Arthur Frazier, pioneered in his industry by creating the store's first elaborate window displays in the 1890's. He imported items from Germany and France and handcrafted many himself. His holiday displays were the most enchanting.

In 1941 his successor, John Moss, designed the first holiday story that went from window to window. It was an adaptation of Clement Moore's poem, "A Visit from St. Nicholas."

The store's Christmas mascot, Uncle Mistletoe, was created in 1946 by Addis Osbourne, an instructor at the Art Institute and husband of a Field's associate.

The fictional characters' Christmas window stories, created in-house, changed yearly with magic carpet adventures that took children around the world. Uncle Mistletoe was later joined by Aunt Holly, Freddie and Martha Fieldmouse, and Mistletoe Bear. He even had his own television show from 1948 to 1952. Within the store Uncle Mistletoe's Cozy Cloud Cottage is still Santa's home away from home, where children can come to whisper their wish lists.

In 1990 Marshall Field's was purchased by Dayton Hudson Corporation, a Minneapolis-based retailer renowned for its own elaborate animated re-creations of classic fairytales. The following holiday season Field's visual merchandising staff joined Dayton Hudson's tradition by designing the story of "Cinderella" in 13 splendorous window vignettes. The display was followed in 1994 by the adventurous tale of "Pinocchio." Each theme is featured for three consecutive Christmas seasons and may subsequently reappear at Dayton's in Minneapolis.

Throughout the interior of Marshall Field's the decorations continue. The most fanciful creations adorn the first floor, where the window theme is elaborated with mechanical figures above the aisles.

The indoor decorations culminate with the famous Walnut Room Christmas tree. Begun in the early 1900's on a grand but smaller scale, it was not until the mid-thirties that the 45-foot "Great Tree" with its 12,000 miniature lights was introduced.

Until 1990 the tree was decorated in a different theme each year using 5,000 handmade ornaments. In-house artists created 27 designs in three sizes, which a staff of five art students from around the country created as summer employment. The ornaments were donated to veterans' hospitals at the end of each season. Though no longer created in-house, the fanciful trimmings are still hand-crafted with the same attention to detail.

For many years the "Great Tree" was a live evergreen. It was well-guarded by two full-time firemen and a specially-installed sprinkler system. In 1962 fire regulations required that the real tree be replaced by an artificial one, which is still being used today. The tree didn't lose its magic, however— customers continued to remark on its lovely fragrance.

Window display: 2nd week of Nov.–2nd week of Jan., 8:00AM–11:00PM (subject to change). For holiday store hours call (312)781–5632.
Between Randolph St. and Washington Blvd.

The Longears bake holiday treats in Carson's window.

28 Carson Pirie Scott
1 South State Street

It's a common sight on State Street to see kids sitting on shoulders, tugging on arms and squeezing under legs to glimpse the enchantment of Carson's four animated holiday windows.

In the 1991 to 1993 exhibit, onlookers were treated to an inside view of Santa's workshop in action. Elves hammered and conveyor belts rolled, as parts of trucks and dolls were somehow pieced together in paint-splattered rooms. "The more movement, the more kids will love it," professes Chuck Luckenbill, vice president of visual store planning and construction and current designer of the window displays.

Before Santa's workshop had run its course, an eager Luckenbill was planning the next display. In January 1994 he presented an idea to Pacific Design & Production, the California-based company that created the previous windows. "I wanted to show from a kid's view what was below the sidewalk and from an adult's view what was above it," Chuck said.

In the initial stages the underground scene featured a variety of burrowing animals—rats, moles, fox and rabbits. Chuck realized early on that as cute as they could make rats look, the critters would not be well-received. After consulting with his children, he decided that bunnies were the most likable choice.

By March the idea was finalized. Drawings for the windows were completed in May, construction was begun in July and by late October the scenes were being readied for installation. Workers from Pacific Design and several of Chuck's staff assembled the displays in a week's time for the November unveiling.

During the holiday shopping seasons from 1994 to 1996, the windows will reveal the Family Longears residing beneath Carson's sidewalk, as unwitting shoppers gaze into store windows overhead. The four burrowed rooms, decorated in exquisite detail, feature members of the animated rabbit family preparing for the holidays; a moustachioed chef decorates a five-layer carrot cake; junior trims the parlor with berry-filled garlands, the older children don their costumes for the holiday pageant; and momma reads a Christmas story to the youngsters in their beds.

At a cost of tens of thousands of dollars per window and months of planning and construction, it is no wonder these elaborate sets are retained for a three-year term. The displays are then sold to a store in a different part of the country, or the mechanical parts are salvaged for another display. Whatever their final fate, the joy these magical windows create remains alive in the memories of all who see them.

1st Fri. in Nov.–2nd Fri. in Jan., 7:30AM–10:00PM (subject to change). *At Madison St.*

The Hyatt's lobby becomes the North Pole for the holidays.

㉙ Clarion Executive Plaza Hotel
71 East Wacker Drive

Passersby can't help but grin at the 14-foot snow dome that tops the entryway of this downtown hotel. The custom-made globe is filled with compressed air to keep snowflakes swirling about the 7½-foot snowman smiling inside.

Thanksgiving weekend–Jan. 1, Day and night. *Between Wabash Ave. and Michigan Ave.*

㉚ Hyatt Regency Chicago
151 East Wacker Drive

There may not be penguins at the North Pole, but there are in the East Tower Plaza of the Hyatt Regency Chicago. Dozens are waddling to the top of a 25-foot castle perched on an iceberg in the hotel's lagoon. Twenty polar bears join the act, while an LGB-scale train travels through tunnels and over bridges tooting all the way. The $150,000 display takes 30 workers three days to assemble. The All Seasons Cafe offers the best seats in the house with an island of tables in the middle of the lagoon.

Thanksgiving–Jan. 8, Day and night. Restaurant: 6:00AM–12:00AM. Casual. Reservations recommended (312)565–1234. *Between Michigan Ave. and Stetson Ave.*

㉛ Chicago Mercantile Exchange
10 and 30 South Wacker Drive

Center of international trade and banking, this twin-towered office complex celebrates the global spirit of the season with its lustrous lobby displays. Within each entrance a wish for "Peace on Earth" greets visitors, while a stunning 8-foot red globe rotates overhead. Holiday customs of nations around the world are elegantly illustrated on enormous banners that hang from the walls. Musicians add to the festivities with lunchtime holiday performances. Salvation Army collection boxes are displayed for donations of clothing and foods.

Dec. 1–Jan. 6, (M–F) 5:30AM–6:00PM, (Sa) 8:00AM–1:00PM. Entertainment: (Every day during Christmas week and other dates to be announced) 11:00AM–1:00PM. *At Monroe St.*

㉜ Sears Tower
233 South Wacker Drive

The world's tallest office building may boast of having 110 stories, 4.5 million gross square feet of floor space, 16,100 windows and 796 lavatory faucets,

A glistening tree lights the atrium of the Sears Tower.

but when the holidays roll around it's the tower's 48-floor Christmas tree that draws the most attention.

Designed for the building's atrium in 1994 by the Becker Group of Baltimore, Maryland, the magnificent shimmering tree flaunts a few impressive statistics of its own. With 7,000 white lights, 1,020 gold and silver ornaments and 192 feet of gold lamé ribbon, it is the largest indoor Christmas tree in Chicago.

Sat. before Thanksgiving–Sat. after New Year's, Day and night. Lobby hours: (M–F) 6:00AM–6:00PM. *Between Adams St. and Jackson Blvd.*

33 The Drake Hotel
140 East Walton Street

When Raul Cuevas began working at the Drake Hotel as a dishwasher 20 years ago, he had no idea his hidden talents would eventually earn him the position of executive pastry chef and creator of a nationally famous gingerbread display.

In 1989 when 100 executives handed him ideas for the first rendition, Raul decided instead to create the village from imaginary pictures that were in his head, and that's the way he's done it every year since.

The work begins on the first of October. Raul draws his original patterns on cardboard. With the help of six other pastry chefs, the walls are cut out of gingerbread sheets and "glued" together with chocolate. A mixture of sugar, egg whites and cream of tartar forms a royal icing for the roofs, while hard candies and cookies add detail to the delectable treats.

When the 24 houses, two bridges and one train station are complete, Raul assembles the town on a 12-foot by 20-foot table surrounded by a curtain until time for its unveiling. The houses are placed at different levels, and a toy train, a mountain and townspeople are added to the scene.

The village houses are completely edible. However, it is recommended that you try Raul's frozen raspberry soufflé instead.

Dec. 1–Jan. 1, 7:00AM–8:00PM. *At Michigan Ave.*

"Festival of Trees"

Christmas trees elaborately decorated with Bulls memorabilia, Frango mints and Scotty dogs have been among those featured in the annual "Festival of Trees" presented by the Easter Seal Society of Metropolitan Chicago, Inc., since 1988.

Local florists, designers and architects create the fanciful displays, while generous sponsors fund the event. Approximately 30 trees are exhibited annually and sold with all their trimmings through silent auction. Proceeds from the festival fund Easter Seal programs, which aid 6,500 disabled Chicagoland residents each year. Though past auctions have taken place at a private opening gala, the society's Women's Auxiliary, which organizes the festival, eventually plans to open the bidding to the public.

5th week before Christmas–1st week before Christmas, Day and night. Downtown lobby location varies annually. For further information call the Easter Seal Society of Metropolitan Chicago (312)939–5115 or the Mayor's Office of Special Events (312)744–3315.

The CTA Christmas Bus

Since 1991 the CTA, seven enthusiastic volunteers and Brach's candy company have been transforming Bus 4436 into the Christmas Bus with lighted candy canes, toy soldiers, gingerbread men and garlands both inside and out. One lucky driver is chosen based on safety record and good attitude to man the craft. "Why catch a regular CTA bus when I can ride this?" a happy passenger remarked. The feeling is contagious as the entire busload often joins in a round of carols.

Two days before Thanksgiving–Christmas, (M–Sa) 7:00AM–7:00PM. For exact route information call (312)836–7000.

Rudolph the Cab

Those who enjoy taxi rides with colorful cabbies will certainly thrill to being driven by a man from the North Pole dressed in a red velvet suit and cap. He's easy to spot—his cab is sporting giant antlers and a flashing red nose. Passengers lucky enough to catch "Rudolph the Cab" receive a free ride and candy as well. Yellow Cab Company donates the amount on the meter to the Cabrini-Green Tutoring Program. Riders are welcome to make additional contributions.

Early Dec.–Christmas, During business hours.

Chapter 2

CHICAGO – NORTH

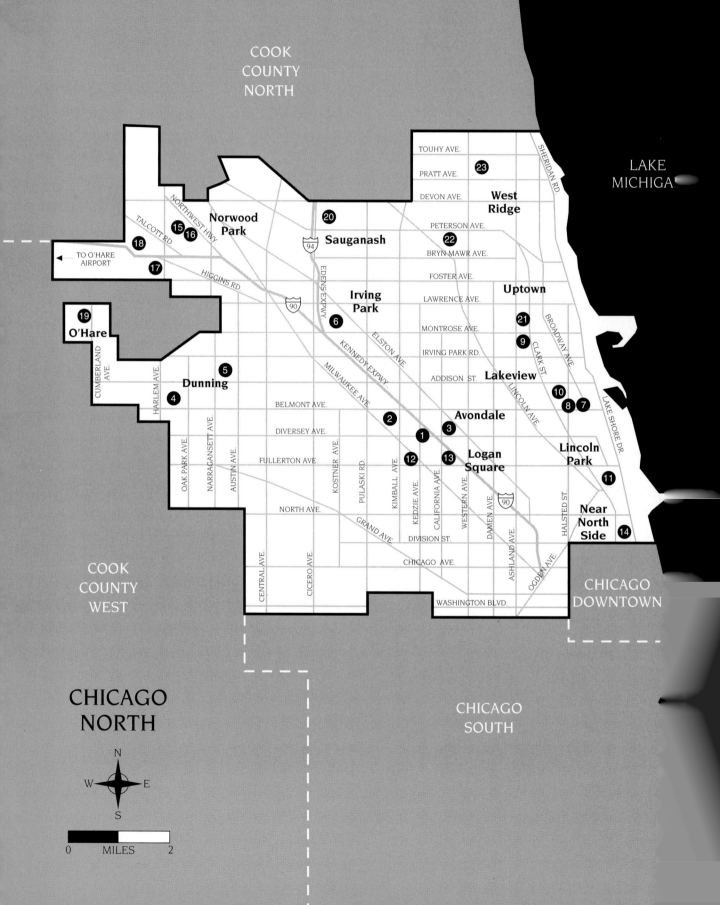

COOK
COUNTY
NORTH

LAKE
MICHIGA

TOUHY AVE.

㉓

PRATT AVE.

DEVON AVE.

West
Ridge

⑳

NORTHWEST HWY.

Norwood
Park

⑮⑯

Sauganash

94

PETERSON AVE.

㉒

BRYN MAWR AVE.

TALCOTT RD.

⑱

TO O'HARE
AIRPORT

⑰

HIGGINS RD.

FOSTER AVE.

Uptown

LAWRENCE AVE.

Irving
Park

90

EDENS EXPWY.

⑥

MONTROSE AVE.

㉑

⑨

BROADWAY AVE.

CLARK ST.

⑲

O'Hare

ELSTON AVE.

KENNEDY EXPWY.

IRVING PARK RD.

ADDISON ST.

Lakeview

⑩

LINCOLN AVE.

⑧ ⑦

LAKE SHORE DR.

CUMBERLAND
AVE.

HARLEM AVE.

⑤

MILWAUKEE AVE.

Dunning

④

BELMONT AVE.

Avondale

②

③

Lincoln
Park

OAK PARK AVE.

NARRAGANSETT AVE.

AUSTIN AVE.

DIVERSEY AVE.

①

KOSTNER AVE.

PULASKI RD.

FULLERTON AVE.

⑫

⑬

Logan
Square

KIMBALL AVE.

KEDZIE AVE.

CALIFORNIA AVE.

WESTERN AVE.

DAMEN AVE.

90

⑪

NORTH AVE.

HALSTED ST.

Near
North
Side

⑭

CENTRAL AVE.

CICERO AVE.

GRAND AVE.

DIVISION ST.

CHICAGO AVE.

ASHLAND AVE.

OGDEN AVE.

CHICAGO
DOWNTOWN

COOK
COUNTY
WEST

WASHINGTON BLVD.

SHERIDAN RD.

CHICAGO
NORTH

N
W   E
S

CHICAGO
SOUTH

0   MILES   2

AVONDALE

❶ 3046 West George Street

Robert and Virginia Holda's cheery Christmas displays have been brightening up the neighborhood for as long as anyone can remember.

Plastic figurines fill the front yard and climb the stairs and rooftop. Evergreen wreaths and garlands covered with lights trim the house and fence. Antique dolls wave from the windows, and outdoor music fills the air.

Dec.15–Jan.10, 5:00PM–12:00AM. *From Kedzie Ave., E on Diversey Ave. 2 bl., N on Albany Ave. 1 bl., E on George St. 1/2 bl.*

❷ Majestic Shell
3181 North Milwaukee Avenue

For a truly complete Christmas decoration adventure, drivers can impress their passengers by starting out the evening with a festive fill-up at Majestic Shell. Brothers Jim and George Sfondeles, who operate the station, trim their pumps with garlands, their storefront with a toy-filled Santa Claus scene, and their lot with cartoon figures and a towering tree of lights. Patrons who visit the weekend before Christmas are treated to free candy, a visit with Santa, and red carnations for the ladies.

The brothers have won first place several years running among nearly 200 local stations that participate in Shell Oil Company's annual decorating contest. Other notable stations include Ontario-Dearborn Shell Auto Care in Chicago and Army Trail Shell at Glen Ellyn Road in Bloomingdale.

Dec.7–Jan.7, Day and night. *SE corner at Belmont Ave.*

❸ 2956 North Rockwell Street

Most customers visit the butcher for fresh cuts of beef, pork or lamb, but it was reindeer that caught the eye of Mark Gehrke at his local meat shop. He was helping his friend Ron Szczech decorate his side yard for the holidays, when he spotted the butcher's display of Santa's reindeer pulling a sleigh. Mark stopped in to ask for the plans, and the butcher obliged.

With the help of their friends Joseph Dohnalik and Lee Hannett as well as Ron's brother Mike, the men got to work enlarging the scene to life-size

Rudolph and a team of homemade reindeer pull a life-size sleigh past Santa's workshop in the yard of Ron Szczech.

proportions. The nine wooden deer were each made of four separate pieces, which easily disassembled.

The sleigh, however, was nailed together permanently. Large enough to seat two adults, it required all five men to lift. "We built it stupid," Ron laughs. The group went on to build a large, but collapsible, Santa's workshop castle and a full-size manger scene.

Though the decorations may have created a storage dilemma for the Szczechs, the neighborhood children anxiously look forward to the holiday yard each year. "The kids keep me on my toes," Ron admits. "If Rudolph's nose is missing or Santa isn't out yet, they always let me know."

Dec.5–Jan.5, 6:00PM–11:00PM. *From Western Ave., W on Diversey Ave. 4 bl., N on Rockwell St. 2 bl.*

DUNNING/SCHORSCH VILLAGE

Candy Cane Lane

"Candy Cane Lane was the big thing when I was a kid," recalls Wayne Basica, who trims his Chicago home with authentic decorations he has collected from the once-famous neighborhood. "Traffic was so heavy, we'd walk up and down the streets with a whole group of relatives. The people who lived in the houses would stand out front and give us cookies and chocolate. When you're a kid…that's seventh heaven. I knew then when I had a house, I would decorate."

"Part of our inspiration comes from the magical memories of Candy Cane Lane which we visited every year as children," reads the sign in the courtyard of Eric and Nancy Mueller's Elmwood Park apartment house, which has become a holiday tourist attraction.

"I remember Candy Cane Lane vividly," remarks Larry Wardzala, whose home is featured on the cover of this book, "I think it was my grooming."

"It was a blast," exclaims former resident Jim Iovino, whose award-winning Elk Grove home is still trimmed with the original candy cane from his boyhood front yard. "I want to pass those memories on to my kids."

Throughout Chicagoland, baby-boomers who decorate their homes for Christmas repeatedly credit their childhood holiday memories of this

COURTESY OF GUS AND LENA GUARINO

The decorating committee that originated Candy Cane Lane proudly displays one of the canes that made their neighborhood famous. (From l. to r.) Bottom row: Ed Minor, John Munao, William Carey, Phil Phillips, John Ogorzalek, Gus Guarino. Top row: Florence Ogorzalek, Veronica Carey, Millie Munao, Marianne Minor, Lena Guarino, Lucille Phillips. (1957)

north west-side neighborhood as the inspiration for their decorating.

Just north of Belmont and east of Harlem, the area was at the height of its popularity from 1953 to 1972. A 1962 feature article in Health magazine called it "one of the wonder spots of Chicago during the holidays." It was a community effort unlike any other at the time. Block after block, neighbors transformed their streets into fantasy lanes, each with a different theme.

A 20-inch wooden letter trimmed with dozens of white lights covered the second floor window of each home on the 7000 block of West School Street, spelling "Merry Christmas" on the south side of the street and "Happy New Year" on the north. A huge three-dimensional silver and blue bell stood on a tall post on the front lawn of each home on the 7000 block of West Henderson. The 6900 block of West Melrose became Choir Lane, trimmed with 4-foot choral singers. The 3200 block of North Nordica was Poinsettia Lane, where giant red blooms were displayed on every lawn, and on Santa Claus Lane at 3300 North Neva the jolly old elf waved from every chimney.

One street west, the 3400 block of Nottingham was Vigil Lane trimmed with 10-foot candlesticks. The 3300 block was Reindeer Lane decorated with 4' x 6' Rudolphs with glowing red noses. And the 3200 block, decorated in 10-foot striped candy canes, became the most famous of them all and the street by which the area was known—Candy Cane Lane.

The huge decorations, which came with two spotlights, were purchased from Frederick's International Advertising Company, a commercial display manufacturer, at an average cost of $20 to each homeowner. Neatly displayed in the same position in each front yard, the matching decorations created quite a dramatic effect in addition to the large outdoor Christmas lights that glowed from every home. Several Nottingham neighbors also constructed wooden frames that would hold the lights neatly around the outline of their houses. Some contend that Commonwealth Edison had to rewire the entire neighborhood because of a transformer blow-out caused by the display.

Individual homeowners added to the block decorations with touches of their own. Many built festive door trimmings. Some rigged outdoor speakers to their record players. "When my neighbor wasn't playing his music, I'd play mine," remembers Candy Cane Lane resident Gus Guarino.

Others created unique displays that left indelible

Ten-foot candy canes on each front lawn transformed the 3200 block of North Nottingham into Candy Cane Lane.

memories for all who viewed them. George Morrison, whose School Street home bore the letter "N," decorated his house with a homemade helicopter, captained by a life-size Santa Claus, and a huge stocking brimming with gifts. Across the street Louis Munao's house was not only decorated with a giant "T," but was famous for its live sheep in a manger. A town of miniature buildings covered the corner lot at Neva. The Guarino home won first place awards for its "Christmas on the Moon" display. And two doors down, George Stumpo, the only hold-out on Candy Cane Lane, good-naturedly wrote "SCROOGE" across his window shade.

The Snyder family on the 3200 block of Newland greeted guests from around the world with holiday messages in a dozen different languages posted across their lawn, while one block north the Duda family's reproduction of a "Swedish Crown" tree of concentric golden hoops was a stunning symbol of the neighborhood's European heritage.

On the 3200 block of Newcastle from 1951 to 1961 LeRoy and Evelyn Hardell completely transformed the face of their brick home into a candy house by covering it with sheets of masonite painted white and covered with glitter. "It fit exactly. No one could see any hardware," Evelyn says proudly. While she did much of the painting, her husband, who had been a mechanical engineer for Stewart-Warner, spent three months meticulously creating dozens of peppermint sticks, pastel cream patties, candy corns, cinnamon hearts, sugar cookies, butterscotch caramels and lollipops using only scrap materials and hand tools.

The couple filled one flowerbed with a garden of suckers and ice cream cones, and another with old-fashioned candies, from gumdrops to peanut brittle, made from cement and rocks. Carols played from a speaker hidden in a handmade steepled church that hung over the doorway. A pink flocked Christmas tree gently rotated in the bay window, like a giant stick of cotton candy. "A lot of people took pictures," Evelyn recalls. "We were picking up flash bulbs all the time."

The entire neighborhood was featured every year on television and radio, and in newspapers and magazines. A local policeman offered horse-drawn sleigh rides down the streets, and the U.S.Marines put barrels on the corners for their "Toys for Tots" campaign. During the two weeks that the displays were lit, cars would fill the streets and families would fill the sidewalks. "As a choir member for many years it was always a gamble whether or not I could get to church in time for midnight Mass," remembers resident Mary Ann Ryan. "Our alleys saved us," recalls Louise Frawley of Choir Lane.

To recreate the magic of a childhood fairytale, LeRoy and Evelyn Hardell turned their Schorsch Village brick home into a homemade candy house every Christmas from 1951 to 1961.

"The area drew a tremendous amount of people. Traffic was horrendous," recalls Don Ferrone, owner of Gray Line Sightseeing Tours. In the mid-fifties his company offered dinner and a tour of Candy Cane Lane, Oak Park, River Forest and Sauganash. "In the other towns it wasn't a joint venture. Candy Cane Lane had the most action. It was mind-boggling," he says. "The city should have paid them."

Old-time residents credit the success of Candy Cane Lane to the pride and camaraderie of the Schorsch Village community, which already had a long history of working together. Most of the homes were constructed by Village Home Builders Inc., which was owned by the six brothers of the Schorsch family, four of whom lived in the neighborhood. "There was a family spirit to begin with," remarks resident John Ryan. The Schorsch Village Improvement Association, the oldest community organization in the United States, had been sponsoring events from snow removal to bowling leagues since it was established in 1931.

In 1939 one of the brothers, Louis Schorsch, established an annual Lawn Prize. "All the lawns in the area were so well taken care of that it was a showplace during the summer months," noted village historian Mildred Losey. In 1940 members established a Christmas Lighting Display contest, awarding prizes to the winning homes. That year Natoma Avenue was the first in the area to begin the tradition of spelling "Merry Christmas" with a letter on every house. Radio stations broadcast news of the attraction, and sightseers were already beginning to tour the neighborhood.

During the war years the displays were discontinued to conserve energy, and the prize money was donated to the U.S.O. The Schorsch Village Improvement Association put its efforts into organizing Victory Gardens, paper drives and a chapter of the Red Cross, among other causes.

In 1945 the Christmas displays resumed and, as more houses were built in the neighborhood, the event grew too. "After World War II there was a sense of public-spiritedness and togetherness," remarks Steve Schorsch, son of one of the developers. So many homes were being decorated that the association expanded the number of awards with categories and block prizes. In 1953 each homeowner on School Street won a prize for the block's giant rooftop holiday greeting. In 1956 Candy Cane Lane was born, and the following year the remaining blocks joined the effort that flourished until the early seventies.

Many hoped that the magic of Candy Cane Lane would never end, but as the organizers grew older, many became less enthusiastic. "How sad it was when a few people stopped putting their letter up," Steve Schorsch remembers. "Some people fought vigorously to keep it going," recalls Mary Ann Ryan. "They would say to a new neighbor, 'I'll put your letter up for you.' Then I guess it just got to be too hard to keep it going."

During the 1973 energy crisis the streets went dark. When the fantasy lanes came alive again in 1974, it proved merely a swan song, as the decorations gradually diminished in the years to follow. "I guess the energy crisis was a good excuse for people to finally bow out," remarks Gus Guarino.

However…a peculiar thing has been happening in the nineties. Large candy canes have been appearing on the lawns of entire blocks throughout Chicagoland. And on every peppermint street, from Schiller Park to Arlington Heights to Des Plaines, there lives a mom or dad hoping to recreate the wonder of a magical childhood memory called Candy Cane Lane. ◆

❹ 6949 West Melrose Street

Though neighborhood streets discontinued their 20-year tradition of elaborate displays in the early seventies, Bob and Louise Frawley have continued to decorate their home in the style that won them numerous ribbons in the days of their own Choir Lane. "We haven't given up yet," Louise says proudly. "We also decorate our home for Valentine's Day, St. Patrick's Day and Easter."

Dec. 6–Jan. 6, 5:00PM–10:00PM. *From Harlem Ave., E on Belmont Ave. 4 bl., N on Sayre Ave. 1 bl., E on Melrose St. 1 bl.*

❺ 3934–6 North Mobile Avenue

"Could we borrow a cup of sugar? Oh, and would you mind if we wrapped the house—you know—like a giant Christmas present?"

To Marge Scott, sharing a duplex with neighbors Dan and Mary Ann Slomiany has posed more interesting questions than the usual next-door fare. Luckily, she shares their Christmas spirit and acknowledges that without her OK, a half-wrapped house just wouldn't have the same effect.

Dan Slomiany has been bundling the brick duplex in its 2' x 140' red vinyl ribbon since 1989 and has cracked ribs to prove it. Though his first designs blew off the house, he readily perfected his system

A giant red ribbon wraps the Slomiany/Scott home.

down to its present science. Masonry nails are driven two to three feet apart into permanent holes in the mortar through grommets installed in the ribbon. Barely-visible copper floral wire is criss-crossed over the top and edges of the ribbon to keep the wind from getting underneath. The 6-foot bow in the center is supported by chicken wire and a wooden base secured with nails and rope. Since devising this method Dan has been able to use the same ribbon year after year.

As one family who posed before the Slomiany home in their Sunday finery will attest, it is also worth getting out of your car to enjoy the other decorations that surround this giant present. Dan, owner of 2nd Dimension art studio in Oak Park, has encircled the front of the house with 20 colorful candy canes and two corner lampposts, which he cut from plywood and painted by hand. A whimsical band of toy soldiers marching through the snow is another delightful product of his handiwork, all of which is available for purchase in his shop. Though Dan takes credit for the house's exterior (with some help from Marge with the lights), he is proud to point out that Mary Ann does an elaborate and beautiful job on the interior as well. In all, they spend three to four weeks decorating, though the hazards of the outdoors sometimes lengthen Dan's task.

One year, while trying to hang lights on a front yard tree, Dan was repeatedly followed up the ladder

The Frawley display is the last from the Candy Cane Lane era.

by the tree's resentful resident—Ebenezer Squirrel. Dan had to spend hours running up and down the ladder distracting the critter with nut bribes so he could complete the decorating. Obviously, not every neighbor is as cooperative as Marge.

Dec. 15 – Jan. 6, 4:00PM – 11:30PM, (Christmas week) – 2:00AM. *From Narragansett Ave., E on Irving Park Rd. 2 bl., S on Merrimac Ave., Follow curve to Mobile Ave.*

The Patano Home

In the southern Italian town of Bari in 1972, Frank and Palma Patano celebrated a traditional Christmas of evening fireworks, visits to neighbors' manger scenes and midnight Mass. The season ended on January 6 when the witch Befana would deliver holiday gifts to the young children. Twenty years later at Christmastime, the front yard of their northwest-side home on North School Street was filled with blinking disco lights, moving figures and electronic music. It was obvious the Patanos had happily adjusted to American tradition.

Frank, a heating and air conditioning specialist, claimed his inspiration was Disneyland, but his obvious affection for his three children was a more likely source.

From the calm of a simple manger scene in Italy, Frank went on to create one of the most inventive and delightful Christmas houses in Chicago. Red, white and green disco lights outlined the house, dancing to-and-fro in the colors of the Italian flag. The Star of Bethlehem glistened at the peak of the roof with 270 alternating lights that Frank individually assembled in a three-month summer project. Old motors from his mother's garage and wire coat hangers were used to devise the mechanisms of a swirling Santa and Frosty. A pulley system and an old record player motor caused teddy bears to jump up and down in the windows, while big red velvet bows attached to the pulley's ropes went back and forth across the top. A manger scene with a rocking cradle and figures that turned in and out were his latest creation. They were the idea of his young son Dominic, who seemed to be following in his dad's imaginative footsteps.

Frank Patano passed away in March of 1994. Of all the homeowners contacted to be included in this book, he was the most excited. He said it was the most wonderful thing to happen to him all year. Somewhere, I hope he is seeing this in print. ◆

JOHN STEDRONSKY

The Patano home was decorated with an imaginative collection of blinking lights and moving figures, which Frank Patano devised from household items and old motors.

IRVING PARK

❻ 4659 North Knox Avenue

Kathy Benson and Joan Sagalow get additional mileage out of their yard ornaments by dressing them up for the holidays. A homemade three-car train, which holds potted flowers throughout the summer, becomes "Santa's Express" in December. It's packed with presents, covered with garlands and pulled by a pair of pink flamingos in boots and Santa hats.

The yard is also adorned with other homemade items, which Kathy and Joan built just for Christmas. Peppermint lollipops and candy canes surround the lawn, and a big smiling snowman stands amid thousands of twinkling lights.

When spring returns Frosty might look kinda' cute with a flowering plant hanging from his broomstick.

Dec. 15 – Jan. 6, Dusk – 1:00AM. *From Pulaski Rd., W on Lawrence Ave. 3/4 mi., S on Kenton Ave. 2 bl., W on Wilson Ave. 1 bl., N on Knox Ave. 1/2 bl.*

The colorful window painting of local artist Chuck Cox has added to the festive decor of Jacqueline's on North Broadway.

LAKE VIEW

❼ 3420 North Broadway

Jacqueline Flynn-Gagen likes to see the patrons of her friendly neighborhood bar in a festive mood, but Christmas, Halloween, Easter and St. Patrick's Day just don't provide enough occasions. Jacqueline adds to the gaiety with a "Christmas in July" celebration on the last Thursday of July, complete with lights, ornaments and a visit from Santa Claus. Each of the bar's events also includes a fundraiser for a local charity.

2nd week of Dec.–Jan. 6, (M–F) 7:00PM–2:00AM, (Sa) 9:00AM–3:00AM, (Su) 11:00AM–2:00AM. (312) 404-5149. *From Belmont Ave., N on Broadway 2 bl.*

**❽ Cornelia's Roosterant
748 West Cornelia Avenue**

The creative nature of "roosteranteur" Tom Talucci is not only reflected in the delicious variety of the restaurant's Italian menu, but in the playful adornments that decorate the building both inside and out.

In an effort "to bring smiles to people's faces," Tom built all the exterior decorations himself. A giant gingerbread man is cleverly outlined in a dotted icing of bathroom caulk and divided into sections to accommodate entry through the front door. Huge glimmering candy canes, colorful wreaths and funky stars, stapled full of tightly packed strands of lights, cover the facade.

Within the restaurant a Christmas tree "in the works," as Tom calls it, is tastefully trimmed with his own collection of antique trucks and marionettes. A ladder with toys on each step is set within the branches, giving the illusion that the tree is still being decorated.

For New Year's a colossal champagne bottle, fizzing with dry ice, covers the back wall. As might be expected, Tom doesn't miss an opportunity to dress the restaurant for other holidays as well. Cherubs fly from the ceiling for Valentine's Day. Easter finds rabbit ears popping out of planters, and Halloween brings out families of pumpkin heads.

Fri. after Thanksgiving–Jan. 7, (Su–T) Dusk–10:00PM, (F–Sa)–11:00PM. Restaurant hours: (T–Su) Dinner 5:30PM–?, (Sa–Su) Brunch, lunch 11:00AM–3:00PM. Appetizers $3–$6, Dinners $10–$14. Reservations recommended. Parking available. (312)248-8333. *From Addison St., S on Halsted St. 2 bl., E on Cornelia Ave.*

Decorations created by owner Tom Talucci make Cornelia's a delightful place to dine for the holidays.

For many years the statue of William Shakespeare at Lincoln Park West and Belden Avenue has been trimmed for the holidays with a changing annual theme by a phantom decorator.

❾ 4249 North Greenview Avenue

With simple decorations owner Doug Gillam elegantly adorns his north-side home. Forty-six window panes on the front porch are laden with artificial snow, as glistening icicles "drip" from above. The shrubbery shimmers with thousands of white lights, while the red bud tree maintains its hue drenched in a thousand bulbs of red.

A little boy once presented Doug with a crayon drawing of his decorated house. "I was real impressed," Doug said. "It made it all worthwhile."

Dec. 15–Jan. 1, Dusk–11:00PM. *From Ashland Ave., E on Montrose Ave. 1 bl., S on Greenview Ave. 2-1/2 bl.*

A Recipe for Artificial Snow

With an electric beater mix 5 parts white laundry powder with 1 part warm water until the mixture has the consistency of cake frosting. Mask window frames. Apply with a stiff paint brush. Dries in one hour.

---

❿ Flashy Trash
3524 North Halsted Street

This northside vintage clothing, jewelry and accessory boutique stocks an unusual array of fashions from turquoise leather chaps to Sonja Henie ice skating costumes. Yuletide wares include a wide assortment of Christmas pins and holiday fashions, available throughout the year.

For the past several seasons, festive clothing has been whimsically displayed in the front window, where owner Harold Mandel and manager Steven Kloepping have demonstrated their flair for the offbeat. Manikins have been dressed in green bell-bottoms for a mod Nutcracker theme, in mirrored gowns as ice princesses, and as formally-attired poinsettia plants standing in flower pots.

Dec. 10–Jan. 6, Window is lit until 2:00AM. Store hours: (M–Sa) 11:00AM–8:00PM, (Su) 12:00PM–6:00PM. (312)327–6900. *From Addison St., S on Halsted St. 1/2 bl.*

LINCOLN PARK

⓫ Lincoln Park Conservatory
2400 North Stockton Drive

Jingle bells, marble and Annette Hegg are among the varieties of red, pink and white poinsettias featured in the Chicago Park District's annual Christmas Show at Lincoln Park Conservatory. Many of the plants are grown in park greenhouses from cuttings made the previous year.

Sat. before Christmas–Sun. after New Year's, 9:00AM–5:00PM. Free admission. (312)742–7736. *From Lake Shore Dr., W on Fullerton Pkwy. 1/4 mi., S on Stockton Dr.*

LOGAN SQUARE

⓬ 2445 North Kimball Avenue

Though Helen and Phil Greco's graystone apartment building is trimmed with Santas, ribbons and thousands of lights, the nativity scene seems to get the most attention. People often stop and leave change near the statue of Baby Jesus. The Grecos use the money to light candles at their church.

One year a father and his three-year-old daughter came to their door. The little girl was upset because

The ceiling of Butch McGuire's whirls and spins with amusing mechanical displays.

it was very cold, and Jesus wasn't wearing a hat. The Grecos found an old scarf and wrapped it around Baby Jesus. The little girl smiled and happily went home.

Dec. 20–Jan. 6, 6:00PM–11:00PM. *From Kedzie Blvd., W on Fullerton Ave. 3 bl., N on Kimball Ave. 1/2 bl.*

⑬ 2656 West Logan Boulevard
(pictured on page 19–photo by Chris Cassidy)

In 1970 Frank Lopez began selling picture frames he had constructed from wire. His business gradually grew to become Chicago Wire Design Co., located on North Kimball Street. The plant now produces a large variety of wire products including Christmas decorations.

With the help of company employees, Lopez directs the holiday trimming of his elegant Victorian home with his wares. On the porch roof, Santa sits in a sleigh full of gifts pulled by a team of eight flying reindeer. From the room above, a golden star crowns a tree of lights. A towering garland Christmas tree stands in the front yard surrounded by a herd of deer and a heavenly trio performing with a trumpet

and glockenspiel. Around the yard, wrought iron fence posts are crowned with busts of reindeer dressed in red ribbons.

Twenty-one acrylic shadow boxes line the fence, each telling a unique Christmas tale. Lopez designed the scenes after receiving a box of miniature figures from a friend. He also designs all the wire decorations on his home. The handsome displays can be purchased from his company, allowing six months for production.

"I entertain myself and my neighbors by decorating the house," Lopez stated, already excited about his secret plans for the coming year.

Dec. 1–Jan. 6, 5:00PM–1:00AM. *From Fullerton Ave., N on Western Ave. 2 bl., W on Logan Blvd. 5 bl.*

NEAR NORTH SIDE

⑭ Butch McGuire's
20 West Division Street

The folks who crowd this north-side restaurant from morning to night throughout the holiday season will attest that dinner or drinks at Butch McGuire's is a real holiday adventure.

Both the restaurant and bar are packed with delightful mechanical displays swinging, twirling and rocking from nearly every inch of the ceiling and walls. Elves fly in a hot air balloon, glide from a swing and balance on a tightrope. Dolls in snow-suits whirl about on a merry-go-round and a snow saucer. Santa sits in an outhouse reading a magazine. Two smiling elves cuddle in the center of a spinning wreath. Stuffed animals, dolls, baseball bats, skates, horns and wagons hang from the ceiling, while over 100 train cars take an endless ride on four levels of track around the rooms. Santa Claus himself appears each evening.

According to owner Butch McGuire, the idea to decorate the restaurant began in 1962. "It was our second year of business. Our Italian porter, Mike, said, 'You've got no decorations up for Christmas. I'll bring you some Italian ones.' The decorations he brought were balloons with sparkles on them. We hung them around and everybody liked them. The customers brought in more things. We hung those around, and that's how it got started."

In his third year of decorating, Butch purchased five huge boxes of remnant store decorations from Marshall Field's at a bargain price. They sold him a second batch a few years later, as did Bonwit Teller. "Every year I'd say, 'Get more,'" Butch recalls.

One of his employees Thomas Sheu, currently owner of Christmas Inn in Lemont, assembled the unique mechanical decorations that became the highlight of the display. Butch now employs an artist to build new displays and repair old ones.

During the Christmas season Butch also hires a "train man," who fixes the broken cars and two of the 12 LGB engines per day. Many of the train cars have been donated by businesses, which display their logos on the sides of the cars.

The decorations reached their current proportion about 15 years ago. Since then the restaurant does as much business in December, as June, July and August combined. Though there is no more room to hang anything else, Butch continues to add to his collection. With a warehouse full of decorations, he is able to change the display every year.

Nov. 7–Jan. 15, (M–F) 10:00AM–4:00AM, (Sa) 9:30AM–5:00AM, (Su)–4:00AM Sandwich menu, $4–$8. Parking available at nearby city lots. (312)337–9080. *From Clark St., E on Division St. 1-1/2 bl.*

The Schreiber lawn is humorously adorned in pink kitsch.

NORWOOD PARK

⑮ 6014 North Nickerson Avenue

Magnolia trees are normally at their loveliest in early spring, flowering with abundant pink petals for a few glorious days. But when Gertrude Miller's magnolia loses its bloom, neighbor Sandra Abrajano is quick to restore its glory with a few decorations of her own.

The tree comes to life at Christmastime with giant red bulbs and inflatable ornaments of Santa and cartoon characters. It is decorated again at Valentine's Day, St. Patrick's Day and Easter. Sandra boasts, "It's the most popular magnolia on the northwest side."

Dec. 15–Jan. 1, 5:00PM–10:00PM. *From Harlem Ave., SE on Northwest Hwy. 2 bl., W on Sayre Ave. (Nickerson Ave.) 2 bl.*

⑯ 6035 North Nickerson Avenue

Bert and Corrine Schreiber's tropical holiday party display features a bit of humorous kitsch, complete with tacky guests, a pink foil Christmas tree and plastic pink flamingos. A favorite of their daughter, Beth, the exotic bird is found in many forms throughout the house. Several even appeared at Beth's wedding, where they danced with the brides-maids, who were dressed in flamingo pink.

Dec. 7–Jan. 14, Day and night. *From Harlem Ave., SE on Northwest Hwy. 2 bl., W on Sayre Ave. (Nickerson Ave.) 2 bl.*

🅱 5340 North Oketo Avenue

"I've got a thing about not throwing away lights," homeowner Rick Hoehn confesses. "I waste hours just to save a $3 strand." His wife, Marge, joins in the tedious task weeks before Christmas, searching for culprit bulbs that cause entire sets to go black.

A 5-foot artificial wreath, which Rick lavishly drenched in nearly 600 green lights, is particularly difficult to repair, since many of the sockets are hidden within the needled branches. But Rick is no stranger to removing the bulbs from these strands. He created them himself by replacing the bulbs in multicolored sets with green bulbs from others. Clusters of red bulbs were added to look like holly berries. "I haven't seen another wreath like it," said Rick. "I don't think anyone else would want to spend the time."

Dec. 15–Jan. 6, 3:00PM–12:30AM. *From Harlem Ave., W on Foster Ave. 1 bl., N on Oketo Ave. 1-1/2 bl.*

🅱 5662 and 5668 North Olcott Avenue

Among the three Christoffel sons, yuletide decorating has become a source of lighthearted sibling rivalry. "We have our own little wars," middle brother Bill jokes. He admits his pop-up Santa at 317 North Harding Avenue in Des Plaines gives him an electronic edge, but chides, "They try to beat me by sheer quantity." Gary, the oldest, lives with his parents at 5662 Olcott. Youngest brother, Brian, lives next door at 5668 with his wife and children.

A towering flagpole Christmas tree in Brian's backyard, which can be seen by motorists on the Kennedy Expressway, gives Bill a run for his money. Above the noise of the traffic, Christmas carols chime from Brian's porch throughout the evening. Gary and Brian's lights and illuminated figurines seem to shine twice as brightly on their adjacent matching Cape Cod homes. The two brothers also have the advantage of being able to suspend Santa and his reindeer between their neighboring roof peaks.

Mrs. Christoffel admits she and her husband may have instigated their sons' hobby by decorating when they were younger. "But not to this extent," she adds.

Meanwhile, the three men continue to exchange huge plastic candy canes and gingerbread men as Christmas gifts. After all, boys will be boys.

Dec. 11–Jan. 8, Dusk–11:00PM. *From Higgins Rd., N on Harlem Ave. 1 bl., W on Bryn Mawr Ave. 3 bl., N on Osceola Ave. 1 bl., W on Olcott Ave. 1/2 bl.*

The adjacent Christoffel homes light up Olcott Avenue.

O'HARE

⑲ 4632 North Maria Court

The precision crafting of the unique homemade display that adorns this northwest-side home unmistakably reveals the occupation of its owner.

Garland hangs in uniform curves about the eaves. Santa's reindeer descend in perfect intervals to the lawn. The yard is surrounded by the symmetrical curves of a golden fence crowned with fleur-de-lis. The walkway is enclosed in a series of glowing Gothic arches. "Lady of Beauty," the statue at the center of the display, is encircled with a wreath of identically-curved flowerets. The "Merry Christmas" sign that sparkles over the garage door is replaced with "Happy New Year" on December 26, followed by "Peace on Earth" when the holidays are through.

Homeowner Antonio Samiotakis is none other than a mechanical engineer. Being a man of his craft he applies the same attention to detail to his Christmas display as he does to the electroplating equipment he manufactures in his plant.

Making use of his shop, Antonio uses steel rods and a bender to form the shapes for his decorations. After welding the pieces together, he dips the figures in vinyl coating to prevent rust. The rods are then wrapped in garland.

Antonio also designed a efficient metal stand to keep his plastic figurines erect. And to hold his lights in place he designed a form for an adjustable and removable metal clip. Over a three year period his wife, Vasiliki, used the form to bend 7,000 clips by hand. "With the clips I can adjust the lights to go in any direction," he demonstrates.

His meticulous display is not only an awesome delight to all who pass, but a holiday tribute to mechanical engineering.

Thanksgiving weekend–Jan.1, 6:00PM–11:00PM.
From Cumberland Ave., W on Lawrence Ave. 2 bl., S on Maria Ct. 1-1/2 bl.

SAUGANASH

⑳ A Post-War Holiday Showcase

Sauganash was known for its multitude of decorated homes when the neighboring Lincolnwood Towers area, now more popular for its displays, was still a glint in a developer's eye.

In the late forties and early fifties the end of the war and the improving economy gave cause for celebration. In Sauganash, as in other neighborhoods, there was a strong sense of community. But in this neighborhood nearly every household added to the gay mood by decorating their homes with lights and homemade creations at Christmastime.

Before the days of plastic figurines, one owner

Santa keeps everyone cheery outside the Stryganek's home.

The Samiotakis display reveals the owner's skill as an engineer.

constructed a wreath around his entire house, and another wrapped his home in ribbons. Neighbors pitched in to trim the homes of the elderly who were unable to do it for themselves. The area was the Christmas showplace of the north side. To accommodate the heavy traffic, the city of Chicago even made all the streets one way during the holiday season.

Though Sauganash residents do not decorate to the degree they had in years past or as elaborately as in Lincolnwood, there are still many well-lit homes. One old-time resident speculated, "I think we're bringing that part back as we develop more community spirit and get everyone working together."
From Bryn Mawr Ave., N to Devon Ave., and from Cicero Ave., E to the C&NW tracks.

UPTOWN

㉑ 4545 North Greenview Avenue

Uptown residents Judy and Casey Stryganek are former adagio acrobats, who performed their stunts on the midway at Chicago's Riverview Amusement Park for 13 years. The couple still enjoys putting on a good show. However, their feats are now more decorative in nature.

During the holidays their front yard is brimming with lights, a nativity scene, a toy train, and animated angels. Encased in an acrylic box, a 50-year-old Santa with bushy eyebrows, rosy cheeks and a cocked cap seems to draw the most attention.

One evening Judy heard two cars collide out front. The drivers jumped into the street and began arguing loudly. One man's small child, begging to see Santa, feverishly tugged at his father's pants. Judy approached the men and scolded, "Santa doesn't want to hear this. Don't argue in front of Santa."

As though dusted by the horn of Dickens' Ghost of Christmas Present, the men suddenly ceased arguing. The first driver quietly got in his car and drove away. The second man happily took his son to see the Stryganek's Santa. And Judy returned to the house laughing, "Our decorations are so good they're causing accidents."

She didn't have the heart to pack Santa away that year. He stood by the bar until the following Christmas with a well-deserved drink in his hand.
Dec. 10 – Jan. 6, Dusk – 2:00AM. *From Ashland Ave., E on Montrose Ave. 1 bl., N on Greenview Ave. 1-1/2 bl.*

Mementos of Candy Cane Lane decorate the Basica lawn.

CHRIS CASSIDY

WEST RIDGE

㉒ 5853 North Rockwell Street

If your nostalgic trips down Memory Lane include Candy Cane Lane, Reindeer Lane and Poinsettia Lane of the fifties and sixties, you will surely enjoy reminiscing at the home of Wayne Basica. Since 1978 he has been collecting Christmas memorabilia from the once-famous northwest-side neighborhood.

The holiday lanes have always been one of Wayne's favorite childhood memories. He recalls excitedly walking up and down the brightly-lit streets, while residents passed out cookies and chocolates to passersby. He knew then he would do the same when he got his own house.

But years later he found that the same plastic figurines he remembered as a child were impossible to buy new, so he advertised in the former neighborhood of Candy Cane Lane for old decorations. His home now bears the delightful results.

The giant ornaments hanging from the eaves, the 6-foot lampposts, the jolly Santas, the lighted star, and Pixie and Dixie elves are all remnants of the famous neighborhood. Three of the roof reindeer are from one family and four from another. Though he has acquired a few too many lampposts, he would still be interested in finding the giant candy canes and reindeer from the lanes so named. He

sometimes wonders if the huge figurines only existed in his imagination as a boy.

Wayne decorates identically every year to make his task easier. He hangs the lights from the eaves, and then goes from one side of the house to the other securing the decorations. He makes sure everything is sturdy, so his only repairs are bulb replacements. He uses 15 to 25-watt bulbs in his figurines, after lighting up the entire block one year with 75-watt illumination. In all, it's a 30 to 40-hour job.

Neighborhood children gleefully watch the decorations go up. Strangers bring gifts and cards of thanks. Even vandals who stole his decorations returned them the next day out of guilt. Wayne Basica has truly re-created the joys of Christmas for many, as Candy Cane Lane once did for him.

Friday after Thanksgiving–Jan. 10, Dusk–11:00PM. *From Western Ave., W on Peterson Ave. 4 bl., S on Rockwell St. 1-1/2 bl.*

㉓ Fluky's Restaurant
6821 North Western Avenue

Abe "Fluky" Drexler opened his first hot dog stand at the corner of Maxwell and Halsted streets in 1929. He probably never imagined that a generation later his son, Jack, would carry on his legacy with three restaurants bearing his nickname. Nor could Jack have realized, when he took over the business in 1964, that the self-service restaurants would become animated holiday attractions.

From one corner of the Western Avenue eatery, Santa and a stow-away mouse look back and forth while being pulled by prancing reindeer in a flying sleigh. A rabbi leans and prays before a 12-foot replica of the Wailing Wall. A band of gnomes decorates trees, bushes and fences with twinkling lights. A cheery snowman nods, while his snowwife playfully shakes her head, and snowflakes dance up and down across the ceiling. "We don't believe in anything sitting still," Jack explains.

The restaurant's other locations in Northbrook and Niles are also decorated with animated figures. The Niles location even has a Christmas tree lot.

Thanksgiving–Jan. 1, (Su–Th) 6:00AM–10:30PM, (F–Sa)–11:00PM. Breakfast, sandwich, salad menu. $3–$5. (312)274–3652. *From Pratt Ave., N on Western Ave. 1/2 bl.*

Chapter 3

CHICAGO-SOUTH

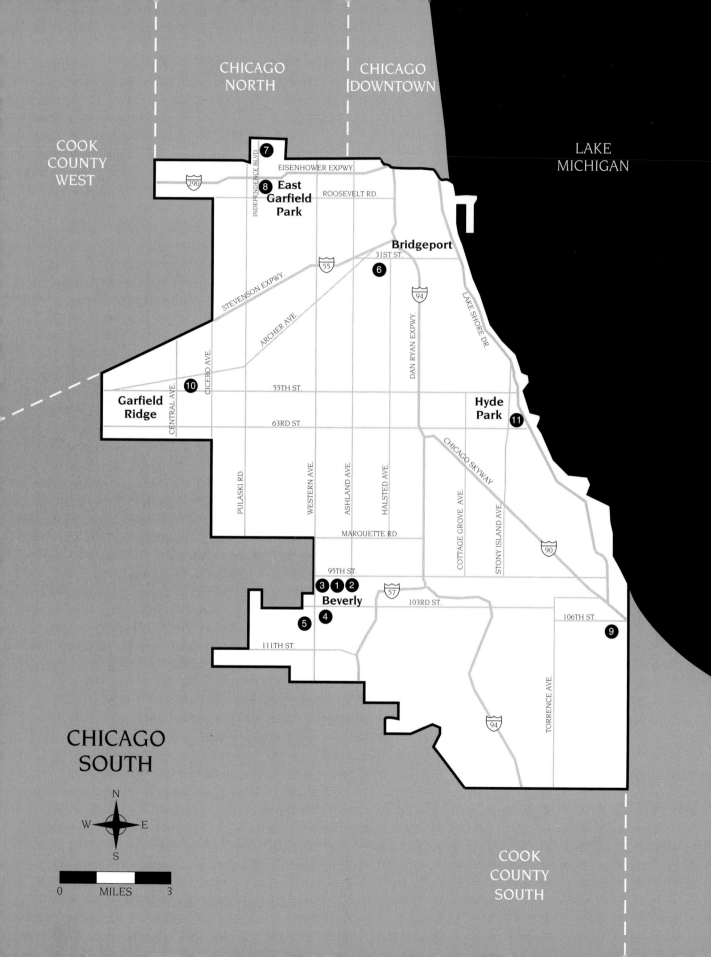

CHICAGO
SOUTH

CHICAGO
NORTH

CHICAGO
DOWNTOWN

COOK
COUNTY
WEST

LAKE
MICHIGAN

COOK
COUNTY
SOUTH

East
Garfield
Park

Bridgeport

Garfield
Ridge

Hyde
Park

Beverly

EISENHOWER EXPWY.

ROOSEVELT RD.

31ST ST.

STEVENSON EXPWY.

ARCHER AVE.

55TH ST.

63RD ST.

MARQUETTE RD.

95TH ST.

103RD ST.

106TH ST.

111TH ST.

INDEPENDENCE BLVD.

CENTRAL AVE.

CICERO AVE.

PULASKI RD.

WESTERN AVE.

ASHLAND AVE.

HALSTED AVE.

DAN RYAN EXPWY.

LAKE SHORE DR.

CHICAGO SKYWAY

COTTAGE GROVE AVE.

STONY ISLAND AVE.

TORRENCE AVE.

290

55

94

90

57

94

N
W   E
S

0   MILES   3

BEVERLY

❶ 9800 South Leavitt Street

Ed Laski has been adding decorations to his Beverly display since 1988. He outlines the entire Dutch colonial frame in multicolored C-9 bulbs, trims the windows and bushes in Italian lights, spotlights his homemade wooden figurines, illuminates his assorted plastic decorations, and animates his window displays. The electric bill increases nearly $200 for the season.

In 1992 when the display first reached this well-lit dimension, the fuse box in the basement began to hum. Ed's wife, Sue, would turn off lights in the house each evening until the noise stopped.

One night Ed found the basement full of smoke. Suspecting it was an electrical problem, he dashed to the fuse box. It was glowing red. Immediately he shut off all the breakers and called an electrician. "He said my main breaker had melted in the open position and that if I hadn't shut down all the breakers, the house would have burned down," Ed recalled.

Though the following day was Sunday, he hired two electricians to completely redo the circuits. Twelve hours later, when the job was complete, the electricians assured Ed that everything was fine and that it would even be ok to add more lights. Sue sighed, "That's the worst thing you could have said to him."

Dec. 10–Jan. 6, 5:00PM–12:00AM. *From Western Ave., E on 95th St. 4 bl., S on Leavitt St. 3 bl.*

The Laski's well-lit home sparkles safely.

JOHN REED

The Beverly home of Concetta and John Fessett is elegantly trimmed for the Christmas season. Many decorated homes can still be found in this area, once well-known for its elaborate displays.

❷ 9757 Longwood Drive

Beverly's hill-top mansions and classic homes on winding tree-lined streets have earned the area recognition as the nation's largest urban historic district. A drive through the neighborhood during the holidays provides a view of many lovely decorations as well as a tour of turn-of-the-century architecture.

Some of the handsomest dwellings can be found on Longwood Drive, which runs along Blue Island Ridge the highest elevation in Chicago. A favorite decorated home on this historic road is the colonial beauty at the corner of 98th Street, trimmed by owners Concetta and John Fessett.

In keeping with the simple elegance of its white clapboards and black shutters, the home is adorned with 10,000 Italian white lights nestled in fragrant wreaths and garlands of balsam fir and colored with 2,000 homemade red velvet bows.

Beneath the columned portico sits a decorated chair. According to Italian tradition, it is a sign of a warm welcome to invited guests for Christmas dinner.

Dec. 20–Jan. 15, Day and night. *From Western Ave., E on 95th St. 3/4 mi., S on Longwood Dr. 3 bl.*

❸ 9822 South Oakley Avenue

Jon Gausselin enjoys Christmas so much, he's willing to climb up on his snowy roof and hang out of second-story windows to prepare his house for the occasion.

A landscaper by trade, he does an artful job of trimming his Georgian home. Thousands of white Italian lights twinkle from hanging swags, evergreen wreaths, sculptured bushes and a 50-foot parkway tree.

Giant bows of red lights glisten from the shutters, while smaller velvet versions accent boughs of greenery. Red bows are also tied about the necks of three delightful snow people, which the family acquired from an old liquor store display.

Most recently Jon has created shadow boxes with animated scenes of children decorating a tree, elves working in their toy shop and a Victorian couple singing carols. He bolts the wooden boxes into anchors' which are permanently installed in the house's brick exterior.

A 5-foot Santa with his bag full of toys crowns the display as it balances on the rooftop. At the start of the holidays, snow-covered shingles are no obstacle to Jon where Santa's concerned. But after the season, a slippery roof is an adequate excuse to keep the old elf perched well beyond his days. Last year Jon lit Santa one last time on Easter Sunday before climbing up on the snowless roof to take him down.

Dec. 5 – Jan. 5, 5:00PM – 9:00PM. *From Western Ave., E on 95th St. 2 bl., S on Oakley Ave. 3-1/2 bl.*

DAVE IRELAND

A trio of snow people greet visitors at 9822 South Oakley.

❹ 10500 South Oakley Avenue

When frost marks the end of the fall planting season and snow settles on wilting flower beds once lush with blooms, what better activity for an inveterate gardener than decorating for the holidays. And…when the green thumb belongs to Chicago's "Gardener of the Year," you can be certain those holiday decorations will be more than a Polk Brothers' Santa and a single string of lights. Such is the story at the Beverly home of Patrick Showalter, winner of the 1991 gardening title, and his proud wife, LaVerne.

What began with a few strands of lights 25 years ago has multiplied as regularly as their 6,000 perennial bulbs. The Showalters' two-story Tudor home is now elegantly decorated with nearly 10,000 colored Italian lights. Patrick directs the three-day operation with help from four workmen and a cherry-picking truck.

Garland entwined with lights and accented with flowing red velvet ribbons outlines the eaves, drapes the windows, and arches the entryway. Four-foot

---

A Landscaper's Tip for Hanging Treetop Lights

A nail partially pounded into the side of a 1"x 1" wooden pole is recommended by landscaper Jon Gausselin as a tool for hanging light strands on tree branches that are out of reach. As the tree grows, the pole can be extended by nailing additional 1x1s to the bottom section of the original pole. Jon has successfully used poles as long as 40 feet to trim the trees for his own display.

evergreen wreaths encircle the bay window and grace the peaks. Thousands of glistening lights color every bush and tree, where over 100 varieties of flowers had painted the landscape only months before.

Inside their home, the Showalters have nine Christmas trees. Each of their nine children is assigned a tree under which their gifts are placed. With the help of friends LaVerne enjoys decorating the silk trees with unique themes. She even matched the wrapping paper to the tree's color scheme.

In the living room is a Victorian tree of lavish pinks. A Santa Claus tree in the den is surrounded by more Santas on every shelf. A tree of crystal adorns the dining room, and a Mickey Mouse tree stands in a nearby alcove. The bedrooms have trees of pastel bows, golden bulbs and lighted hearts. The bathroom is home to a patriotic tree of wooden flags, stars and Uncle Sams, while a tree of homemade ornaments is assigned to the basement. Even the family pet, a Dalmatian named Cricket, is decorated with a red bow about his neck. **Thanksgiving weekend–Jan. 6, Day and night.** *From Western Ave., E on 103rd 2 bl., S on Oakley Ave. 2 bl.*

Cork and Kerry's holiday mice have donned their gay apparel for a cheesy feast.

⑤ Cork and Kerry Tavern
10614 South Western Avenue

On the evening of the Friday after Thanksgiving, Chad and Scott Weiler dim the lights in their Morgan Park tavern and offer a holiday toast in thanks to their loyal patrons. When the ceremonial switch is flipped, nearly 15,000 lights glisten from every corner of the room, while over 30 mechanical displays twirl and rock on the ceilings and walls.

The "Morgan Park Ski Lift" transports snowmen back and forth above the bar. The "Double A Choo-Choo" travels in a figure-eight around the back room. Snow babies play in a wintery scene and elves saw and hammer to build toys.

Chad and Scott have acquired over 80 boxes of decorations for their tavern from garage sales and flea markets. The two brothers build all the mechanical displays themselves. Chad learned many of his techniques while employed for eight years at Butch McGuire's, an elaborately decorated restaurant/bar on the city's north side.

In addition to the atmosphere, the Cork and Kerry features a variety of "winter warmers," including Irish coffee and cocoa with peppermint schnapps. Red grenadine is a favorite non-alcoholic holiday beverage for kids, who are welcome to see the decorations with their parents before 5:00PM and receive a free candy cane.

Fri. after Thanksgiving–Jan. 6, (M–F) 2:00PM–2:00AM, (Sa–Su) 12:00PM–12:00AM. (312) 445–CORK. *From 111th St., N on Western Ave. 1/2 mi.*

JOHN REED
Visitors to this lovely Beverly home may find owners LaVerne and Patrick Showalter waving in the window or handing out candy canes.

The proud residents of West Flournoy Street stand in the glow of a canopy of lights that decorate both sides of their entire block.

BRIDGEPORT

❻ 1035 and 1041 West 34th Place
(pictured on page 35)

The Arizzis, the Myers, and the Guerreros were next-door neighbors who picnicked together in the summer and decorated together in the winter. On the Friday after Thanksgiving they started their weekend decorating task by sharing a warm potluck dinner. Together they trimmed their houses, front yards and cyclone fences with Italian lights, homemade wreaths and illuminated figurines.

When the Myers and the Guerreros filled their parkway trees with white lights, Mario Arizzi, whose front yard was treeless, wanted to keep the houses uniform. He built a tree from dead branches, conduit and duct tape and happily trimmed it to match.

The Myers have now moved away, but the Arizzis and the Guerreros hope that by surrounding their new neighbors with decorations, they can entice them to join the party.

Sun. after Thanksgiving–Jan.15, 4:00PM–11:30PM.
From 31st St., S on Halsted St. 1/2 mi., W on 34th Pl. 2 bl.

EAST GARFIELD PARK

❼ Garfield Park Conservatory
300 North Central Park Boulevard

A paradise of over 4,000 poinsettias and other wintery blooms are featured in the Garfield Park Annual Christmas Flower Show. The lustrous holiday plant is grown by staff floriculturists from cuttings in several varieties.

In the midst of a blustery Chicago winter, the conservatory is a wonderful place to escape for an early breath of spring.

Sat before Christmas–Sun. after New Year's, 9:00AM–5:00PM. Free admission. (312)746–5100.
From the Eisenhower Expwy. (I-290), N on Independence Blvd. 1 mi., E on Lake St. 1/4 mi., N on Central Park Blvd.

❽ 3300 Block of West Flournoy Street

In the midst of the crime-ridden west side, the 3300 block of Flournoy lights up the neighborhood as a gleaming sign of hope. From the second floor of all the block's 36 two-flats residents hang strands of colored lights that stretch across the sidewalks to the parkway trees. Many decorate their homes as well.

It's a magical experience to walk down the street under the sparkling canopy. Most of the residents come out each night to enjoy the glow. They are often stopped by passing motorists who ask how they are able to achieve such spirit in an area that has the highest crime rate in the city.

The effort began in 1973 when a group of residents, who "just wanted to have a nice neighborhood," joined together and formed the 3300 West Flournoy Block Club. The club's first accomplishment was having new sidewalks installed. The group went on to sponsor an annual tea, a Saturday clean-up program, a 4th-of-July children's party, numerous cook-outs and a children's activity program. They established rules to discourage car maintenance on the street and began a program to deliver fruit to the children of Flournoy on Christmas.

Most recently the group purchased new sod for all the parkways, using treasury money collected from their $5 monthly dues. "Some people didn't want the sod, but when the truck got here everybody wanted it. People just got out there, dug it up and put it down," said Eli Blair, president of the club for the past 20 years.

The same spirit initiated the Christmas lighting idea in 1974. "We all got together and decided we'd do this, and we just went on and did it," the no-nonsense block president added.

At first a committee of men drilled screws into the face of each building and hung lights from one side of the street to the other. After a few years the residents decided they wanted to decorate their own homes. With many of the same families living on the block, 100 percent of the homeowners still participate today.

"We had so much traffic through here this past Christmas you'd think it was the expressway," Blair said proudly. When passersby ask how they do it Blair responds, "You get the people together, and you just get out there and start working." Drivers tell him, "It's the best looking block in the city." And in many ways, that's really true.

Dec. 10–Jan. 1, 7:00PM–12:00AM. <u>Note</u>: It is advisable to visit this display only if you are familiar with the neighborhood. *From the Eisenhower Expwy. (I-290), S on Independence Blvd., E on Harrison St. 4 bl., S on Homan Ave. 1 bl., E on Flournoy St.*

EAST SIDE

❾ 10741 Avenue L

One summer in the midst of housecleaning, Audrey Wilocki came across a pile of old Christmas cards. A cute one with four elves, matching the number of people in her family at the time, was all the excuse she needed to stop cleaning and turn her energies to a more creative task.

She enlarged the figures freehand. Her husband, Jim, cut them out of plywood, and she painted them. The following Christmas Audrey, Mike, Jim and Melissa Elf decorated the front lawn.

The birth of their youngest child, Stacey, and an extended family of nieces and nephews prompted Audrey to add 17 gingerbread people around the front window—one for each child.

Over the years the small front yard and face of the Wilocki's Georgian home have become delightfully crowded with homemade replicas of cartoon figures dressed for the holidays—proving that it's much more fun to let the vacuuming wait.

Dec. 5–Jan. 3, 5:00PM–10:30PM. *From Torrence Ave., E on 106th St. 1 mi., S on Avenue L 1-1/2 bl.*

Santa's sleigh parks in a holiday garden of poinsettias and evergreens at the Garfield Park Conservatory.

GARFIELD RIDGE

⑩ 5554 West 54th Street

Jimmy and Syrena Ficaro, ages eight and ten, are two very lucky children when Christmas rolls around. They tell their dad what is the "hottest thing out," and he builds a holiday version to decorate the front lawn. With a new addition to the collection each year, the display now includes dozens of figures from fairyland castles to dinosaurs.

James Sr. freehands the cartoons onto plywood from pictures on glassware, matchbooks, paper cups or anyplace else they appear. The figures are then cut out with a handheld jigsaw.

Dad lets Jimmy, Syrena and Mom help with the painting. He makes it easy by labeling the figures like a paint-by-number set. When the coloring is complete, James outlines everything with markers.

The whole family helps put up the display, and Jimmy and Syrena get to turn on the lights. It's their job to turn them on and off all season. Sometimes they stay on all day.

Fri. after Thanksgiving–Jan.1, Dusk–Dawn. *From Archer Ave., S on Central Ave. 1 bl., E on 54th St.*

COURTESY OF THE MUSEUM OF SCIENCE AND INDUSTRY

Holiday trees from around the world decorate the science museum.

HYDE PARK

⑪ The Museum of Science and Industry 57th Street and Lake Shore Drive

Chicago is a town of many cultures and holiday traditions, which the Museum of Science and Industry has been celebrating since 1941 in an exhibit entitled "Christmas Around the World."

Three crèches and 42 trees decorated by various ethnic community groups are displayed throughout the museum. A tree from Wales is adorned with Welsh "love spoons" which suitors traditionally carve upon proposing marriage, a Native American tree is trimmed by the young and old of 30 tribes with handmade natural ornaments, and a Japanese tree is decorated with the intricately folded figures of origami, to name but a few.

Throughout the holiday weekends, performers from many of the countries entertain with traditional yuletide songs and dances. In 1994 the museum added the "Holidays of Light," an exhibit depicting festive traditions of cultures that don't celebrate Christmas.

Fri. before Thanksgiving–Mon. after Jan.1, (M–F) 9:30AM–4:00PM, (Sa–Su) 9:30AM–5:30PM. Admission fee. (312)684–1414. *From Lake Shore Dr., W on 57th St.*

Ficaro's choirs also decorate the 83rd St. toll plaza on I-294.

Chapter 4

COOK COUNTY–NORTH

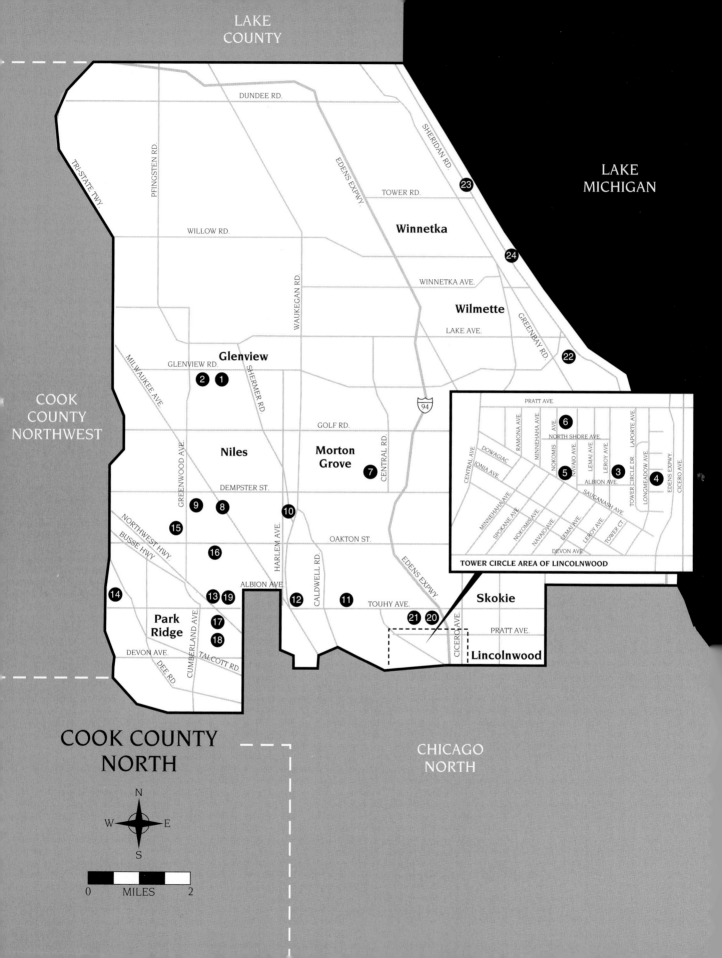

LAKE
COUNTY

LAKE
MICHIGAN

DUNDEE RD.

PFINGSTEN RD.

TRI-STATE TWY.

SHERIDAN RD.

EDENS EXPWY.

TOWER RD.

㉓

WILLOW RD.

Winnetka

WAUKEGAN RD.

㉔

WINNETKA AVE.

Wilmette

LAKE AVE.

GREENBAY RD.

㉒

Glenview

GLENVIEW RD.

MILWAUKEE AVE.

SHERMER RD.

❷ ❶

COOK
COUNTY
NORTHWEST

GOLF RD.

Niles

**Morton
Grove**

CENTRAL RD.

❼

GREENWOOD AVE.

DEMPSTER ST.

❾ ❽

❿

HARLEM AVE.

⓯

NORTHWEST HWY.

BUSSE HWY.

⓰

OAKTON ST.

CALDWELL RD.

EDENS EXPWY.

ALBION AVE.

⓭ ⓳

⓬

⓫

TOUHY AVE.

Skokie

⓮

❶⑦

**Park
Ridge**

CUMBERLAND AVE.

⓲

㉑ ⓴

CICERO AVE.

PRATT AVE.

DEVON AVE.

TALCOTT RD.

DEE RD.

Lincolnwood

PRATT AVE.

RAMONA AVE.

MINNEHAHA AVE.

NOKOMIS AVE.

❻

NORTH SHORE AVE.

LAPORTE AVE.

CENTRAL AVE.

DOWAGIAC

IONIA AVE.

NOKOMIS

NAVAJO AVE.

❺

LEMAI AVE.

LEROY AVE.

❸

TOWER CIRCLE DR.

LONGMEADOW AVE.

CICERO AVE.

ALBION AVE.

❹

EDENS EXPWY.

MINNEHAHA AVE.

SPOKANE AVE.

NOKOMIS AVE.

NAVAJO AVE.

LEMAI AVE.

SAUGANASH AVE.

LEROY AVE.

TOWER CT.

DEVON AVE.

TOWER CIRCLE AREA OF LINCOLNWOOD

**COOK COUNTY
NORTH**

CHICAGO
NORTH

N
W ✦ E
S

0 MILES 2

EVANSTON

Rudolph's Home

From the fifties through the seventies the May family's front lawn was the holiday home of the season's most popular reindeer. With a red nose visible from a block away the life-size papier maché Rudolph stood mid-air with reins of white lights leading his way to the rooftop. When the family moved from their Evanston home on Hamlin to Avers Avenue near Church Street, the lovable deer came too, like one of the family. And no wonder—the father of the household was no other than Robert L. May, the creator of Rudolph, the Red-Nosed Reindeer.

A copywriter for Montgomery Ward & Co., Mr. May was known for his humorous puns and poetry written for office parties. As a lark he was asked to write a holiday story to be used as a toy department give-away.

He began writing about a reindeer, who at first had bright eyes instead of a shiny nose and was named Rollo and then Reginald before becoming Rudolph. May would read the tale to his daughter and her friends to get their reaction.

The initial story was rejected by May's boss, who felt that the red nose would be associated with alcoholism and inappropriate for Christmas. Determined, May headed for Lincoln Park Zoo to recreate his character from live models. With the help of the company art department he was able to create a reindeer that pleased enough Ward executives to sway his boss.

May's poem with illustrations by staff artist Denver Gillen was printed in 1939 as a 32-page booklet and given to 2.4 million children. In 1946, after World War II, the booklet was reprinted and 3.6 million copies were distributed.

Ward's then felt that Rudolph had played out its usefulness, but Robert May recognized the enormous popularity his reindeer had gained. He requested ownership of the copyright, which was granted, and took a seven-year leave of absence to manage Rudolph. The character that earned him a byline and a Christmas bonus its first year provided a business opportunity that is still helping to support May's family today.

The story has sold millions of copies in over 20 languages. The song "Rudolph, the Red-Nosed Reindeer," written by May's brother-in-law, Johnny Marks, and recorded by Gene Autry in 1949, not only was a best-seller but forever engraved the story of

Creator Robert L. May attaches the famous glowing red nose to his front yard Rudolph with daughters Betsy and Martha at his side. (circa 1964)

Rudolph in children's minds. The 1964 television special continues to delight audiences yearly. May's six children operate the Robert L. May Company to satisfy the demand for licensed Rudolph products from stuffed animals to boxer shorts in the United States, Japan, New Zealand, Australia and the UK.

Robert May, an unassuming man who eventually returned to his job at Montgomery Ward's, considered the success of Rudolph to be good luck and an amazing blessing. Recalls his daughter Elizabeth, "You could tell it thrilled him every year when people would pay attention to Rudolph. He would really feel proud and special at Christmastime."

He enjoyed sharing his pride each season by mailing hundreds of reindeer Christmas cards with red noses individually hand-colored by his children. During the holidays a parade of cars would pass to view Rudolph at the May home. Children would have their pictures taken on Rudolph's back, and carolers would come to sing the famous deer's theme song.

After Robert May's death in 1976, the family donated the life-size Rudolph to May's alma mater, Dartmouth College, where it is displayed with other Rudolph memorabilia in proud memory of a loving man who gave a simple gift to the children of the world.

This display is now at Dartmouth College in Hanover, New Hampshire.

A homemade collapsible Christmas tree made of PVC pipe glows amid dozens of lit figurines and thousands of lights that decorate the flowerbeds of the Olsowski home.

GLENVIEW

❶ 2557 Glenview Road

It's a little rough being a pine tree on the lawn of admitted yuletide fanatics Pam and Dick Dorband, but never dull. At Christmastime the tree and the neighboring shrubbery are covered with thousands of white Italian lights in an annual human ritual all evergreen trees have come to accept. But, when it alone is draped in hearts and red and white lights for Valentine's Day, green derbies and matching lights for St. Patrick's Day, fluorescent eggs and lighted carrots for Easter, flags and star-covered garlands for the 4th of July, and witches and vampires for Halloween…a self-respecting evergreen may be tempted to uproot.

But, alas, faith was restored at the beginning of one school year when Dick rejected Pam's plan to trim the boughs with lunch boxes, rulers and crayons. After all, even a tree needs time to relax before the holidays.

Dec.1–Jan.1, 4:30PM–12:00AM. *From Shermer Rd., W on Glenview Rd. 1/4 mi.*

❷ 940 Huber Lane

The sprawling front yard of this brick ranch home with its manicured shrubs and landscaped flower beds provides the perfect setting for a Christmas wonderland, and homeowners Lee and Grace Olsowski certainly do it proud.

Brightly-lit peppermint canes, holiday candles and lollipops march in alternation around the circular drive. Frosty the Snowman and his wife and kids fill center stage, while elves, Santas, gingerbread men, reindeer and penguins appear among bushes and trees that dance with over 8,000 lights.

Dec.10–Jan.1, Dusk–1:00AM. *From Greenwood Ave., E on Glenview Rd. 4 bl., S on Huber Ln.*

LINCOLNWOOD

Long-time residents of the Lincolnwood Towers neighborhood in this north-side suburb recall area homeowners drawing crowds of visitors to their holiday displays clear back to the 1950s.

Jim and Irene Archambault on LeMai Avenue created the most popular attraction by disguising their two-car garage as a manger. The outside of the garage was camouflaged with boughs. Life-size statues of the Holy Family shared the cave-like interior with live sheep, a rooster and a donkey, which the couple brought from their Wisconsin farm. The attraction drew such large crowds that businessman and Lincolnwood neighbor Andy Frain offered to send ushers.

On Nokomis Avenue, Mary Kriengberg decorated her yard with a magnificent choir of 16 boys in white gowns, a gilded pipe organ surrounded by a forest of lighted trees, two white reindeer with golden antlers and a Victorian couple hanging a wreath—all of which she sculpted herself. The choir is now displayed on the lawn of the George family at 5246 West Pratt.

Mary's daughter, Ruth Miles, who lived on Ramona Avenue, joined her mom's efforts by displaying a large elf, who was keeping Santa's records at his desk. Dr. Vladimir Skul, a Croatian immigrant, celebrated his freedom on LaPorte Avenue with a patriotic display of flags and toy soldiers that surrounded his entire yard.

Animated dolls and life-size movable Santas in suits of gold and red velvet appeared in picture windows throughout Lincolnwood Towers, as residents of this affluent neighborhood shared their good fortune with all who passed.

By the mid-sixties three families at the intersection of Sauganash and Nokomis avenues were again causing traffic jams—over 300 cars an hour. The LiPomi home on the northeast corner is best known for its animated scene of elves in a candy cane factory. Across the street the Cascio family had a seal on the front porch that spun a ball on its nose, a mechanical Santa in the window, giant ornaments hanging from the eaves, soldiers lining the driveway and a wreath over the entryway that encircled a huge elf, which once decorated State Street. The Bongiovanni family on the southwest corner displayed a life-size nativity scene, four animated elves constructing toys, a golden angel swinging on the porch, a clown performing flips and a snoring Santa snoozing in his chair.

Contrary to rumor each family owned their decorations and assembled the displays themselves. For over two decades that the families decorated, they were featured regularly on television news programs.

The LiPomis are still decorating (see page 50). The Cascios moved away in 1990. And though the Bongiovannis discontinued their display in 1992, they sold all their decorations to the Stefani family, who display them with some added attractions of their own at their home on the southeast corner of LeMai and Albion avenues.

A younger generation of Lincolnwood Towers residents, many of whom remember the area from their childhoods, have taken over with elaborate displays of their own, which are featured on the following pages. Viewers are encouraged to drive up and down all the streets of the neighborhood to look for additional surprises that these fun-loving neighbors have displayed, such as Mr. and Mrs. Santa kissing in a window, a giant Santa cuckoo clock, and a decorated tree house. ◆

Santa Loses His Head

Several years ago, the central shopping district of Evanston was decorated with a huge 16-foot Santa Claus. On an unusually blustery day, the firm that supplied the enormous display received an emergency call. It seemed Santa's head had come loose and was rolling down the middle of the street.

---

❸ 6601 North LeRoy Avenue

When the teacher asked her students to name a family holiday tradition, Kevin Noonan responded, "We get a Christmas tree." The class was unimpressed until the proud youngster added, "And it's so big that it goes through the roof!" With wide-eyed admiration his classmates gasped, "Wow, that's your house!"

Children and adults from miles around have come to know the famous 24-foot tree, too large for its 20-foot house. Its base, which measures 11 feet in diameter, takes up the entire living room picture window. The tree begins to taper off as it rises to the second floor, but none too soon, as its last three feet burst through the ceiling and out to the roof.

It takes Mary and Mike Noonan and their six children two weeks to decorate this enormous tree with 25,000 lights, 450 ornaments, hundreds of feet of garland, 60 stale candy canes, several strands of plastic (thank goodness!) popcorn, and a tree skirt that barely covers half the base. Though the Noonans really enjoy the end result, they admit that the tradition of decorating the Christmas tree, which might find the perfect family bonding in love and togetherness, wreaks havoc when the task is this overwhelming. Mike jokes, "Our family is bound together by one thing at Christmastime—we all hate decorating."

The colossal Noonan family tradition began in 1982 when Mike brought home the first Christmas tree for their new home. It was much taller than their 8-foot ceiling. Mike tried smashing it into the room until it looked like it was cracked in two. It was then that the idea struck him—the tree would ascend into the second-floor bedroom, where the top would show through the window. Though the family was happy with dad's solution, it was not big enough for Mike. He proclaimed, "Next year it will go through the roof!" And it has ever since.

For several holiday seasons the family had the tree special-ordered and delivered from Michigan. In the spirit of Christmas, Mary dutifully vacuumed the endless needles and cleaned the sap. However, the year that a chain saw was used in her well-kept living room to shorten the trunk, the smell of fresh pine somehow lost its appeal. The following season a custom-ordered artificial tree replaced the live one.

From the first year the tree was displayed, the family has heard the sound of passing motorists who stop and back up in a baffled double-take. Those convinced that the tree actually goes through

The Noonan's Christmas tree bursts through the roof.

the roof have been known to wager bets, mistakenly thinking the Noonans would resolve their dispute. But Mary and Mike simply reply, "It's the magic of Christmas," and the children (who are all sworn to secrecy) respond, "The ceiling has a hole in it and the roof has an insulated louvered trap door."

Another attraction of the Noonan display is the life-size Santa and sleigh pulled by two stuffed reindeer. Mike bought the antique figures from a museum in Union, Illinois. He acknowledges that the services of a taxidermist will be needed to repair both animals' weathered hooves, but the Noonan children are more concerned with adding a red nose to one of them.

Mike adds lights to the bushes and moving figures in the windows each year. Mary, a former school teacher, also sets up a special window display, which she attributes to her "bulletin board mentality." Life-size carolers sing on the balcony and are often joined by the youngest Noonans, who won't be seen without their Santa hats. An electrical supply salesman, Mike is able to store the decorations in a warehouse at work and move the large pieces in a company truck.

With crowds of spectators arriving late at night to see the display, it had become increasingly difficult for Mike to turn off the lights without boos and hisses

from late-night visitors. At first he attempted to sneak behind the bushes to reach the connections and avoid the jeers, but finally resorted to using timers.

Often sitting near the front window of the Noonan home is Mary's dad enjoying the passing crowds. In the fifties he would take the family from Rogers Park to Lincolnwood to see the decorations. Mary fondly remembers the "long ride" and glistening displays but never knew exactly where she had been. During the first holiday season in her Lincolnwood home, Mary suddenly realized she was in the midst of her childhood dreamland. Oh, the magic of Christmas!
Dec. 15 – Jan. 2, (Su – Th) 5:00PM – 11:00PM, (F – Sa) – 1:00AM. *From Cicero Ave., W on Pratt Ave. 4 bl., S on LeRoy Ave. 2bl.*

❹ 6601 Longmeadow Avenue

As a young typist for a local publishing firm, Pat Domanik was given the assignment of decorating the company bulletin board for Christmas. While searching books and magazines for a fitting holiday phrase, she found a poem entitled "To Believe in Christmas." Pat printed it on parchment and hung it on the office

The Domanik residence glows with the joy of the season.

board. Fellow employees, as well as the president of the company, were deeply moved by its message. Pat kept the poem and committed it to memory.

As the years have passed she has displayed the genuine love of the holiday that the poem inspired. Standing amid shelves of decorations that fill two rooms of her basement and the garage, Pat admits, "My heart flies out of me when I have to put these things away. I kiss everything good-bye with a promise to see it again next year."

In a town where the holiday traffic is so heavy some neighbors choose to leave town, Pat Domanik revels in the excitement of the crowds. "That's the fun of the whole thing," she exclaims. The first year she moved in, Pat and her nieces sang carols and gave away candy canes to passersby. Another year, sick and unable to get her decorations up in time, Pat yelled out to a busload of touring senior citizens to please return the following week.

Owner of an hors d'oeuvre catering company that began in her kitchen as a special occasion cake business, Pat is no stranger to decorating. She exhibits her flair in an elegant Christmas display that tastefully combines a variety of unique decorations.

A 9-foot antique Santa Claus greets visitors on the north end of her front yard. One of Pat's decorating helpers spotted it collecting dust in a storage attic and knew immediately where Santa would find a good home. It now stands nestled among Pat's pine trees with a burlap bag full of gifts.

At the center of her yard a huge evergreen strung with Italian lights towers over the display like a star-filled sky. Her white brick home and the surrounding shrubbery glow with thousands more lights expertly hung by her friend Ken Sowizrol, a city electrician who decorates the Daley Center tree. The two met by fate when Pat sold him her previous house.

Greeting visitors at the front walk, Mr. and Mrs. Goose sport four different holiday outfits throughout the season. Wire mesh angels, which Pat included as fixtures in the purchase of the home, blow their horns in the glisten of white lights. A giant picture window is divided into dozens of snow-filled panes as backdrop to a porch trimmed with enchanting holiday surprises. And at the center of all the decorations shines a verse encased in plastic that relays the heartfelt message of a woman who truly believes in the spirit of the season.

Dec. 1–Jan. 8, 5:00PM–12:00AM. *From Cicero Ave., W on Devon Ave. 2 bl., N on Longmeadow Ave. 3-1/2 bl.*

❺ 6601 North Nokomis Avenue

The LiPomis are the last remaining "old-time" decorators from Lincolnwood's glory days of the 1960s. Theirs is also the last of the three outstanding displays that caused a gaper's block at the intersection of Nokomis and Sauganash avenues for over 20 years.

The family's decorating tradition goes back further still to their former home in Sauganash, where Salvatore and Connie LiPomi lived with their three daughters from 1954 to 1963 and elaborately trimmed their lawn with lights and figurines. The Sauganash area, adjacent to Lincolnwood, had been famous for its many lighted homes in the post-war years. It seems, however, that when the LiPomis moved to their new suburban neighborhood the tradition of elaborate displays came with them. In the years to follow, the number of decorated homes in Sauganash began to decrease, as the displays in Lincolnwood grew more grand each year.

Connie was not fond of the cold and left the decorating to her husband. Salvatore, a precision machinist, was a creative man who appreciated fine workmanship. He had seen many animated figures displayed in picture windows, but imagined a scene of animated figures on his new front lawn.

He acquired the services of Silvestri Corp., a manufacturer of custom indoor displays. Using weather-proof materials and a 100-watt light bulb to keep the motor from freezing, an artisan at the company created Salvatore's first outdoor moving figurine—a little elf that bends over laughing. It was followed by an elf putting candy canes in a wheelbarrow and another trying to budge a stubborn donkey. Together with seven other unique inanimate figures, the candy cane factory run by elves, that Salvatore had envisioned, came to life.

The side of the house was also trimmed with choir boys and a huge wreath that bore the names of all the members of the family. Candy canes lined the circular drive and flanked the garage door. "And dad had so many lights, my mother was afraid the house would burn down," remembers Salvatore's daughter Stella. "On the weekends we'd set the alarm for 1:00AM, so we could get up, put our boots on and go out to the garage to turn off all the lights."

Since her father passed away, Stella, her cousin Peter Fontana and her neighbor Ira Lauter have continued to assemble the candy cane factory every year in Salvatore's memory.

Sat. before Christmas–Sat. after New Year's, (Su–Th) 6:30PM–10:30PM, (F–Sa) –12:00AM.
From Central Ave., E on Devon Ave. 3 bl., NE on Nokomis Ave. 3 bl.

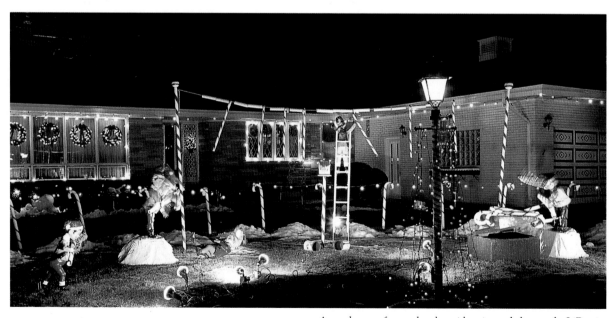

A candy cane factory bustles with animated elves at the LiPomis.

Art Miner and his daughter, Arden, huddle close in their festive front yard filled with Art's homemade creations.

❻ 6719 North Nokomis Avenue

Nine-year-old Arden Miner pointed to the neighbor's Christmas decorations and sweetly suggested, "We should do something like that, Dad." With a father's soft spot for his little girl's desires, Art Miner decided to build a display for her.

As an architectural and interior designer, his creativity and construction skills equipped him well for the task at hand. Over the next several years he built one of the most delightful, original and easy-to-assemble displays in the area.

Seven glittering arches of conduit, garland and lights, flanked with peppermint candy canes, form a magical tunnel through the front yard. Eight flying reindeer whirl beneath a twinkling canopy in a holiday merry-go-round, while an 8-foot ferris wheel spins gaily in another corner of the yard.

Art built the mechanical decorations of lightweight copper tubing to lessen wear on the 3-rpm motors. He used his daughter's old bicycle gears on the ferris wheel and a unique electrical system that employs a copper contact disk to prevent the lights

from getting tangled in the moving parts. Both displays are cleverly assembled in a few hours with bolts and wing nuts securing the modular framework.

Art also constructed some of his decorations from wood. Using a pattern from a 1985 issue of Family Circle Magazine, he enlarged the design and stained pieces of oak and walnut various colors to create a handsome three-dimensional crèche.

A four-car train bearing the greeting "N-O-E-L" is the latest colorful product of Art's handiwork. In addition several store-bought animated figures wave from the windows indoors, soldiers march along the drive, wreaths glisten from the garage, holiday flags line the street and lights abound.

For his efforts Art has won an achievement award from the town, has been featured on the local news and has lit the eyes of many a child. But his biggest thrill is knowing that his daughter Arden, now a grown women, is just as tickled as always to see his decorations.

Dec. 15 – Jan. 1, 6:00PM – 1:00AM. *From Central Ave., E on Pratt Ave. 4 bl., S on Nokomis Ave.*

MORTON GROVE

❼ 9040 North Mason Avenue

Those afraid of heights are advised to simply enjoy this rooftop display and dismiss any thoughts of how the decorations got up there. The curious may read on.

In past years when Jeff Huber hung the lights at the highest peak of his two-story brick home, the extension ladder wouldn't quite reach. To compensate he backed his Blazer onto the grass and rested the ladder on the tailgate. "I thought that was more sturdy than the uneven lawn," Jeff defended. "But my wife always panicked a little, dialed the first six numbers of the Morton Grove Fire Department, and stayed on the phone until I made it down."

Last Christmas Kathy Huber wisely bought her husband a larger 32-foot extension ladder. Since the Blazer has been sold, she may have thought she could hang up the phone. However...Jeff still boosts himself onto the roof and climbs to its 24-foot crest to hang lights from the chimney. He also wires a 4-foot Santa to the smoke stack along with a sleigh and nine reindeer that fly to the garage. 9-6-5-2-1-2...

Dec. 10 – Jan. 6, 5:00PM – 12:00AM. *From Dempster St., N on Central Rd. 3 bl., W on Davis St. 7 bl.*

Lights abound at the Baluszynski home on West Amelia Drive.

NILES

⑧ Town Decorations

Thanks to the Public Works Department, the town of Niles annually becomes a holiday winter wonderland regardless of Mother Nature's degree of cooperation. Every lamppost on Milwaukee Avenue from Albion north to Golf Road wears a 4-foot snowflake glimmering with white lights and garlands. As the road winds through town it's a sight to be seen. Parkways of sparkling trees add to the charm at the intersections of Albion, Touhy, Harlem and Howard.

The Building and Grounds Department decorates the parks with 40 Christmas trees and 50,000 lights, a task that often requires more than a month to complete. Six men from the Department of Forestry and Lighting install the snowflakes in four days with the help of two snorkel trucks. The 150 steel-frame flakes slide into brackets permanently attached to the poles and are connected electrically with extension cords to the light heads.

Department managers Ken Piwko and Tom Oleksy admit that these repetitive tasks can get tiring on a cold winter day, but the residents' enthusiasm makes the crew happy to add to the joy of this special time of year.

Fri. after Thanksgiving–Jan. 31 (Tree decorations may not be complete until a few weeks later.) Dusk–Dawn. *Milwaukee Ave. between Albion Ave. (Niles' southern border) and Golf Rd.*

⑨ 8423 West Amelia Drive

Christmas is the favorite holiday of Jozef Baluszynski. He delights in buying new Christmas items each year and filling his front yard with lights and figurines.

This native of Poland does not limit his decorating to his suburban home, however. When his brother Eddie and cousin Ted came to visit from the family's hometown of Nowy Sacz, he sent them off with lights and decorations.

Thanks to Jozef, this small Polish mountain village may soon resemble a glistening corner of Niles.

Dec. 8–Jan. 6, 5:00PM–12:00AM. *From Greenwood Ave., E on Dempster St. 3 bl., S on Cumberland Ave. 6 bl., W on Amelia Dr.*

⑩ 7100 Block of West Lill Street

Nearly 35 years ago, the residents of this suburban cul-de-sac decided to make Christmas decorating a block project. The "Season's Greetings" message spelled out with a big red letter on the front lawn of each home has created a feeling of warmth among the neighbors and become a part of holiday tradition in Niles.

2nd Sun. in Dec.–Jan. 6, 5:00PM–11:00PM. *From Dempster St., S on Harlem Ave. 5 bl., E on Lill St.*

⑪ Leaning Tower YMCA
6300 West Touhy Avenue

The world's only replica of the Leaning Tower of Pisa is an exact half-size reproduction of its Italian counterpart with four exceptions: 1) In 1933 the Niles tower was built as a water tower by Robert A. Ilg to supply three swimming pools at this former park. The Pisa tower was built as a bell tower for the town cathedral. 2) The Niles tower is a concrete and steel structure on a concrete foundation. The Pisa tower is a marble structure on wood pilings. 3) Each level of the Niles tower is a separate floor connected by stairways from the balconies. The Pisa tower is hollow with steps inside the walls. 4) The Niles tower is adorned in lights of red, white and green for the holidays, which happen to be the colors of the Italian flag. The Tower of Pisa just continues to lean.

The YMCA and the city of Niles usually celebrate the lighting of the tower on the second Friday of

Niles' own Tower of Pisa leans festively for the holidays.

December. The Mayor does the honors, Santa arrives by fire truck, and there are free refreshments and group caroling.

Dec. 15–Jan. 15, Dusk–11:00PM. For more information call (708)647–8222 *From Milwaukee Ave., E on Touhy Ave. 1 mi.*

⑫ Fountain View Condominium
6980 West Touhy Avenue

Thanks to the residents of this 40-unit condominium, the busy intersection of Milwaukee and Touhy is aglow with the spirit of the holidays. Bushes and trees are dressed in 17,000 white lights, while four stories of balconies on both sides of the building are decked in bulbs and bows and wreaths according to the owner's fancy.

Rumor has it that residents are already drawing up plans for next year in a friendly effort to outdo their neighbors. Passersby may soon find out just how much will fit on a 6′ x 24′ balcony.

Day after Thanksgiving–Jan. 6, 4:00PM–11:00PM. *NE corner of Milwaukee Ave. and Touhy Ave.*

PARK RIDGE
⑬ Shopping District

Victorian homes, quaint shops and gas street lamps flavor the city of Park Ridge with the charm of an era past. In like fashion, the holiday season finds the town trimmed with traditional greenery, while residents enjoy celebrations that have gone on for the past 35 years.

On the main streets nearly 100 gas lamps are circled in wreaths, draped in garlands and trimmed with bright red bows. In Hodges Park at Prospect and Touhy, a 30-foot evergreen is decorated with ornaments, handmade by members of various local organizations.

On the Friday after Thanksgiving the two local merchants' associations sponsor a holiday open house. Four double-decker buses take one-way scenic tours north on Prospect and south on Cortland from one shopping district to the other. Despite the cold, riders vie for open-air seating on the upper level of the bus for a better view along the route of homes competing in the town's decorating contest. Shop owners at both ends stay open past regular business hours and treat their customers to holiday treats such as pfeffernüsse and gluwein. In the uptown area, there's added excitement as shoppers compete for prizes in a hunt for Parker Penguin, a 16-inch town mascot hidden in several store windows.

Fri. after Thanksgiving–Jan. 1, Dusk–Dawn. Open House: Fri. after Thanksgiving, 6:00PM–9:00PM. *Northwest Hwy. at Touhy Ave. and Devon Ave. at Cumberland Ave.*

Fountain View Condominium lights up Milwaukee and Touhy.

⑭ 408 North Dee Road
(pictured on page 43)

Throughout the winter Murphy Lake glistens with the reflection of the home of Don Schumacher. He and three of his friends, Bill McDonald, Jim Lange and Tim Delana spend a few weeks of their spare time decorating this sprawling two-story home. Using 750 strands of white Italian lights, they outline every corner, window, eave, roofline and chimney, along with the bushes, trees and gazebo.

For once, rumors that the owner has his own electric company are true. Don is the president of Schumacher Electric Corporation in Chicago.

Dec. 1–Feb. 15, 4:00PM–4:00AM. *From the Tri-State Twy. (I-294), E on Touhy Ave. 3/4 mi., N on Dee Rd. It is permissible to use the private drive for viewing.*

⑮ 1120 North Delphia

The women of the family take over decorating at this household, inside and out. Florence Panuce and her daughter Sandra, both in the clothing business, display their flair for style in a home that glistens with class. Thoughtfully-placed white lights glimmer from bushes, trees and large wreaths framing the windows. Bright red bows, which Florence makes herself, accent the greenery and put the final touch on the gaily-ribboned garage door.

Often the recipients of decorating honors in their former home in Edgebrook, the Panuces cherish their most recent prize from a group of caroling neighbors. The singers chose their home as the favorite and awarded them a blue ribbon, a bottle of champagne and a round of "Jingle Bells."

Dec. 10–Jan. 6, 4:30PM–12:00AM. *From Greenwood Ave., W on Oakton St. 1 bl., N on Delphia 1-1/2bl.*

"Draping" Lights

Sandra Panuce discovered that drapery hooks are ideal for securing lights to bushes. The narrow side of the hook holds the light strand tightly, while the wider end is just right for grasping branches. To reach high places, she found her weeder to be a useful extension pole.

Fastening Lights

Angelo Velasquez of Park Ridge fastens his lights to the gutters and brick walls using rubbery suction cup hooks smeared with petroleum jelly. They hold the strands surprisingly well throughout the season.

⑯ 613 West Oakton Street

The sign on the chimney proclaims, "Jesus is the Reason for the Season." Below, a simple manger cradles the Christ Child, while Mary and Joseph kneel at His side. They are joined by the three wise men—no, wait, it's not three wise men, and it's not a shepherd with his flock. It's just a flock—that is, a flock of geese, and they're dressed for the occasion.

Mr. Goose wears a furry red coat and hat with a full white beard about his beak. The Mrs. hides her feathers in a red shawl, bonnet and muff. One gosling poses as a reindeer—or is it a reindeer posing as a gosling? The other is an angel with a golden crown and an extra set of wings.

The true identities of this deftly-disguised family of fowl are Lester and Lucy, the 2-foot 70-pound adult geese, and their ten-pound cement children Linus and Lulu. Since 1989 their playful owners, Doris and Bob Kyllingstad, have had a ball outfitting them for Christmas and many other holidays to the delight of motorists on this well-traveled street.

The Kyllingstads originally purchased one goose with a 4th of July Uncle Sam costume. A few months later they bought him a mate and several matching outfits. Much to Doris and Bob's surprise, drivers began slowing down and were even mailing notes of thanks for brightening their day.

A truck driver confessed he had altered his daily route just to pass the geese. A mother was grateful that the amusing fowl, especially in their Ninja Turtle outfits, had made her reluctant six-year-old look forward to attending his school across the street. Another thankful woman bought the geese French navy clothing to celebrate Bastille Day.

Buoyed by the attention, Bob decided it was time Lester and Lucy had a family. On April Fool's Day he introduced Linus and Lulu with goose family members appropriately dressed in pink and blue.

At their Oakton Street home Lester, Lulu, Lucy and Linus Goose spread good cheer by dressing for the holidays.

Signs announced their arrival, proclaiming "It's a Boy" and "It's a Girl." It didn't take long before a congratulatory plant with a shower card was delivered by a passing motorist.

Doris and Bob now devote a section of their closet to goose clothing, with outfits from raincoats to negligees for over 20 occasions. Hangers are bent into "A" shapes to accommodate the unusual goose form. The Kyllingstads purchased their feathered friends and many of their clothes from Kinn-Shaw of Joliet. This outdoor lawn ornament company's main business is selling four sizes of geese and 45 garments from an $8 bikini to a $22 fur coat.

Doris and Bob are also favorite customers of Goosey Gander Creations of Bradley, Illinois, a mail order goose clothing company. Sisters Dorothy and Rilla Hammond offer a catalog of nearly 90 original outfits and patterns. They have had a thriving national business since 1988, selling nothing but goose clothes. Dorothy, who began sewing women's clothing out of her home, is surprised and delighted with the fowl phenomenon. She tells of a women who bought eight geese and had them dressed up like her daughter's bridal party, and of a store in Ohio that is selling 400 geese and 300 outfits a week. "My whole life is geese now," she says with some trepidation.

Fri. after Thanksgiving–Jan.1, Dusk–11:00PM.
From Milwaukee Ave., W on Oakton St. 1 mi.

⑰ 325 South Prospect Avenue

Annual prize winners Christ and Betty Nicholas use their grandchildren's old toys, among other holiday items, to create a colorful window diorama. Their closed-in front porch with recessed ceiling lights makes an ideal setting for the display.

Fri. after Thanksgiving–Jan.1, Dusk–11:00PM.
From Cumberland Ave., E on Touhy Ave. 1/4 mi., S on Prospect Ave. 1-1/2 bl.

⑱ 516 South Prospect Avenue

The Pientka family changes their decorations every year by voting on various ideas mom sketches in September. A giant lighted "Merry Christmas" sign attached to the roof and a 30-foot Christmas tree have been among her winning ideas, but the favorite of passersby was a walkway of lighted arches made of conduit and flexible pipe. The glimmering canopy was so inviting that the Pientka's never knew if people were visiting or just "passing through."

Day after Thanksgiving–Dec.25, Dusk–10:30PM.
From Cumberland Ave., E on Touhy Ave. 1/4 mi., S on Prospect Ave. 1/2 mi.

The yuletide diorama at the Nicholas home is a highlight of the Park Ridge Holiday Open House.

⑲ 235 North Wisner

Helen Pintor's former cottage-style home became famous in Lincolnwood as "The Gingerbread House" for its elaborate lighted display. But fame had preceded Helen to the Park Ridge home she now shares with her husband, Angelo Velasquez. The two-story brick house is known as the former Rodham residence—the childhood home of first lady Hillary Rodham Clinton.

As the designer of Helen's Lincolnwood display, Angelo seems less impressed by the reputation of their new residence than by its potential for Christmas decorations. "The house has a glass sun room with a good view from all sides. It will be perfect for animated displays," he said, "and I also hope to incorporate the garage."

Italian lights drenched the bushes, trees and windows of their former home and striped the roof dotted with lighted snowflakes. With the help of Helen's son-in-law, Glenn, Angelo hopes to outdo the spectacular display.

It seems the Rodham residence's former claim to fame may soon be surpassed by "The Gingerbread House–Part II."

Dec.19–Jan.6, 5:00PM–11:00PM. *From Northwest Hwy., E on Touhy Ave. 2 bl., N on Wisner 2 bl.*

This Linden Avenue home is alive with holiday magic thanks to the creativity of owner Warren Perkins.

Steve Bramati's simple decorations glow with elegance.

SKOKIE

⑳ 5030 West Farwell Avenue

All six members of the McAuley family come in the front way during the holidays, so they can see the Christmas decorations up close. A manger scene, candy canes, snowmen, soldiers and candles cover the house and lawn. Lights glow from bushes, trees and windows. A giant star beams from the chimney, and Santa stands on a rooftop full of blinking white lights. Even the antenna is decked out for the season.

Dec.6–Jan.6, 5:00PM–10:00PM. *From Cicero Ave., W on Pratt Ave. 3 bl., N on Lavergne Ave. 1 bl., W on Farwell Ave.*

㉑ 5037 West Farwell Avenue

Steve Bramati is quite the grandpa. At age 65 he decided to start decorating his home for his seven-year-old grandson, Mike. He spent two weeks neatly trimming the front of his ranch home with 6,000 lights, four evergreen wreaths, garland ropes and velvet bows. He built a giant "NOEL" sign to hang over the garage and lined the walks with a fence of glistening bulbs. "When Mike started bringing his friends home from school to see the lights, I knew it was worth the effort," Steve beamed.

Dec.6–Jan.6, 5:00PM–10:00PM. *Same as above.*

WILMETTE

㉒ 631 West Linden Avenue

At the corner house on Linden and 7th Street, a sleighload of toys pulled by five prancing reindeer climbs 30 feet into the sky, as a railroad gate drops and flashing lights warn, "Stop Reindeer Crossing." A giant Christmas tree spins a path of dancing colored lights, a gazebo of carolers fills the air with the melodies of the season and messages of peace and joy alternately flash from the garage. Sixty-four cascading snowflakes blink in a magical flurry across the front of the house, while a side sunroom becomes a winter diorama with Mr. and Mrs. Santa and their busy elves.

Homeowner Warren Perkins has combined his skills as an industrial arts teacher with his love of entertaining children of all ages to create this unique, delightful and well-made Christmas display.

Mr. Perkins built the sleigh and reindeer in 1949. His father, Warren Sr., later created the motor and pulley system that has pulled Santa's crew to the treetop an average of 20,000 times per season for nearly 40 years. The sleigh returns by gravity and has a heating system and an automatic thermostatically-controlled manual override, which prevents icy ropes from causing a malfunction when the temperature dips below freezing.

Perkins' snowfall originated in 1960 as six blinking snowflakes and gradually developed into a sparkling blizzard. Eight rows of eight different snowflakes, stenciled on translucent plastic and lit from behind, appear to descend as a homemade timing device with a 9-rpm motor trips eight cam-operated switches to alternately light the display.

Warren Perkins built his display to last. The original electromechanical devices are still being used and have required only minor repairs. Mr. Perkins' only problem is whether or not to touch up the sleigh and reindeer for the first time. They just don't make paint like they did 45 years ago.

Dec. 4–Jan. 6, 5:00PM–10:30PM. *From Green Bay Rd., E on Lake Ave. 3/4 mi., S on 7th St. 4 bl.*

WINNETKA

㉓ 825 Glenoak Drive

In 1982 when Rocco Fiore surprised one of his best landscaping customers with a decorated 12-foot blue spruce, he had no idea what he was starting. Homeowner Bill O'Donnell and his wife Nicky

The stunning display at the Winnetka home of Bill O'Donnell twinkles brighter every year thanks to the efforts of landscapers Rocco Fiore & Sons, Inc.

To owners Richard and Patricia Kent their Sheridan Road mansion is "an ideal Christmas House."

enjoyed the sparkling tree so much that Bill installed outdoor electrical receptacles and hired Rocco's landscaping company to expand the display.

The beautiful yard, already resplendent with trees and hedges, now dazzles in the glow of 60,000 lights with 440 amps of available power. Lindens, boxwoods, hawthorns, magnolias, crab apples, serviceberries, arrowwoods, black haws and hicks yews are each covered in red, green, blue, white or mixed lights. The colors are alternated every year for variety.

Michael Fiore, Rocco's cousin and the landscaper in charge of decorating the O'Donnell home, has perfected his technique since his neophyte days. He wraps each branch with lights top to bottom from the trunk to the twigs. When moving past the display the lights appear to sparkle, as they hide behind branches.

The 12-foot tree that started the tradition is still the focal point of the display. It is hand-picked annually from a Wisconsin tree farm. Michael trims it to size, sets it in the front yard fountain, and anchors it to the ground with cables. One-and-a-half-inch bulbs make the tree especially bright.

Michael enjoys this challenging departure from his normal craft. "I've always wanted to do this, since I was a little kid, " he gleams. He's happy to take on the six-day task, especially when his generous employer is not as concerned that the "electric meter goes flying" as Michael would need to be.

Though Bill O'Donnell has left the difficult work to the pros, he has enjoyed the boyish thrill of flipping the switch that turns his home into a stunning winter wonderland.

Dec. 1–Jan. 1, 6:00PM–11:00PM. *From Tower Rd., N on Sheridan Rd. 1/4 mi., E on Glenoak Dr.*

24 191 Sheridan Road

A winding path of glittering white lights on sculptured shrubs, manicured hedges, and stately pines adds to the magic of this storybook mansion of gables and stone on the shores of Lake Michigan.

Fri. after Thanksgiving–Jan. 2, (Su–Th) Dusk–11:00PM, (F–Sa)–12:00PM. *From Winnetka Ave., N on Sheridan Rd. 1/2 bl.*

Chapter 5

COOK COUNTY–NORTHWEST

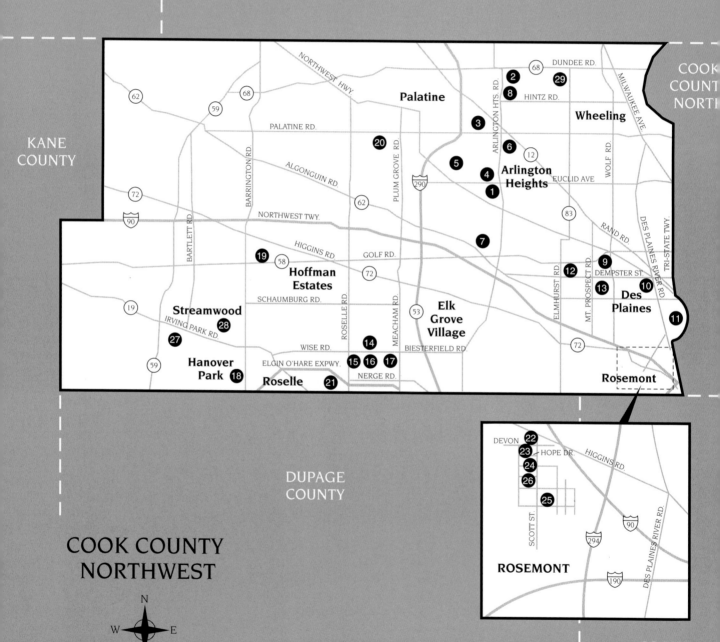

COOK COUNTY
NORTHWEST

MCHENRY
COUNTY

LAKE
COUNTY

KANE
COUNTY

DUPAGE
COUNTY

COOK
COUNTY
NORTH

COOK
COUNTY
WEST

Palatine

Wheeling

Arlington
Heights

Hoffman
Estates

Streamwood

Hanover
Park

Roselle

Elk
Grove
Village

Des
Plaines

Rosemont

ROSEMONT

NORTHWEST HWY.

PALATINE RD.

ALGONQUIN RD.

NORTHWEST TWY.

HIGGINS RD.

GOLF RD.

SCHAUMBURG RD.

IRVING PARK RD.

WISE RD.

ELGIN O'HARE EXPWY.

NERGE RD.

BIESTERFIELD RD.

DEMPSTER ST.

DUNDEE RD.

HINTZ RD.

EUCLID AVE

RAND RD.

BARRINGTON RD.

BARTLETT RD.

ROSELLE RD.

MEACHAM RD.

PLUM GROVE RD.

ARLINGTON HTS. RD.

MILWAUKEE AVE

WOLF RD.

ELMHURST RD.

MT. PROSPECT RD.

DES PLAINES RIVER RD.

TRI-STATE TWY.

DEVON

HOPE DR.

HIGGINS RD.

SCOTT ST.

DES PLAINES RIVER RD.

MILES

0   4

ARLINGTON HEIGHTS

❶ Village Decorations

Clink, pop, beep, boop...the sounds of Santa's workshop are heard coming from inside the maintenance building of the Arlington Heights Park District. Though evidence seems to indicate that employees Louis Nagy, Mike Spilotro, Richard Knox, Slim Beaudry, Alan Welk, Richard DiCanio and Angelo Capulli may be elves working here part-time, there have yet been no sightings of green tights or jingle-belled toes.

It's only known that since 1991 on many a rainy day, manikins, motors, polyester fiberfill, steel rods, chicken wire, garden hoses and other scrap materials have gone into the building and, unseen for several months, have magically reappeared at Christmastime transformed into North School Park's delightful holiday displays.

Like an enchanted road to fairyland, 10 lighted arches form a path to a stunning collection of welded forms drenched in lights that glisten throughout the park—an old-fashioned locomotive with a coal car and caboose, Santa and four reindeer flying though the air, a Gay Nineties couple twirling on an ice rink, and a turning windmill. A wooden gazebo sparkles with lights, and three giant Hanukkah dreidels spin a twinkling trail. In the center of the park fountain, a 30-foot Christmas tree majestically stands, surrounded by a colorful choo-choo train.

Though the park staff has built and maintained all the decorations in recent years, local sculptor Fran Volz, famous for his snow sculptures down the street, was one of the original elfin crew who designed and constructed many of the first figures.

At one end of the park his 8-foot snowman welcomes visitors, while at the other a furry teddy bear twirls upon a brightly wrapped present. "Season's Greetings" spans five flag poles that surround the bandstand, which is adorned with a 10-foot wreath. Santa Claus waves from a rooftop chimney, a little drummer boy plays atop a giant tin drum, and a life-size wooden gingerbread house is trimmed with peppermints, chocolate chip cookies, an assortment of candies and gobs of icing.

Thanks to the imaginative crew's continuing efforts the display grows from year to year and may soon expand onto Northwest Highway and Lake Arlington Park.

Last weekend in Nov.–Jan.6, Dusk–11:00PM.
From Euclid St., S on Arlington Hts. Rd. 2 bl., At Eastman St.

North School Park glimmers with holiday surprises.

The Massa home is elegantly trimmed in reds and greens.

Greg's displays have earned first place in the town decorating contest and the admiration of friends and neighbors. They annually gather in the street for the official "flipping of the switch" the Saturday after Thanksgiving.

Sat. after Thanksgiving–Jan. 7, 4:30PM–12:00AM. *From Hintz Rd., N on Arlington Hts. Rd. 4 bl., E on Burr Oak Dr. 1 bl.*

❸ 1414 Cambridge Street

Though Christmas lights may come in blue, orange, yellow and white, Art Massa has always been a traditional red and green kind of guy. As a teenager in Cincinnati, he decorated his parents' home in red and green lights for six years. As an adult he has continued the motif on his own home since 1985.

Art explains, "The entire house is done in alternating red and green lights. Nine hundred Italian lights outline 16 windows across the front of the house. Five hundred ten C-9-1/4 lights line the gutter on three sides of the house and trim three groupings of bushes. Each of four large trees in the front feature either two green or two red 150-watt flood lights illuminating the bare branches above. A separate green spot light illuminates a large wreath next to the garage door, while a white spot light shines on a green foil-wrapped front door sporting a smaller wreath. Two sets of porch lights also are converted to red and green bulbs."

Art continues to add new lights to his display each year—red and green ones, of course.

Dec. 7–Jan. 1, 6:00PM–11:00PM. *From Arlington Hts. Rd., W on Palatine Rd. 800 ft., W on Frontage Rd. 1/2 mi., N on Yale Ave. 4 bl., W on Cambridge St.*

❷ 719 East Burr Oak Drive

As a student at the University of Indiana, Greg LaBonar earned a reputation during the holidays for trimming his dorm room, then his frat house and later his off-campus housing with Christmas decorations both inside and out. While other students cut classes a few days prior to Thanksgiving to go home and party, Greg did so to allow himself enough time to decorate his family's home in Arlington Heights.

At the LaBonar household, no one else has shared Greg's desire to brave the cold, so he has been in charge of outdoor decorations since he was nine years old. His parents have supported his effort by allowing him to buy one new item each season. "If Greg had his way, he would have something going 200 feet in the air, so you could see it from Arlington Heights Road," his mom jokes.

Hanging Lights Around Windows

To achieve perfect lighting on the windows indoors, Art Massa originally secured each light in place with masking tape, but the tape would dry out, fall off and remove the finish from the wood. He now uses plastic light holders designed for roof shingles. When cut 2-1/2 inches shorter, they can be wedged between the window frame and the trim.

❹ 818 North Highland Avenue

Janine Karkow is a talented craftsperson who creates lovely works in fabric and wood. For the holidays she decorates her family's historic Arlington Heights farm house in traditional style with evergreen swags and big red bows. Candles shine from the windows, and on the porch an old pair of skates hangs over an antique sleigh. Beautifully crafted wooden figures of a Victorian family dressed for the holidays fill the front lawn. The Karkow home exudes the charm of a quiet Christmas from an era past. But behind the scenes…

Janine spent two months laboriously working full-time to create the five detailed figures of the Victorian family. The task of painting hundreds of tiny checks, stripes and floral patterns on their clothing kept her so absorbed she quit smoking.

For several years she insisted on making the garlands by hand from the branches of the blue spruce trees that grew in the front yard. The family would use the top of the evergreen for their Christmas tree, and Janine would cut off the bottom branches and wire them together to make garlands and wreaths. After using as many trees as the front yard could spare, she bought more from a nursery.

Janine refers to this period of avid decorating as her "neurotic days." She was doing a lot of crafts while staying at home with her two small children. But now the kids are older, and Janine has more time to herself. The greenery is artificial. The decorations haven't changed in a couple of years. And the old farm house with its quiet country charm is calm and quiet inside as well.

Dec. 1–Jan. 1, Dusk–10:00PM. *From Arlington Hts. Rd., W on Euclid St. 3 bl., N on Highland Ave. 3 bl.*

Janine Karkow's hand-painted Victorian figures accent the charm of her turn-of-the-century home.

❺ 1308 North Kennicott Avenue

David Lienau sneaks cases of discounted white lights from the trunk of his car. Carole Lienau waits until he's gone to turn on outdoor music for the "singing" choir boys. Though the couple may not agree on all the details of their Christmas decorations, the collaboration of a husband who's an expert rose gardener and a wife who's an interior designer has resulted in a stunning display.

Over 7,000 white lights adorn the peaks, eaves, trees and bushes of this sprawling split-level home. An ivory-colored manger scene nestles among the evergreens, and a trio of straw deer with wreaths about their necks amble in the distant snow. Sixteen wide-eyed choir boys, handmade from an original by Dave's father, are sometimes heard "singing" near the drive.

Unable to use their clothes dryer or dishwasher in past years while the decorations were lit, the Lienau's look forward to next season. They've added 12 circuits and upgraded their electrical service to 200 amps. Now Dave may not have to tiptoe so lightly with that new case of white lights, as strains of "Silent Night" echo from Carole's choir boys.

Sun. after Thanksgiving–Jan. 10, 4:30PM–11:00PM. *From Euclid St., N on Arlington Hts. Rd. 1/2 mi., W on Oakton St. 3/4 mi., N on Kennicott Ave. 1/4 mi.*

Weatherproofing Wood

Janine Karkow discovered that oil-based varnish used over acrylic paint to preserve outdoor wooden decorations will gradually yellow, causing an antique look. The tint worked well on her Victorian family, but if this is not the desired effect, a water-based breakthrough provides a lasting clear finish.

The plastic figurines that fill the Chiappetta yard create a magical playland for children.

❻ 210 East Maude Avenue

At the start of each holiday season, Ashley, Jenna, Brent and Matt excitedly huddle on grandma and grandpa's front porch waiting their turns to light the Christmas decorations.

Matt flips the first switch—on come 38 toy soldiers guarding the front sidewalk. The children laugh with delight. Brent flips the second switch—nine snowmen, three elves and five Santas spring from the darkness. The little boys run to see Santa and his reindeer flying across the roof. Jenna flips the third switch—28 carolers come to life as Christmas music begins to play. She waves her arms before the choir leading them in song. Ashley flips the fourth switch—the Christmas story unfolds as three kings, their camels and a shepherd stand before Joseph, Mary and Baby Jesus.

Edward and Virginia Chiappetta beam with joy as they watch their grandchildren jumping about in the holiday playground. The children's laughter makes all their efforts worthwhile.

Easily visible from Arlington Heights Road, the Chiappetta's display is a favorite among neighborhood children as well. One little boy, who had been looking at decorations with his dad, awarded the couple a box of candy because he liked their house the best.

Ed doesn't mind if youngsters walk up the path to the manger scene. They really enjoy being in the middle of 150 lighted figures. He recalls his happiness as a little boy when his dad decorated the house for him. For the last thirty years he has been happy to share this memory with his children, his grandchildren and all the little people who visit his display.

Dec. 1–Jan. 6, Dusk–10:00 PM. *From Palatine Rd., S on Arlington Hts. Rd. 2 bl., E on Maude Ave.*

❼ 1506 South Princeton Avenue

"This is the house! This is the house!" cried the elderly grandma, as though she had found a missing treasure. When her two small grandchildren discovered the source of her excitement, all three stared at the house on Princeton Avenue beaming with delight.

Young and old alike are thrilled to see the unique assortment of holiday characters that adorn the lawn of Donald and Dolores Tasch. Three cheery elves mix a brew of egg nog, while their elfin friends

Two Candy Canes for the Price of One

To make his candy canes sit flat against the house, Don Tasch cautiously cuts them in half. (A Dremel® tool with an emery wheel is recommended for the task.)

He then cuts half-inch plywood to fit the inside outline of the candy cane. A large hole is drilled into the wood to accommodate a 7-watt bulb, and several smaller holes are added to prevent over-heating. The wood is screwed into the candy cane at the sides with sheet metal screws.

The canes are attached to the house with two pieces of perforated strapping, screwed to the outside edge of the cane a few feet apart. The other end of the strapping is screwed to the house. With aluminum siding the strapping can be twisted and screwed to the underside of the panels.

load a sleigh full of toys. A pair of reluctant reindeer stand by, anticipating the work ahead. Santa and Mrs.Claus check over their list, which includes the names of the Tasch's seven children and eighteen grandchildren. Two soldiers stand guard on the garage, and a gingerbread couple smile hand in hand.

Don builds all the delightful wooden displays in his workshop. He does such an outstanding job, that even the company which designed the original patterns was impressed. "You wouldn't want to come out and do ours would you?" wrote Ken Williams of Wooden Memories®.

Using a band saw and a power sander, Don enhances the company's patterns by making them larger and adding several layers of wood for a three-dimensional effect. Some of the figures have as many as six layers and take as long as one month to build. For durability he uses a weatherproof wood glue and two coats of bright enamel craft paint.

The yard is also home to a waving snowman Don made from three wire wreaths welded together and backed with plexiglass. It glows amid the bushes and trees, which are covered with colored lights. In the background the Tasch's house looks good enough to eat, decked in candy canes, lollipops and gingerbread men.

Since 1990 Don has earned first place in the Arlington Heights decorating contest every year. He and Dolores were also honored by a choral group from Rolling Meadows High School, who appeared at the door to sing carols in thanks for their efforts.

Dec. 1–Mid-Jan., Dusk–2:00AM. From Golf Rd., NW on Algonquin Rd. 1/4 mi., R on Kennicott Dr. 1 bl., L on S. Princeton Ave.

❽ 2727 North Vista Road

On a snowy day this lovely home outlined in glimmering white is picture perfect as it peeks through the barren trees. Its cathedral windows reveal a stunning 18-foot Christmas tree. Trimmed with over 5,000 colored lights and 500 ornaments, it is the Green family's pride and joy.

Bruce and Janet special order the giant wild balsam each year from a nursery in Upper Peninsula Michigan. Even with the help of their three children it takes an entire week to trim. A pole is needed to hang decorations toward the top.

Getting a tree this large into the house is one thing, but getting it out, once the branches have dried and fallen open, is another story. The Greens strip all but the top five feet and throw the branches out the window. The uppermost section is left to dry

Delightful handmade wooden figures decorate the Tasch home.

Santa pops up from his chimney at the Christoffel's.

for the summer and covered with snakes and spiders for Halloween. The trunk is cut into pieces and burned as a yulelog the following Christmas.

In a tradition begun by Janet's father, the family saves a slice of the trunk, woodburns the date in it and dips it in polyurethane. The slices hang on the wall each holiday season as a reminder of all the happy Christmases the family has shared together.

Dec. 14–Jan. 7, Dusk–10:30PM. *From Arlington Hts. Rd., E on Hintz Rd. 1/4 mi., N on Vista Rd. (Douglas Ave.)*

DES PLAINES

❾ 317 Harding Avenue

What becomes of a corporate electronic engineer who formerly expressed his wild creative side by designing pyrotechnics, black lights and chaser spots for bands such as the Spit Balls, Crash and the Moody Blues?

At the suburban residence of Bill Christoffel, now a happily married father of three, the black lights have been replaced with bulbs of red and green, the chaser lights are rotating about a Christmas tree and the closest thing to fireworks is a cheery Santa popping up and down out of a red brick chimney. Though "Nights in White Satin" has

been replaced by "Jingle Bells," Bill has found that delighting his neighbors can be just as much fun as causing a hippie to yell, "Party, man."

The first Christmas after Bill and his family moved into the area, the neighbors watched curiously as he spent two weeks covering his house with lights. They were amused when the glass block windows blinked in a sequence of reds, yellows and greens. They were impressed when the nativity star beamed a light to the manger through a tube of plastic. They smiled at the two little skaters balancing on a glittering pond. But when they passed by the house and caused music to play and Santa to emerge from a chimney and shout, "Ho, Ho, Ho," they were truly awestruck by Bill's electronic wizardry.

With an elevator-like chain-driven system, the 3-foot "pop-up Santa," as the neighborhood kids have dubbed him, rises from a chimney equipped with ice scrapers and a heater. His sudden appearance is triggered by a passive infrared sensor. A dual-channel tape system allows Santa's message to be reset without repeating the entire chorus of the music. In 1995 Bill intends to add a penguin sliding out of an igloo to begin the sequence.

At the suggestion of Bill's oldest son, Santa's innards recently doubled as the workings of an Easter Bunny jumping out of his basket. This has inspired the possibility of a pop-up character for every occasion. Neighbors have only one response—"Party, man."

Dec. 11–Jan. 15, Dusk–12:00AM, (Christmas week)–3:00AM. *From Wolf Rd., W on Golf Rd. 1 bl., S on Warrington Rd. 3 bl., W on Harding Ave. 1/2 bl.*

Assorted Decorating Tips From Arlington Heights Sculptor Fran Volz

Cardboard tubes, used for building cement posts, make ideal candles or peppermint sticks when covered with contact paper.

To disguise light strand wiring, slice the length of an old rubber hose and drill holes for the sockets to fit through.

Polyester fiberfill sprayed with paint makes authentic-looking fur and withstands winter weather.

Parishioners Barbara Dopp and David, Candice, Camille and Dawn Gerald take part in the living nativity scene at Christ Church in Des Plaines.

⑩ Christ Church
1492 Henry Avenue

A life-size crèche stands in the front yard of this colonial church with the figures of the Holy Family, shepherds standing watch and kings bearing gifts. It is a scene familiar to all the Christian world, depicting the birth of Jesus.

But these figures are not carved in wood or cast in plastic or stone. In the manger at Christ Church they are members of the parish who volunteer an hour of their busy lives to experience the hush of a straw-filled manger.

Joseph wears hiking boots under his tunic. One shepherd holds her staff with ski mittens. Another's furry hood protrudes from her garb. Cars pull up and

The First Crèche

Saint Francis of Assisi was inspired with the idea of a manger scene as a means of telling the story of Christ's birth. After acquiring the Pope's permission in 1223, he hired local craftsmen to construct a stable, where real people and animals depicted the holy scene.

parishioners chat over hot cocoa. Yet, somehow, it doesn't seem to take away from the feeling in the air of a holy time when a Child was born in Bethlehem.

Dec. 17–Dec. 23, 6:00PM–8:00PM. *From Des Plaines River Rd., W on Algonquin Rd. 2 bl., N on Cora St. 2 bl.*

⑪ Lake Mary Anne

Drivers on the Tri-State Tollway have a brighter commute during the holidays thanks to a giant snowman that glows across Lake Mary Anne at Golf Road. The 27-foot decoration adorns the home of Gerald and Arlene Kane, whose son Todd and son-in-law Doug helped build the colossal figure in 1987.

The snowman's top hat and arms, and the seven, eight, and 10-foot "snowballs" that form his body are made of 10-foot lengths of conduit, screwed together with couplings for easy storage and assembly. After being wrapped with strands of C-9 bulbs, the snowballs are hoisted into position with a pulley and screwed separately to the house.

The Kane's home is also completely outlined in multicolored bulbs. The reflection on the lake makes the already lustrous display appear twice as bright.

Dec. 1–Jan. 6, 4:30PM–12:30AM. *This display is best viewed from the expressway. Drivers are cautioned not to slow down or stop. E of the Tri-State Twy. (I-294), N of Golf Rd.*

Doug and Arlene Kane's 27-foot snowman sends a cheery greeting to drivers on the Tri-State Tollway.

Surprise, Surprise

At 5:00AM one November morning in 1982, Al Thomas was in a cab returning from a trip to Palm Springs. While turning the corner, the driver exclaimed, "My God, look at that house!" Al looked to see a two-story home, completely outlined in large colored bulbs from roof to shrubs. "That's MY house!" he replied in shock. His wife, Charlene, wanted to surprise him while he was on vacation, and that she did.

The family has continued to decorate every year, but plan to move in the near future. Many will remember their brightly lit home, which is visible from the Tri-State Tollway off Golf Road. Its approximate 7,050 C-9 bulbs, which were taken down yearly and stored in barrels, required twelve 20-amp, 120-volt circuits. The 18,750-watt usage costs $15 per day to light. The electrical drain would often cause fuses to blow— a frequent decorating problem even for Al, an electrical contractor.

⑫ 445 West Millers Road

When Art and Pat Lukowicz began decorating their home in 1961, they trimmed the little evergreen in front of the house with one strand of seven lights. In every season that followed they added more lights to the growing tree. At last count, the 35-foot evergreen required over 1,400 lights and was visible from a block away.

Keeping with tradition the couple uses the large C-9 bulbs. Lighting the tree alone requires five 20-amp electrical circuits and more wattage than their summer air conditioning. A bucket truck is rented to reach the top of the tree. At a cost of $60 an hour, the truck is only kept long enough to decorate what can't be reached with a pole. The lights are wrapped around the branches, and each plug connection between strands is tied in a knot to keep everything secure in heavy winds.

Candy canes and lollipops circle the base of the tree. Toy soldiers, teddy bears and gingerbread men line the walks and drive. A magnificent 8-foot lighted wreath frames the porch of the front entryway, where families often pose for Christmas photos.

Art covers the garage door with heavy-duty aluminum foil taped around the edges of each panel. He then glues on decorations cut from half-inch styrofoam insulation. By cutting the material where the door panels come together, he is still able to use the garage. The door has been a giant present covered in gift tags, a fireplace trimmed with stockings and surrounded by elves, and a collection of snowmen. Though the display on the garage door changes every year, it is always decorated with the names of Art and Pat's nine grandchildren.

Sun. after Thanksgiving–Jan. 6, Dusk–10:00PM.
From Dempster St. (Thacker St.), N on Elmhurst Rd. (Rt.83) 2 bl., E on Millers Rd. to 1st cul-de-sac on rt.

Amanda Wozny and Stephanie and Scott Howard convinced their parents to turn Westfield Gardens into Candy Cane Land.

*The lighted evergreen that towers over the Lukowicz home
draws visitors to a yard full of surprises.*

⓭ Westfield Gardens

During the holiday season of 1991, Amanda Wozny and Scott and Stephanie Howard went looking at Christmas decorations with their parents. They visited Schiller Park, where many of the streets have a common yuletide theme. When the youngsters returned home, there was more than hot chocolate and Christmas cookies on their minds. "We should do that around here," they said. Inspired by their children's enthusiasm, the parents agreed to the plan, and Candy Cane Land was born.

At first the idea was discussed among a few of the neighbors. The response was favorable, so Jim Wozny and Tom and Debbie Howard sent letters to all the households in Westfield Gardens inviting them to join in the effort. A local store owner agreed to discount the price of 30-inch plastic candy canes to those who presented the letter.

In its first year, over 70% of the residents participated in the project. At last count, 307 candy canes lit the five-block area in front of over 80% of the homes. Non-participants seem to be moving away, leaving the door open for greater numbers still.

The idea has not only lit up the street, but the community spirit of the area as well. "We have gotten to know everybody. It has really brought the neighborhood together," Jim commented.

Elderly residents, unable to assemble their own displays, are assisted by generous neighbors and delighted to see the block aglow. Eighty-year-old Herb Long, who holds the record for the best-decorated house in the area, uses his charm to convince the senior ladies to participate in the project.

Twice a week Scott, Amanda and Stephanie accompany their parents as they drive through the neighborhood in a decorated station wagon to replace burnt-out bulbs. "They've been a big part of it—all three of them," Jim Wozny says proudly. The children's parents now distribute a neighborhood newsletter about the decorations and other community concerns four times a year.

In Westfield Gardens the simple notion of a child has created a spirit of neighborhood camaraderie among the young, the old and everyone in between. And wasn't that the plan of another little child from the start?

Sun. after Thanksgiving–Jan. 1, Dusk–10:00PM.
*From Algonquin Rd., N on Mt. Prospect Rd. 1/4 mi.,
E on Walnut Ave.*

Mary Hoffman has all the tools needed for a winning display.

ELK GROVE VILLAGE

⓮ 1703 Biesterfield Road

Seventy-six-year-old Mary Hoffman loaded two sheets of quarter-inch plywood on the top of the car with the help of her 72-year-old sister, Marge. They were bringing materials to Mary's basement workshop for a Christmas display she was building for her son, David, and his family.

It seems that her daughter-in-law, Cindy, had discussed the neighborhood Christmas decorating contest with her and hinted, "You're good at this. Why don't you help us?" Cindy, David and their five little boys could handle the lights and the plastic figurines, but they needed something extra special. Mary, a talented handywoman, obliged adding, "I'll help you win first place."

So, for the Christmas of 1991 the Hoffman's corner lot was not only covered in lights and figurines, but adorned with Mary's homemade wooden figures of a choir of angels, Santa and his reindeer and a "Happy Holiday" sign held by Rudolph. The Hoffman family won first place in the neighborhood contest. Grandma had come through.

Mary has since built figures of a little girl playing an organ, two drummer boys, a snowman, three choir boys and a 5-foot Santa with a band of elves— all from patterns cut out of plywood. She also made a sign reading "Peace on Earth" with a star outlined in 150 lights, which were individually mounted in holes she drilled into the wood.

Mary Hoffman obviously does not engage in the typical hobbies of a petite woman in her seventies.

"I took up hairdressing…but I preferred machinery," she explained.

During World War II, she was a top-ranked machinist for Douglas Aircraft, where she set up, operated and tore down her own milling machine— skills uncommon to women at the time.

After the war Mary and her husband, Carl, were roofing and insulation contractors and owned several buildings. Often when a tenant would call with a problem, Carl would ask her to go see what was wrong. When she would return with the details he would tell her, "Go fix it." She still does much of her own home repair, including electrical and plumbing work.

In addition to her son's Christmas decorations, she enjoys making egg ornaments with miniature dioramas and table-top Christmas villages. She also hopes to find the time to build some feeders and bird houses for her yard.

However, with the recent birth of David and Cindy's first daughter, Grandma is bursting with new ideas

Using Patterns to Create Two-Dimensional Figures

Mary Hoffman buys patterns from local craft stores or mail order catalogs. She traces the figures onto quarter-inch plywood sheets and cuts them out with a scroll saw. The back and sides of the wood are painted with two coats of outdoor paint.

The patterns are then either traced onto the wood and painted by hand or glued directly to the plywood. For gluing, plastic resin glue brushed on the wood or a glue solution made with corn starch seems to adhere best. The patterns should be rolled or rubbed down with a soft cloth. Mary outlines the figures in glitter sprinkled on a bead of white glue.

Whether painted or glued, the figures are then protected with two coats of outdoor varnish or clear lacquer. Mary cautions that the colors of the glued patterns are apt to run, so brushing should be done with care. She prefers spraying two thin coats of varnish.

Granny's homemade decorations trim the Hoffman home.

she could not have created for her five grandsons. On Easter she made the four-month-old, who still had no hair, a straw bonnet covered in flowers and ribbons with blonde bangs and long flowing curls glued to the inside. Brittany, meet your Grandma.

Thanksgiving–Jan.14, (Su–Th) Dusk–10:00PM, (F–Sa) –11:00PM. *From Meacham Rd., W on Biesterfield Rd. 1/4 mi., At Wise Rd.*

⑮ 807 Galleon Lane

Taryn Ross was quite surprised when her husband, Marty, suddenly began painting Christmas characters for the outside of their home. She joked, "He's a CPA. They have no artistic talent."

Marty, using pictures from his children's coloring books, drew the figures freehand on plywood, cut them out and painted them. The results proved he had more than accounting skills.

He began with the Cookie Monster stuffing himself with Christmas treats and went on to create the entire cast of Sesame Street characters decked for the holidays. Bert and Ernie, wrapped in scarves, sing carols arm in arm, while Big Bird, wearing earmuffs, decorates a whimsical tree. Oscar the Grouch, inside his garbage can adorned with a big red stocking, smiles at the "Sesame St. Express" as it pulls a trainload of toys. Even the Ross' house gets in the act with a cartoon chimney.

On the other side of the yard Marty created a winter town complete with a gingerbread house, a log cabin, an igloo with penguins and a steepled church with stained-glass windows. Overhead, where the basketball net used to be, flies a helicopter with a propeller that blows in the wind.

Marty's creations not only earned second place in the competitive Elk Grove Village decorating contest, but a little boy was so convinced with his painting of the igloo that he wanted to go inside.

Dec. 6–Jan.15, 5:00PM–10:30PM. *From Meacham Rd., W on Nerge Rd. 2 bl., N on Cutter Ln. 1 bl., W on Galleon Ln. 2-1/2 bl.*

Living Room Furniture Dioramas

By cleverly using her living room wall unit as a backdrop for her window scene, Taryn Ross saved space and was still able to access the cabinet's drawers and shelves. She placed the backsides of the unit a few feet in front of the window and decorated it with aluminum foil and home-made paper trees.

Using tables of varying heights, Taryn created a multi-level platform, which she covered with fake snow. She then posed the kids' toy animals around the scene. A stuffed dog, which went round and round chasing his tail, was actually sitting on the turntable of the record player.

16 1843 Oriole Drive

Jim Iovino's childhood address is probably the envy of every kid who grew up on the northwestside of Chicago in the fifties and sixties. He lived in the Schorsch Village neighborhood on the 3200 block of North Nottingham Avenue, otherwise known as Candy Cane Lane (see pages 21–24) "Christmastime

was pure joy," Jim recalls. "It was like living in the Land Of Oz." Every house on his street was glowing with lights and 10-foot candy canes. Carloads of people lined the street, and families crowded the sidewalks, all coming to see the display.

"The anticipation was so much fun. It was really an event to look forward to," Jim says, still reveling in the memory. "I have clear visions of seeing my block on the news and staring out the window watching all the cars go by. It was especially fun when my cousins would come over, and I could take them down all the streets with me. It was like a storyland."

Having lived on Nottingham Avenue from 1949 to 1978, Jim experienced the thrill of this holiday phenomenon during its 20-year history from start to finish. "Christmas isn't the same without it," he remarks. So as an adult with his own house and family, he has tried to recreate the magic of his childhood holidays for his three children.

At Christmastime, with the kids' help, Jim turns their ranch home into a candy cottage that has been an annual winner in the town's decorating contest since 1990. Giant foil-wrapped hard candies and peppermint canes trim the sides of the house and the garage. Candy canes, plastic lampposts and colorful all-day suckers, big enough to last a month, cover the lawn. In the center of them all proudly stands the faithful reminder of the wonderful

The tasty trimmings in Jim Iovino's front yard surround the 10-foot candy cane from his childhood home.

The Polich home shines brightly on Schooner Lane.

HANOVER PARK

⑱ 6831 Hickory Street

The festive roof of this two-story home can be seen a block away. "Happy Holidays" glistens from the peak. A cross of lights shimmers on the shingles. Yuletide candles shine from two aerials. And a 4-foot star is perched high atop a CB radio antenna.

It may appear that homeowner, Vernon Moore, is a daredevil of sorts, but he actually does not relish heights. He just likes to decorate his entire house—roof and all. So Vernon and his family trim the lawn by day, and he does the roof at night. He reasons, "As long as I can't see the ground, I'm all right."

Dec. 1–Jan. 2, 5:00PM–11:00PM. *From Irving Park Rd., S on Barrington Rd. 3/4 mi., W on Walnut Ave. 3/4 mi., N on Hickory St.*

Christmases of Jim's youth—the original candy cane from his family's front yard.

Perceptive passersby often stop to ask if the familiar peppermint is from the famous display. When Jim happily confirms their suspicions, it's certain that the aging candy cane still holds its magic as the visitors drive away fondly recounting their memories of Candy Cane Lane.

Dec. 15–Jan. 6, 4:00PM–12:00AM. *From Meacham Rd., W on Nerge Rd. 1-1/2 mi., N on Plum Grove Rd. 1/4 mi., E on Oriole Dr.*

⑰ 779 Schooner Lane

The Christmas spirit is bursting from the homes of the Windemere Subdivision, and this Schooner Lane residence is one of the brightest. When asked exactly how many lights are used to cover the trees and bushes, and line the eaves, windows, roof and sidewalk, homeowner Barbara Polich simply answers, "To the point of frostbite."

She and her husband, Michael, recently began decorating for Halloween as well. No sooner do they get the graveyard cleared away and Mike free of his moldy mummy gauze, than they are crawling up on the roof with lights.

Dec. 16–Jan. 6, 7:00PM–11:00PM. *From Meacham Rd., W on Nerge Rd. 1/4 mi., N on Cutter Ln. 2 bl., E on Schooner Ln. 1/2 bl.*

Lights abound from the roof to the ground at the Moores.

Homemade holiday cartoons decorate the Hiser lawn.

HOFFMAN ESTATES

⑲ 1450 Caldwell Lane

Since 1975 Gene and Jeannie Hiser have been creating two-dimensional Christmas characters out of plywood. Jeannie's oldest brother, Artie, started the family tradition years ago using designs from Popular Mechanics.

With a painting contractor's old opaque projector, used for copying patterns onto walls, Jeannie traces figures onto 3/4-inch plywood. Gene cuts them out with a jigsaw. The figures are then painted with two coats of exterior latex paint. It usually takes about two hours to complete one character.

The Hisers add to the display each year, which now includes a penguin, bunny, goose, lamb and chipmunk dressed for the holidays; two elves helping Santa out of a chimney; a group of reindeer hoisting bags of gifts to the roof; Santa engineering a trainload of toys; elves carrying packages, untangling lights, painting candy canes, loading a train and building a snowman; and two eskimos being pulled in a dog sled. Because the decorations are easy to stack, the Hisers still have plenty of room to store the other set of characters that decorate their lawn for Halloween.

Sun. after Thanksgiving–Jan.1, Dusk–11:00PM.
From Barrington Rd., E on Higgins Rd. (Rt.72) 1-1/4 mi., S on Oakmont Rd. 1 bl., E on Caldwell Ln. 1 bl.

PALATINE

⑳ "Festival of Trees"

Fifty decorated balsam trees, representing every state in the union, line the corner of Palatine Road and Smith Street for this annual event organized by the local chamber of commerce.

Each tree is sponsored by one of its members. A few of the businesses choose to decorate their own trees, but most are done by local children's groups. "The kids love to drive by and look at 'their' tree," says Debbie Lee, whose brownie troop trimmed the Delaware tree. Some ornaments are contributed by

Enlarging Drawings onto Plywood

Though an opaque projector, available at art supply stores for about $70, is a handy tracing tool for enlarging drawings, the grid method works as well. Draw a grid of small squares over the original drawing. On the plywood draw the same grid enlarged to the desired size of the decoration. Copy the drawing one square at a time onto the plywood. This works especially well when the drawing is upside down.

out-of-state natives, and many are made from recycled materials. Every year at the center of the display, a special 18-foot "angel tree" is trimmed with paper angels, each bearing the name and age of a needy child.

On the Sunday after Thanksgiving, the village has a lighting ceremony. The mayor and Santa Claus arrive by firetruck, and there is hot chocolate and caroling. Children proudly point to the ornaments they made, and 100 families choose an "angel" from the center tree for whom they will buy a Christmas gift.

Sun. after Thanksgiving–1st weekend in Jan., Dusk–12:00AM. *From Plum Grove Rd., W on Palatine Rd. 4 bl., At Smith St.*

ROSELLE

㉑ 500 Block of May Street
100 Blocks of Albion and Arthur Avenue
(pictured on page 59)

The glow coming from south of the Elgin-O'Hare Expressway near Roselle Road might appear to be the opening of a new theme park, but it's actually the delightful consequence of a square block of Roselle neighbors getting in the mood for the holidays.

It all started in 1985 when Gene and Carol Orrico, who live at the corner of May and Albion, decorated

Richard Rhode's homemade wooden cartoon characters add to the fun on May Street.

their home for the new block's first annual neighborhood Christmas party. The house was trimmed with garlands. There was a snowman on the chimney and a couple of soldiers out front. On the roof were two teddy bears, one for each of their children. The nine families on the block attended the party, and one of the dads dressed up as Santa Claus.

In the years since, the street has grown to fifteen homes, and the Orricos display has expanded in all directions. There are four teddy bears on the roof, 105 soldiers guarding the house, tens of thousands of lights, 14 trellises over the walk, a glowing two-story turret archway over the driveway and an electric bill that soars to $500 for the season. To accommodate the cars of sightseers, sometimes over 4,000 a night, the village makes the streets one way. And to accommodate the electrical usage, the Orricos have added outlets all around the exterior of the house.

The family's annual block party has grown to nearly 200 guests. Six high school girls dressed as tin soldiers greet visitors at the door. Santa and Mrs. Claus arrive by horse-drawn carriage. An Elvis impersonator sings Christmas carols. Victor and Wally Elf perform a song and dance routine. Caricature artists draw cartoons of the guests, and crabs wearing Santa hats race for prizes.

Gene Orrico, a fit man in his fifties, likes to do all the outdoor decorating of his home himself. He begins with the roof work two weeks before Thanksgiving, while the weather is still good, and works on the display every night, often until 2:00AM. He even takes a few days off from his regular job as a general contractor just to decorate.

Gene first attaches the wooden frames that support the soldiers surrounding the top of the house and gradually decorates his way to the ground. Right up to Christmas Eve he adds a little more each day and makes repairs throughout the season. "I'm going out to maintain," he announces nightly. Yet this avid decorator never seems to tire of the holidays. One year he dressed as Santa Claus to pass out candy canes to the crowds. After standing in the cold for an hour and a half, Gene had to be dragged into the house, waving to passersby all the while.

Carol, whose aunt lived on Chicago's famous Reindeer Lane (see page 22), shares her husband's zeal. In 1987 she ordered a truckload of 60 toy soldiers to decorate May Street. She tied a couple to the mail boxes of the new vacant homes, sold one or more to each of her neighbors, and Toy Soldier Lane was born. Though the Orrico home is still the most elaborately decorated, other homes in the neighborhood have joined in the fun with charming features of their own:

527 May – Two 5-foot toy soldiers, custom-made from half-inch pipe and mini-lights, stand at attention at the Yentes household.

534 May – Owner Richard Rhode designed and built the adorable toy soldiers guarding the entryway, the impish elves lining the lawn and the timid reindeer hiding in the bushes.

537 May – "When you said you decorate, you really meant it," reacted the Murphy family when they first moved onto the block in 1988. They have since joined forces with the Orrico's across the street to suspend Santa and his sleigh pulled by nine reindeer from their chimneys. Roselle makes them sign a waiver of responsibility each year, so the town can't be held liable if Rudolph loses his way.

On the ground below, two homemade miniature houses feature Victorian living rooms with wreaths over the fireplaces and animated dolls.

540 May – Children sneak a peek at Santa's Workshop and Victorian dolls decorate a Christmas tree in two delightful dioramas that add to the splendor of the Pesole family's home.

151 Albion – Known for their frightening Halloween display, the Gallaghers come through for Christmas as well. A delightful fireplace scene, a giant 30-foot candy cane, a collection of huge brightly-wrapped presents, wooden reindeer, a choo-choo train riding through a tunnel and a penguin display right out of the South Pole ornament their front lawn.

109 and 110 Arthur – The Reillys and the DiMarias decorate their yards in homemade gumdrops and lollipops. It's a delectable entryway to their street's Candy Cane Lane, where many homes are catching on to the theme.

To avoid the traffic and experience the holiday spirit these neighbors work so hard to convey, dress warmly, park your car on Lincoln, Arthur or Schreiber and take an enchanting walk down the trellised sidewalks of May Street, as well as Arthur and Albion.

2nd Sun. in Dec.–Jan.4, 5:00PM–11:00PM. *From the Elgin-O'Hare Expwy., S on Roselle Rd. 2 bl., W on Schreiber Ave. 1 bl., N on Marion St. 1 bl., W on Arthur Ave. 1 bl., N on May St., W on Albion.*

ROSEMONT

㉒ Village Decorations

The Village of Rosemont barely covers two square miles. Criss-crossed by expressways and corridors of commercial facilities, the population of the small residential area is only 4,000 people. Judging from the glitter that brightens I-90 every Christmas season, it seems safe to say that the inhabitants of Rosemont have the highest per capita holiday wattage of any town in northeastern Illinois.

Credit for this phenomenon most likely belongs to longtime mayor Don Stephens. His son Brad recalls the family's past holidays, "My father has always loved Christmas. He would take us four kids to my grandmother's, and when we'd come home, Santa Claus would be at the end of the street waving to us. Our house was decorated with a moving snowman that wiped the snow off the window, flocked trees, a big train and a winter village. Only dad was allowed to place the cotton that made the village look like it was covered with snow."

To the mayor's delight, he now has a real village to decorate. He even lets his son Brad, carpenter and general foreman of O'Hare Expo Center, do most of the work.

Exiting north on River Road from the Kennedy Expressway, the mayor's decorations begin with dozens of trees bathed in Italian lights. At the corner

Donald E. Stephens Park becomes a festive playland with giant balloons, holiday dioramas and Santa himself.

The Syzdek's sugary house looks good enough to eat.

of Higgins Avenue a giant snowman offers the town's first yuletide greeting from inside his snowy dome. To the southwest Dunne Park at Willow Creek and Glen Lake joins the fun with an assortment of giant inflated holiday figures.

Further west on Higgins Road at Scott, visitors are treated to the delightful decorations at Donald E. Stephens Park, which has been catching the eye of tollway travelers since 1980. Three 30-foot illuminated hot air balloons of two toy soldiers and a cheery snowman tower over the one-acre site. The central Christmas tree, constructed of several smaller trees, rises 25 feet from the park's fountain. It is surrounded by a ring of life-size skaters carved in styrofoam by town resident Bonnie Geren.

Paths throughout the park lead to six little houses, just the right size for children to peek at the Christmas scenes within. Each house contains a Christmas tree decorated by Rosemont's primary school children.

During the week before Christmas, live barnyard animals graze in a petting stable. The farmer who owns them assures animal lovers that the sheep, goats, donkey, geese, pig and cow are treated better here than at the farm. "If they're cold they can go into a heat-lamp manger," he says.

Santa appears the same week. His schedule is posted outside his colorful home, a salvaged prop from the movie "Home Alone."

After walking through the park, visitors won't want to miss a drive through Rosemont's well-decorated residential area to the south, where homeowners have caught on to the mayor's spirit.

2nd Sun. before Christmas–Jan.6, Dusk–Dawn. Parking is available across I-90 in the lot off Higgins, in the health club lot 1 bl. west or on side streets near the park. *From the Kennedy Expwy. (I-90), W on I-190 towards O'Hare, N on River Rd. 1/2 mi., W on Higgins Rd. 1 mi.*

㉓ 10021 West Devon Avenue

"When we were buying this home all I could think of was what a great gingerbread house it would make for Christmas," Marie Syzdek confessed. No sooner was the furniture in place than she and her husband, Darryl, started a "candy shop" in their house, building peppermints, hard candies, suckers and Christmas cookies to merrily disguise their home.

Giant cherry and lime lollipops were cut from styrofoam, primed in latex, spray-painted with a swirl,

John Frank's 1993 display invited guests to make a wish.

and covered in cellophane with a dowel rod for a stick. Translucent hard candies were cleverly designed from clear plastic salad containers wrapped and tied in grape, lemon, lime, strawberry and blueberry-colored cellophane. Empty cardboard rolls from food wrap and toilet paper were painted, tied in cellophane and strung together to form ropes of candy garlands. Gingerbread cookies were cut out of half-inch plywood, painted brown and trimmed in white caulk.

Since they began their "confectionery" in 1991, the Syzdeks have created new candies annually to add to the display. So when their gingerbread house comes to life each holiday season, it's always a little bit sweeter than the last.

Dec. 7–Jan. 1, 5:00PM–12:00AM. *From Higgins Rd., S on Scott St. 1 bl., W on Devon Ave. 1/2 bl.*

㉔ 10007 West Hope Drive

Residents of Rosemont know Steve Dahlke not only as one of the village landscapers, but their only professional pumpkin carver. The two 400 to 800 pound pumpkin gargoyles that have graced the entrance to Donald E. Stephens Park the past several Halloweens were Steve's handiwork. He also carves a similar pumpkin for his own front yard each year.

For the Christmas season, Steve exercises his craft in a medium more appropriate for the holidays—ice. He has taken culinary classes in ice sculpture at Triton College, where he is a fine arts student. For his

family's display, Steve has a 400-pound block of ice delivered to his home at a cost of $50. Using a chain saw and chisels he has carved a reindeer, a Christmas tree, a toy soldier and the greeting "Merry Christmas." When the weather has stayed above freezing, he has carved as many as four sculptures in one year to replace those that melted.

Occasionally, Steve is lucky enough to find discarded ice sculptures left over from hotel parties. After a slippery ride home in the back of his station wagon, the sculptures can often be repaired, or the ice can be salvaged for a new design.

During a warm spell, visitors are likely to miss Steve's carvings. However, it will hardly be a total loss. He also trims the house and six evergreen trees exquisitely in lights.

Dec. 6–Jan. 1, 5:00PM–10:30PM. *From Higgins Rd., S on Scott St. 2 bl., W on Hope Dr. 1/2 bl.*

㉕ 6111 North Scott Street

John and Diane Frank enjoy decorating their house so much for Christmas that the lights never seem to be in the basement for long. The twinkling bulbs just move to the back yard where the trees, bushes and rock garden are decorated for parties in the summer.

A hobbyist woodworker, John has been adding to the lights with homemade holiday creations since his retirement. His first display of "Wishing Trees" was inspired by a children's story and a free load of wooden skids he salvaged from a construction dumpster. As the story goes…good little girls and boys who come upon the forest can make a wish and their Christmas dreams will come true.

However, like most magical places that never stay for long, the wishing trees vanished at the end of the season, as do all John's decorations. He gives them to his daughter in Wauconda and gets to work creating something even better for next Christmas.

Dec. 10–Jan. 6, 5:00PM–10:00PM. *From Higgins Rd., S on Scott St. 4-1/2 bl.*

㉖ 6236 North Scott Street

When Lori Anderson was a little girl, she seldom joined her sister in baking bread and cupcakes. She preferred to help her dad with his projects, such as building their garage. In her own first home, she helped gut the building to the studs and installed much of the wiring, plumbing and drywall.

So when she wanted to put Christmas decorations on the new home she and her husband, Tim, purchased in 1983, it was no surprise that Lori climbed to the peak of the roof and hung the 6,000 lights herself. She's been doing so ever since, and has recently been joined by her daughter, Becky.

In a society that has been making great strides in equality of the sexes, the vast majority of exterior holiday decorating, in particular the roofs, is still being done by men. Isn't it heartwarming to know that at least one woman has crossed the roof-lighting barrier, and that her husband is secure enough to feel no threat to his masculinity? Tim thinks so. As Lori and Becky put the ladder away, he and his son lean back on the couch and watch the hockey game.

Dec. 1–Jan. 1, 4:30PM–1:00AM. *From Higgins Rd., S on Scott St. 2-1/2 bl.*

STREAMWOOD

㉗ 42 Evergreen Drive

When Joseph Laflamme was a child he and his brother, Mike, would help their Aunt Rita decorate the outside of her home for Christmas. She had no children of her own, and the boys loved to decorate, so this annual event was a special treat for them all.

Now that Joseph has his own home, he continues the tradition his aunt inspired. A skating pond, a North Pole scene and a "Happy Holidays" sign fill the yard, which is outlined in candy canes. Snowmen smile from the window boxes, and lights abound.

Nov. 29–Jan. 1, Dusk–10:00PM. *From Bartlett Rd., W on Irving Park Rd. (Rt. 19) 1/2 mi., S on Merryoaks Rd. 1 bl., W on Evergreen Dr. 2 bl.*

㉘ 619 Wicker Avenue

Sam Ragano has been decorating for Christmas since he bought his first home in 1956. Nearing his eightieth birthday he continues to do so. "And I get better and better as the years go by," he says proudly. In 1991 when a neighbor told him about Streamwood's decorating contest he replied, "What do you mean? I never knew there ever was a contest. I always did this because I enjoyed it."

A lighted pegboard greeting sign welcomes visitors to the Laflamme display.

A cheery snowman shares a grin with his creator, Sam Ragano.

devised a rectangular conduit framework to fit over the shrubbery so lights could hang neatly in rows. Above the garage door, Santa and his reindeer fly over a glowing moon that Sam made from three hula-hoops lit from behind and covered with white plastic. "Mostly when I'm in bed I think about ideas, and I don't get any sleep," Sam said. "Though sometimes I get an idea in the daytime too."

One day when he received an advertisement on adhesive-backed phosphorescent paper, Sam knew he'd found a material he could use for stars to surround Santa and his sleigh. He called the funeral home that sent the mailing and traced the paper to its source. The paper company sent him some sample sheets. He got to work cutting out 100 stars, using the one on his flag as a guide.

Before the season is over, Sam is already excited about new things he'll try next year. "I just have the Christmas spirit. To me it's fun." If the town judged on enthusiasm, he'd be a sure winner every year.

Dec. 10 – Jan. 1, 5:00PM – 10:00PM. *From Barrington Rd., W on Irving Park Rd. 1 mi., N on Sunnydale Blvd. 1 bl., W on Wicker Ave. 1/2 bl.*

He entered that year and was one of 30 finalists. The lure of competition had him hooked. "The next year I got a letter from the village congratulating me for coming in fifth place. I was really proud of myself. I am trying for at least fourth place or more this year," he confides.

Though nearly blind, Sam does all his decorating himself. He has even invented a few gadgets to ease the process. Though he will not divulge the details, he has designed an extension pole that allows him to hang all his lights on gutters two stories from the ground, without using an extension ladder. Another device removes Italian light bulbs from their sockets, preventing broken fingernails.

A former precision grinder for Bell & Howell, Sam enjoys creating new decorations each year. He built a "Merry Christmas" sign over the front door from peg board laced with Italian lights and made a 7-foot snowman out of plywood. To line his sidewalk and driveway with lights, he made peppermint sticks out of conduit and drilled holes at the tops so a wire could be laced through to hold the strands. He also

WHEELING

㉙ Kingsport North Subdivision

For the past several holiday seasons the glow from the Kingsport North Subdivision has been attracting spectators to its well-lit displays. "It wasn't an organized effort," says resident Karen Wilson, whose home at 533 Briarwood is famous for its icicles of lights. "Neighbors see one house decorated, and then everybody else starts to do it."

Dec. 15 – Jan. 1, Dusk – 11:00pm. *From Elmhurst Rd. (Rt. 83), W on Hintz Rd. 1/4 mi., N on Longtree Dr. Travel up and down the streets west to Schoenbeck Rd.*

Icicles of Lights

The icicles that sparkle from the Wilson's eaves are as easy to make as they are attractive. Simply form loops of various sizes with white mini-lights and secure them with twist ties.

Chapter 6

COOK COUNTY–SOUTH

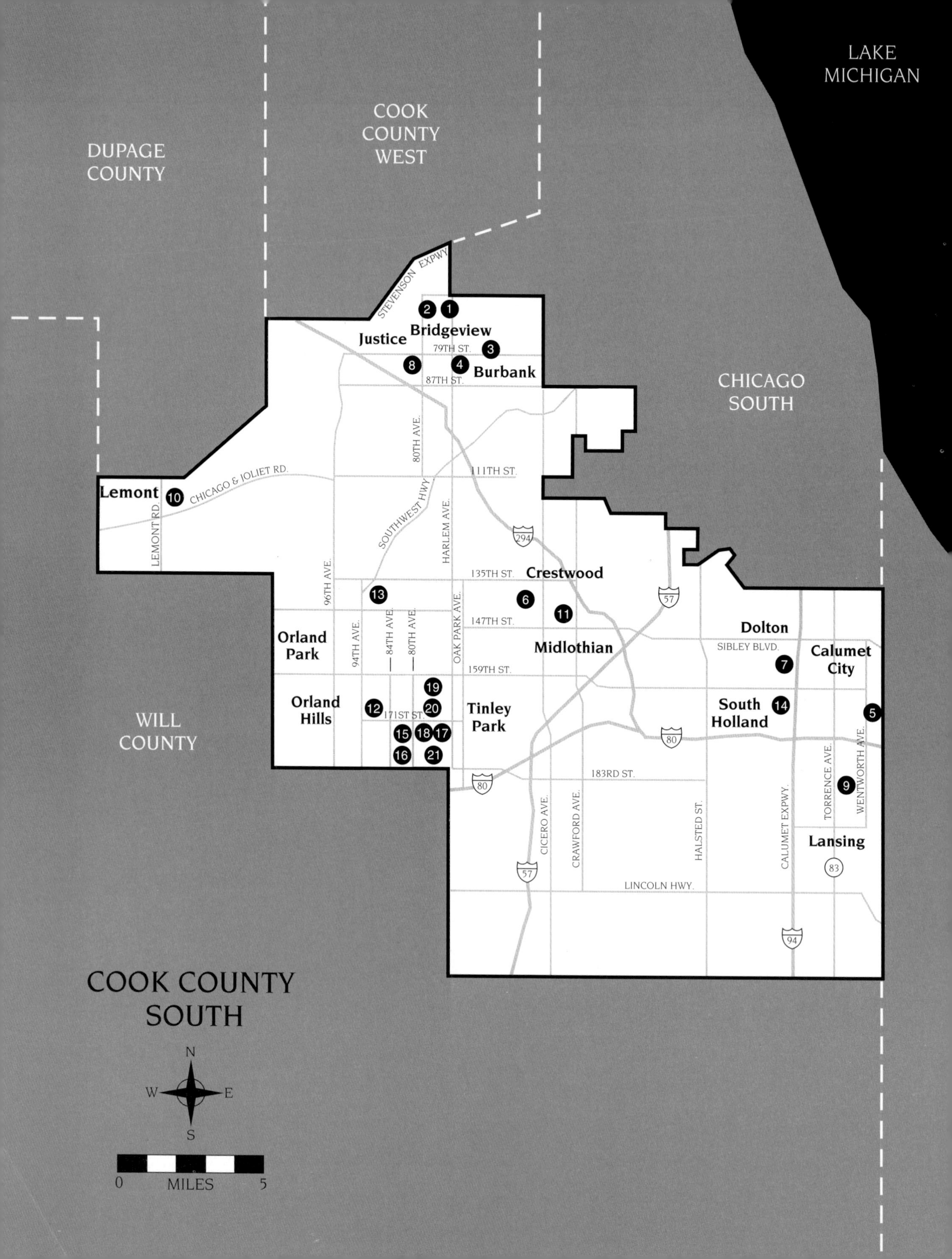

LAKE
MICHIGAN

DUPAGE
COUNTY

COOK
COUNTY
WEST

CHICAGO
SOUTH

STEVENSON EXPWY

② ①
Bridgeview
Justice
79TH ST.   ③
⑧   ④ **Burbank**
87TH ST.

80TH AVE.

CHICAGO & JOLIET RD.

Lemont ⑩
LEMONT RD.

SOUTHWEST HWY.

HARLEM AVE.

111TH ST.

294

135TH ST.   **Crestwood**

96TH AVE.

⑬
**Orland
Park**

94TH AVE.
84TH AVE.
80TH AVE.

OAK PARK AVE.

147TH ST.
⑥
⑪

Midlothian

159TH ST.

57

Dolton

SIBLEY BLVD.
⑦

**Calumet
City**

⑤

**Orland
Hills**

WILL
COUNTY

⑫ ⑲
171ST ST. ⑳
⑮ ⑱ ⑰
⑯ ⑳

**Tinley
Park**

**South
Holland** ⑭

WENTWORTH AVE.
TORRENCE AVE.

80

⑨

80
57

CICERO AVE.

CRAWFORD AVE.

183RD ST.

HALSTED ST.

CALUMET EXPWY.

Lansing
83

LINCOLN HWY.

94

**COOK COUNTY
SOUTH**

N
W   E
S

0   MILES   5

BRIDGEVIEW

❶ 7416 South Octavia Avenue

Charles was the first generation of Christmas decorators in the Pavel family. His former home on the 7400 block of Oketo was remembered for, among other decorations, a large mechanical Santa Claus that peeked in and out of a rooftop chimney.

Robert, Charles' son, carried on the family decorating tradition with his wife, Nancy, after they moved to their Octavia Avenue home a block away. His father's mechanical Santa Claus became a part of their elaborate display.

Santa eventually wore out and was replaced by other decorations, which were made by Robert, Nancy and their son, Jim. "I'm sure I'll continue decorating when I get my own house," Jim says. According to Robert, the family enjoys having a display that is "different than most you see," so the decorations are primarily homemade. A few items, such as Santa losing his pants to a big dog and Santa's burning pants being extinguished by a reindeer, were made from woodcraft patterns purchased from a Michigan-based company called The Winfield Collection. Most of the other decorations, however, are original designs.

The three large oilcloth stockings, brimming with gifts, that hang outside the living room window were built with plywood backs and newspaper stuffing to hold their shapes. The 8-foot candy canes that flank

The elves stay toasty in their Christmas tree lot at the Pavel home, where many of the displays are homemade.

It's a "Kool Yule" at the Jansen's, where new, used and homemade decorations fill the windows and yard.

the stairway were made from 8-inch-diameter metal ductwork painted white and striped with red vinyl ribbon. Though these two displays have appeared annually for the past 16 years, the family likes to change at least three items each season.

Viewers may see 3-foot snowflakes made from two intersecting pieces of plywood, a rooftop star beaming lights onto a manger scene, a miniature Christmas tree lot, penguins ice skating around an igloo, rows of 3-foot candy canes, a brightly-lit "Season's Greetings" sign or something completely different. The holiday spirit of Grandpa Charles certainly lives on.

Dec.6–Jan.7, 4:30PM–10:30PM. *From Harlem Ave., W on 74th St. 1 bl., S on Octavia Ave. 1/2 bl.*

❷ 7444 South Thomas

Like the Whos of Whoville in Dr. Seuss' storybook "The Grinch Who Stole Christmas," Robert and Laurie Jansen have managed to keep the spirit of the holiday alive despite a few misfortunes.

In 1989, after working days to assemble their decorations, the couple looked outside and found that their entire Christmas display had been stolen from the front of their home. "We're just going to go out and buy more," Robert said resolutely. They went to the store the very next day to replenish their collection.

The following December their home was under major construction. They had no living room ceiling, no plumbing and their four children were sharing a bedroom, but they still decorated for Christmas. When the lights were lit in the evening, passersby were awed by their display. "During the day, when you could see the construction, it looked horrible," Laurie confessed.

With the house nearly complete, the Jansens are now able to enjoy the holidays with a bit more calm. Their display changes and grows from year to year. "People like seeing new things," Laurie claims.

Robert, who owns a hardware store and is quite handy, makes many of the unique decorations. A moving carousel, a tree farm and a ferris wheel are among his most ambitious creations.

The Jansens have acquired most of their unusual items from want ads, garage sales and auctions. The life-size animated Santa that turns in the front door and checks his list was from an original Marshall Field's display, though the couple has added the names of the neighborhood children to his list. Numerous other animated dolls are part of delightful scenes in every window. Outdoors, a miniature train gives stuffed animals a ride around a Christmas tree, while illuminated figures, old and new, fill the front yard and fly through the air. A glistening star shines high upon the roof, leading spectators to the Jansen house from blocks away.

Though the home has won first place two years running in the local decorating contest, it has enjoyed equal fame for its extensive Halloween display. Robert has constructed a guillotine, a torture rack, animated coffins and an electric chair. Now that should discourage a would-be grinch.

Thanksgiving–Jan.15, 4:00PM–11:00PM (All day Christmas and New Year's). *From 79th St., N on Harlem Ave. 4 bl., W on 75th St. 5 bl., N on Thomas 1/2 bl.*

BURBANK

❸ 7819 South Natoma

A furry teddy bear rides the engine of a battery-powered train past Barney, Baby Bop, a skiing penguin, tobogganing Ninja Turtles, and dozens of other assorted stuffed toys. While a spare battery, charging when the other is in use, keeps the train running smoothly all evening, the inanimate toys in the scene seem to cause more problems.

When homeowners Debra and Douglas Klein attempt to use their children or grandchildren's favorite stuffed animals in the display, they often hear protests of "No, no, no, you can't take that one." The couple relents to the sentimental attachments of their offspring and purchases many of the furry creatures new. After all, the toys will be outdoors for a month and a half. However, Debra defends, "The stuffed animals hold up in the wet weather when left untouched. The wind dries them out really well."

In addition to the children's toys, the front yard also features an elf house, a snowbaby igloo, an ice skating pond and a manger scene. Santa and his reindeer fly through the air among twinkling lights, while animated dolls tell their own stories from windows all around the house.

The Klein display is so elaborate that during a recent season while the family was decorating, a couple walked into the house thinking it was a store.

Thanksgiving–Jan.1, 5:00PM–11:00PM. *From Harlem Ave., E on 79th St. 3/4 mi., N on Natoma 1/2 bl.*

Stuffed animals frolic on the Klein's snowy hill.

In 1993 John Cassidy's house was hard to miss.

A Burbank House Aglow

To say that John Cassidy is zealous about Christmas decorating is probably an understatement. At the age of four he was already dragging Christmas lights out in June. As a teenager he was nearly arrested in Willow Springs Woods for attempting to cut down a tree to build a manger scene. And as an adult he gave Clark Griswold a run for his money in 1993 by covering his entire house in lights. Although John has moved from his Rutherford Avenue home, his unique display certainly merits mention and may appear again someday lighting up another street for the season.

John contends that the red, white and green pallet he used on his former Burbank home did not look as garish as the white lights that covered the Griswold home in "National Lampoon's Christmas Vacation." As an electrical engineer for ComEd, John assuredly installed his display more safely than his counterpart's sparking wad of interconnected plugs. In fact passersby lucky enough to have seen his short-lived display agreed that the Cassidy house looked "really cool."

Contrary to public belief at the time John got no break on his electric bill, but his training did help him limit the bill's increase for the holidays. "Spread the usage among several circuits and use as few extension cords as possible," he recommends.

Though he shares his electrical tips he will not divulge the secret method he devised to attach the 10,000 lights that striped his siding, roof and awnings. He will only say that no hardware penetrated the roof.

With all his decorations in storage, John is sure his display will appear again someday along other innovations. He admits that the thrill of decorating for him is the challenge it presents. "If I think of an idea, can I make it work?" he says. Now there's a ComEd employee for you—always walking around with a light bulb over his head. ◆

❹ 8410 South Rutherford

It's all smiles at the south suburban residence of Clem and Jackie Hojnacki during the holidays. A giant yellow smiley face dressed in a furry red Santa hat shines his enormous grin over a dozen mini-smileys that dot the front yard with their sunny faces. But the smiles don't stop there.

A family of happy snowmen extend wishes for the New Year, while a trio of smiling dogs scamper alongside, toting doggie bones wrapped in big red bows. Jovial snowpeople slip and slide on an ice pond. Cheery gingerbread men dance atop a glistening evergreen tree, and a jolly Santa waves from the window. Even a mechanical melting snowman seems to accept his demise with a grin, knowing that in seconds he'll magically come to life again.

It's all smiles at the Hojnacki residence.

The Hojnackis, who have been decorating since 1970, make most of their decorations themselves and try to add something new to their display each season. "This is a time of year when we can give back a little happiness to others," explains Jackie. "When we make people happy, we all are happy too!"

During the week-and-a-half the family spends decorating their front lawn, they manage to keep their cheerful dispositions as well. When Clem slid off the roof and safely landed in the bushes, even he laughed. And when everyone works in the freezing cold to set up the display, Jackie directs the operation from inside her heated car—with a smile.

Dec. 1–Jan. 1, Dusk–12:00AM. *From Harlem Ave., E on 84th St. 7 bl., S on Rutherford.*

CALUMET CITY

⑤ 110 167th Street

The Schultz family has won so many prizes in the 6th Ward decorating contest in Calumet City, town officials decided to make them judges and give other homeowners a chance to win.

Dan and Arlene Schultz and their three daughters take their judging quite seriously as they drive throughout the neighborhood. All note their own impressions of the displays. When they arrive home,

the family has a discussion to choose the winners before presenting their votes to the other judges.

The Schultzes admit favoring homemade displays. Having made most of their own decorations, they understand the creativity and work involved. Dan's father began the family trend when he built a sleigh in 1956 so the kids could pose for pictures in it. The entire family has since contributed their talents to create a variety of colorful wooden decorations.

One of the most popular is a rooftop Santa stepping out of the chimney with his pants afire. A reindeer squirting him with an extinguisher appears quite effective when the chimney is smoking.

Fri. after Thanksgiving–Jan. 2, 4:30PM–10:30PM. *From Torrence Ave. (Rt.83), E on 159th St. 1-1/2mi., S on Wentworth Ave. 3/4 mi., E on 167th St.*

CRESTWOOD

⑥ House of Hughes
14300 South Cicero Avenue

The House of Hughes may be as renowned for its Christmas display as it is for its barbequed ribs. Perhaps because one of its cooks is as skilled at hanging lights as he is over the restaurant's open pit.

Antonio Garcia and his helpers trim the sprawling restaurant and surrounding bushes and trees with tens of thousands of miniature lights creating a dazzling spectacle. "It takes patience," Antonio recommends. And as for the ribs—Hughes' special BBQ sauce.

Thanksgiving–Mid-Jan., Dusk–2:00AM. Restaurant hours: 11:00AM–(at least)10:30PM. Lunch $6–$9, Dinner $15–$23. Reservations recommended. (708)389–4636. *From 147th St., N on Cicero Ave. 4 bl.*

DOLTON

❼ 15145 Blackstone Avenue

After JoAnne Lipinski drags nearly 100 boxes of decorations from her crawl space, her fiance Bill, her sister Janet, her granddaughters Roxanne and Nicole, and her neighborhood friends and their dogs join in the "fun" to decorate her one-acre wooded lot.

The job takes nearly a month and, in spite of all the help, has left JoAnne sometimes decorating on Christmas Day or never finishing at all. In an attempt to be more organized, she has recently labeled all the boxes. She also hopes that avoiding past mishaps, such as Bill dangling from high atop an evergreen tree, will speed the task.

At its most complete stage, nearly 300,000 lights cover everything from the highest oak to the smallest shrub, dozens of figurines fill the yard, and animated scenes dress each window. Visible from I-94, the display attracts many onlookers, including television

Even the oak trees are trimmed on the Lipinski's corner.

reporters, who have featured the well-lit home on every local station. JoAnne's display also won honors in city-wide and national contests.

"It's our Christmas present to the world," says Bill. And it's a gift that goes on giving as the couple continues to turn the lights on for snowfalls and special occasions throughout the year.

Dec.1 (something will be lit)–Jan.15 (intermittently thereafter), Dusk–11:00PM. *From the Calumet Expwy. (I-94), W on Sibley Blvd. 2 bl., S on Dorchester 2 bl., E on 152nd St. 2 bl.*

JUSTICE

❽ 8107 Christeen Drive

When Dave Dvorak learned that his bride-to-be was a Christmas fanatic, his first reaction was "uh-oh." But over the years he has equaled his wife Donna's enthusiasm and admits, "I like to go bonkers."

Donna decorates the interior, where even the archways are trimmed with lights, and Dave fills the front yard with nearly a hundred plastic figurines and many innovations of his own.

Dozens of candy canes and lollipops, a collapsible display case, a teddy bear slide and a stable for the manger scene were all built of wood. Icicles dripping from the eaves were cut from styrofoam, and a North Pole sign was made from a cylindrical cement form.

The House of Hughes glimmers inside and out with tens of thousands of miniature lights.

Snowflakes hanging on the garage door were fashioned from salvaged strips of plastic venetian blinds. Dave likes them so much, that they are also hanging from his ceiling at work. Uh-oh.

Dec. 10–Jan. 6, Dusk–12:00AM. *From Roberts Rd. (80th Ave.), W on 79th St. 2 bl., S on 82nd Ave. 5 bl., E on Christeen Dr.*

LANSING

❾ 3049 186th Street

Mark Foster's 30-foot spruce trees are the perfect shapes for two Santa heads wearing their pointed caps. Mark creates the figures using thousands of red, white and blue lights wrapped around the tree branches. It's no wonder Mark has a unique display—he is the owner of Holiday World, a Christmas decoration store.

Thanksgiving–Jan. 1, Dusk–10:00PM. *From the Kingery Expwy. (I-80), S on Torrence Ave. 1-1/2 mi., E on 186th St. 1 mi.*

LEMONT

❿ Christmas Inn
107 Stephen Street

Whether the holiday mood strikes after a winter tour of decorated homes or a June day at the beach, Christmas Inn provides yuletide dining year-round in an old-fashioned room brimming with festive displays.

From the tin-plated ceiling hang dolls in snow-suits spinning on teeter-totters, wooden rocking horses, giant ornaments, rotating snowmen and playful elves. A mosaic fireplace decked for the season stands beside rows of shelves packed with reindeer, carved horses and stuffed dolls. Christmas trees, wreaths and lights galore adorn the country-blue wainscotted walls. Above the wooden bar an electric train winds along a garland-covered track. Lucky children may even get to blow its whistle.

Christmas songs by artists from Bing Crosby to Dolly Parton are standards on the juke box, and hot cocoa is available all year. Owners Shirley and

After the holidays Dave Dvorak faces the overwhelming task of cramming 93 plastic figurines and a collection of other homemade decorations into the ceiling of his garage.

Homemade candies and cartoons gleam on Kenton Street.

the holiday silhouettes. The towering rooftop star as well as the angels, bells, candles and wreaths are made from welding rod he bends into the festive forms, which Jan has chalked on the garage floor as a pattern. The figures are then spruced up by wrapping them in garland and lights.

Jan makes the two-dimensional wooden decorations with the help of her friend Nancy Gamauf, who lends her artistic skills. Jan cuts out the figures with a scroll saw, and the two childhood companions share the painting task.

Though the brick bungalow and city lot seem full to the brim, the Mondscheans seem to find room for new displays each year. One of their latest additions is a miniature Christmas tree lot complete with a strand of skewed colored bulbs suspended around it and a sign overhead reading "Trees for Sale." When a passerby asked to purchase a tree, the Mondscheans knew their latest creation had made the grade.

Dec. 8 – Jan. 2, 5:00PM – 10:30PM. *From Crawford Ave., W on 147th St. 3/4 mi., N on Kenton St.*

Thomas Sheu, who also run a commercial Christmas decorating company, simply love the holiday season. "Christmas is a time when everybody seems to have the most fun," Shirley says. "We thought, 'Why can't we be that way all the time?'"

Open year-round. (Tu – Th) 11:00AM – 8:00PM, (F – Sa) 11:00AM – 9:00PM, (Su) Breakfast buffet, 9:00AM – 2:00PM. Casual. $3 – $7. (312) 257 – 2548. *From the Stevenson Expwy. (I-55), S on Lemont Rd. 3 mi., E on Illinois St. 2 bl., N on Stephen St. 2 bl.*

MIDLOTHIAN

⓫ 14648 South Kenton Street

A colorful choo-choo train runs along a tall wooden fence beneath a sign that reads "Candy Cane Crossing." Further down the tracks, the station's ticket booth looks so realistic it fools a spectator who asks if she must pay to see the rest of the display. Though it is worth the price of an admission, there is no charge to view the elaborate decorations that cover all four sides of Michael and Jan Mondschean's home and yard.

Since 1985 the couple has been adding to the display with their homemade creations. A pipefitter by day, Michael uses the tools of his trade to build

A spruce tree makes an ideal Santa in the Foster's front yard.

ORLAND HILLS

⑫ 9337 170th Place

Resourcefulness, imagination and love for children are the ingredients that make John and Mary Porter's Christmas display so appealing. As a young couple they enjoyed looking at other people's decorations and dreamed, "When we get a house and have kids, we want to decorate like that."

With their own home, five children and one income, the Porters have used their talents and resources well to make their wish come true. The windows of the house are trimmed with lights, backed with wrapping paper and decorated with children's toys. Candy canes lining the walk, a reindeer on the roof, a Santa shop and a manger scene were all handmade from plywood. Empty boxes wrapped in plastic and trimmed with vinyl ribbon were used to make giant presents.

Mary crafted 3-foot Christmas trees from triangular wire wreath stands wrapped in garland. Three sizes of straw wreaths attached together and covered with white garbage bags became a snow couple with smiling faces of black electrical tape. Wreaths were again used to make colorful lollipops covered in cellophane. With the addition of a few store-bought items and 30 strands of lights, the house is decorated without extravagant expense.

Each year when John and Mary Porter are ready to turn on their Christmas display, all the neighbors come to watch. When the switches are flicked, lights twinkle from the house and dance upon the trees. Windows sparkle with holiday scenes. The lawn comes alive with snowmen, presents and candy canes. And the children's faces light up with amazement, just as the Porters had dreamed.

Dec. 15–Jan. 9, 6:00PM–10:30PM. *From 171st St., N on 94th Ave. 1 bl., E on 169th St. 1 bl., S on Hobart, Follow curve to 170th Pl. 1 bl.*

ORLAND PARK

⑬ 13823 Coghill Lane

When Tony and Carrie Calderone stop at garage sales they glance past the roller skates, push mowers and percolators with hawk-like vision that darts directly to any hint of red and green where a Santa Claus, reindeer or snowman might be hiding. It has become a hobby for the couple to collect unique holiday decorations, and other people's cast-offs have proven to be a treasure-trove.

The Calderone's largest purchase was from Orland Park residents Ed and Dorothy Albrecht, who were retiring their famous display on 86th Avenue at 135th Street (see next article). Familiar with the young couple's growing display, Mr. Albrecht knew the Calderones would continue his 36-year tradition. He sold them half of what he owned.

After more than a decade of bargain hunting, Tony and Carrie have accumulated several hundred items, both old and new, from animated characters that fill the display cases lining their driveway to a 1978 Sears Winnie the Pooh in its unopened box. The collection is more than their front yard will hold. So the Calderones have expanded onto both their neighbors' lawns, who are delighted to have someone else decorate for them.

Sat. after Thanksgiving–Sun. after New Year's, 5:00PM–12:30AM. *From Southwest Hwy. (Rt.7), E on 135th St. 2 bl., S on Lincolnshire Dr. 3 bl., W on Timber Trails 1 bl., S on Coghill Ln. 1/2 bl.*

The Albrecht Home

During the holiday season of 1992, 18 angels, 15 Pooh bears, 65 ceramic Victorian houses, 30 candy canes, 14 gingerbread men, five Santas, 38 choir boys, 23 Frosty snowmen, 30 toy soldiers, 5,000 lights, one Noel sign and 30 miscellaneous illuminated figures decorated the home of Dorothy and Ed Albrecht, as they had in varying numbers for the past 22 years. But in 1993, to the regret of all who annually visited this holiday home at 86th Avenue and 135th Street, a sign amid the lights announced that this would be the last year of the couple's Christmas display. The Albrechts were moving to Arizona.

Before residing in Orland Park, Dorothy and Ed decorated quite elaborately at their Chicago home on 52nd and Spaulding for 13 years. One of their three children, Ronald, who also decorated nearby Saint Gaul's Church, had bought his family an outdoor manger scene. There the tradition began. Sadly,

Ronald died in a accident in 1964. The Albrechts decided to continue decorating in his memory.

Ed added to the display yearly. Retired and in his seventies, he continued to decorate the entire house on his own. He would begin the first of October and work daily from 11:00AM to 3:30PM. Two months and 200 trips up and down the ladder later, the task would be complete.

Not surprisingly, this former armored car messenger established quite an efficient system. He drove wooden dowel rods fitted with brass screws into the mortar six inches apart up and down the perimeter of the house. Two hundred strands of lights were then easily secured by winding them around the screws. The 30 angels that lined the housetop were fastened to plywood boards that screwed into the roof. A rubber roofing material under the shingles closed up after the screws were removed to prevent leaks. Santa and his reindeer flew through the air on the same wire cable for 35 years.

Ed constructed the glass display cart, which stood in the driveway, housing a Christmas village of 65 ceramic miniatures. He also rigged the lighting of the little houses, a far easier task than that of his own home. Nine circuits and 96 amps of the Albrecht's 100-amp electrical service, along with electricity borrowed from their daughter and neighbor on either side, were devoted to illuminating their display. The couple was unable to use their microwave throughout the season and were cautious about turning too many things on at the same time.

Dorothy added to the interior decorations with teddy bears she had been collecting since 1986. Numbering over 300, they were attached to a chain link cable and draped in a garland-like fashion throughout the living room, dining room and entryway. She recalled one evening when friends were invited to their home. They came to the door accompanied by a foreign-speaking family. She invited them all in and gave them a tour of the bears throughout the house. When they returned to the living room, the second family, to the surprise of all, smiled thankfully and walked out the door. Both guest and host had assumed they were the other's friends. The strangers must have thought it was an open house.

The Albrechts received much recognition over the years from newspapers and television. But simple notes from passersby meant the most to them, such as that from a little boy who enclosed three baseball cards as a thank you. The couple admits they will truly miss decorating their home, but they will be taking 1,400 lights to Sun City. ◆

The Albrecht home delighted holiday visitors for 22 years.

SOUTH HOLLAND

🄬 16320 Prince Drive

West of the Calumet Expressway at 159th Street gleams the home of Gordon and Patricia MacDonald, abundantly trimmed in multicolored C-9 bulbs. In spite of a $160 monthly increase to the electric bill, Gordon, an electrical contractor, enjoys the result and is happy to pick up the tab. "I had plans for the house even before we bought it. I thought it was perfect for decorating," he said.

In addition to the lights, the MacDonald's front lawn is adorned with a homemade stable. On a windy night several years ago, the structure fell down and was resting on Joseph's head. Gordon found it humorous that an electrician was getting even with a carpenter for a change.

The manger scene also came in handy to wean the MacDonald's seven-year-old daughter from her security blanket. "Baby Jesus needs your blanket to keep warm," Gordon and Patricia coaxed. The blanket has been Baby Jesus' "woobie" nearly 20 years.

Dec. 1–Jan. 6, 5:30PM–10:30PM. *From the Calumet Expwy. (I-94), W on 159th St. (Rt.6) 1 bl., S on Prince Dr. (frontage road).*

TINLEY PARK

🄯 8050 Chippewa Trail

When Mark and Caryl Joritz go on vacation, it's not ashtrays, thermometers or backscratchers they bring home as souvenirs, but Santas, snowmen and elves. In a quest for decorations that can't be found

---

Decorating in Tinley Park

In 1984 several Tinley Park residents called the police about a pair of suspicious-looking men, who were driving a truck slowly around the neighborhood shining a flashlight on people's houses. No reason to fear, it was only the mayor, Ed Zabrocki, and village trustee Greg Hannon copying the addresses of the best decorated houses in town so they could award them certificates of recognition.

A few evenings later several residents were startled by a group of men ringing their doorbells. Not to worry, it was just the mayor and a group of trustees with a token from the village to honor the top holiday displays.

And so began the "Tinley Park Christmas Decorating Festival," an annual event that now awards hundreds of certificates and historical ornaments to the unusually large number of elaborately decorated homes in town, and no longer alarms its residents.

The mayor, who has since turned his judging duties over to a committee, attributes the magnitude of the town's spirit to its young population. Over 75 percent of the 40,000 residents are under 45 years of age. "A lot of young kids and families get involved in it," Zabrocki says. "When we were driving around, we saw families putting their decorations up together."

The expansive suburb, which covers 12 square-miles, is now divided for the contest into six sections with a committee of volunteer judges assigned to each. First, second and third place and 10 honorable mentions are awarded in every area, along with 100 certificates of merit.

The recognitions were limited in number after judging committees one year turned in over 3,000 addresses worthy of prizes, nearly 25 percent of the residences. Secretary Jeanie Condon, who must reference the water bills to find the homeowner's names to complete the certificates, joked, "It would probably be easier to give something to all the people who don't decorate."

Recently a growing number of residents have also been decorating for Halloween. This prompted the mayor to re-initiate his judging duties. He and his wife, Emily, drove around the village to find the best displays. Outstanding homes were sent a certificate of recognition signed "Count Zabrocki"—there goes the mayor scaring the residents again.

A collection of snow people fill the Joritz lawn.

in Illinois, the couple has made holiday shopping as much a part of their itinerary as swimming in the hotel pool. Yellow bucket luminaria, 30-inch lighted garland bells and a collection of 17 different snow people are a few of their unusual finds.

Some of their travels are even planned to places where Christmas shopping is the main activity. Frankenmuth, Michigan, is a favorite destination, where the Joritzes spend one weekend every other year shopping at Bronner's Christmas Wonderland.

And while some folks fantasize about trips to Maui, the Joritzes dream of Pigeon Forge, Tennessee, home of The Christmas Place, the largest holiday store in the southeast.

Sat. after Thanksgiving–Jan. 1, 5:00PM–10:00PM.
From 171st St., S on 80th Ave. 1/2 mi., W on Chippewa Tr.

⓰ 17630 Cloverview Drive

Though dozens of plastic figurines decorate the front lawn of Chuck and Diana Favero's home, they don't look quite like anyone else's. Diana sews hats for the teddy bears, crochets little scarves for the gingerbread men, and ties big red bows beneath the penguins' beaks.

The characters aren't just standing around in the snow either. Chuck built a teeter-totter, a swing and a spinning snow saucer for the teddy bears and

is working on a ferris wheel. Together with his son, Michael, he has turned the roof into a snowy hill, with Santa and a cast of warmly dressed critters tobogganing and sliding in saucers down its face.

The family adds to their collection of figurines every year, but is still searching for the elusive but darling Winnie the Pooh that is no longer manufactured by Sears. Anyone willing to sell this item to the Faveros can be certain Winnie will have a good home and warm clothing.

Dec. 6–Fri. after New Year's, 5:00PM–1:00AM.
From 183rd St., N on 84th Ave. 1/2 mi., E on Cloverview Dr. 1/4 mi.

⓱ 17120 South Oketo Avenue

"Barb, look what I bought to put in the front yard," 61-year-old Esther Drwal announced to her daughter proudly as she and her husband John, 75, returned from their shopping trip with a giant waving Santa Claus and four reindeer in their arms. The next week they arrived with a five-piece manger scene, followed a few days later by six toy soldiers, then a wreath, two gingerbread men and finally ten lighted candy canes. "We got a little carried away," admitted Esther.

The Faveros give special attention to their plastic figurines.

When Barb Meller and her husband Roy moved into their south suburban residence with her parents, they didn't realize that their sprawling front yard would be irresistible to a retired couple who love Christmas. "We just told them to buy whatever they wanted, and we'd put it up," Barb said.

Now every fall Esther and John travel to the patio store waiting for the swimming pools and outdoor furniture to disappear, so they can begin the fun of bringing home their weekly holiday surprises.

Sun. after Thanksgiving–Jan.1, 4:30PM–12:00AM. *From Harlem Ave., W on 171st St. 3 bl., S on Oketo Ave. 1/2 bl.*

⓲ 17331 South Osceola Avenue
(pictured on page 81)

Ed and Lori Kulik have won a prize every year since the Tinley Park decorating contest began in 1989. And if a special award was given for "Best Use of a Front Porch," it would certainly be theirs as well.

Normally, the Kulik's brick portico has an arched entryway with two matching window wells, but during the holidays Ed transforms it into a delightful snow scene. He fills in the bottom half of the doorway with a decorated wooden partition and hangs divided window panes trimmed with lights in each archway. The enclosed area provides ample space for the fun-filled display of skiing, skating and tobogganing snowmen. As general manager for a major Chicago food retailer, Ed was able to acquire the figures, originally "Strohsmen," from an outdated 1970s point-of-purchase display.

The large window in the front of the house is also cleverly disguised. A homemade shadow box of Santa's Workshop is bolted to the exterior frame. Santa checks his list, and busy elves hammer and paint, while the Kulik's living room remains undisturbed.

Ed has been a busy little elf himself, building these and many of his other decorations. His three-dimensional "Christmas Express" train, the gingerbread mailbox, the candy tree, the choir people and the reindeer are all his handiwork.

As a child, Ed was always intrigued by the idea of decorating a house. Now that he has been doing it for nearly 20 years, he relates, "We enjoy watching people and how they react to our home." During a recent visit to Michigan they were speaking to a stranger who, when learning that they lived in Tinley Park, asked if they were near "that house that decorates so well for Christmas." They were thrilled to discover that the woman was referring to their house.

Dec.1–Jan.6, Dusk–11:00PM. *From Harlem Ave., W on 171st St. 1/2 mi., S on Oriole Ave. 1 bl., E on 173rd Pl. 1 bl.*

⓳ 16423 South Parliament Avenue

"We always decorated an average amount. Then I made two dozen candy canes and it mushroomed from there." In what sounds like a statement at a meeting of Christmas Decorators Anonymous, Rick Esposito describes the beginnings of his addiction to trimming his home. "I enjoy the lights, the colors and the fantasy of it all," he explains.

In only a few years his holiday habit has resulted in one of the most elaborate displays in town. In addition to the original 24 candy canes, dozens of toy soldiers line a front yard brimming with over 90 illuminated figurines, dozens of homemade creations and nearly 4,000 lights.

Party Ball Ornaments

Rick Esposito discovered that plastic party balls, sold as beer containers, make wonderful giant ornaments when empty.

He sprays them with one coat of primer, followed by a coat of fluorescent paint (orange and red work well on the brown plastic). For each ornament, Rick cuts a 2-inch diameter circle out of 1/4-inch plexiglass, and drills a hole through the center large enough to snugly hold a candelabra-size light socket. He prefers to replace the socket wiring with sturdier extension cord wiring. To secure the socket he inserts it into the hole and sandwiches the plexiglass between the male and female fittings that come with the lamp. He then screws in the bulb. With the bulb facing the inside, the disk is screwed in place over the hole in the party ball. The giant illuminated ornaments look terrific hanging in trees and are a clever means of recycling as well.

Ingenuity rings from the Esposito display.

Throughout the year Rick is on the lookout for items to add to his display. Discarded stage props in a dumpster were his most recent find. He intends to use them to build guard houses for his nutcrackers.

A professional carpenter, he spends a good deal of time perfecting his decorating techniques as well. The lights that stripe the roof and siding are wound around brass hooks in the wood trim and stainless steel screws that are permanently installed in 3/16-inch plastic plugs in the brickwork. Santa and his nine reindeer are suspended from an 8-foot steel structure bolted to the roof. A pulley system allows Rick to attach Santa's team one at a time before hoisting them skyward.

Rick employs another clever technique to draw the swirls on his peppermint candies. He attaches a string to the side of a cup that he places in the center of a circular piece of plywood. A pencil, tied to the other end of the string, is pulled around the cup. An even curve is drawn as the taut string gets shorter.

While Rick is credited with decorating the outside of the house, his wife, Cindy, adds to the display by creating a three-tiered snow village of 20 miniature buildings in the living room window.

She has also begun to exhibit her husband's zeal by carrying not only pictures of their four children in her wallet but a photo of their holiday display as well. Christmas addiction is obviously contagious.

Dec. 10–Jan. 6, (Su–Th) 5:00PM–11:00PM, (F–S)– 12:00AM. *From 171st St., N on 80th Ave. 3/4 mi., E on Nottingham Rd. 3 bl., N on Parliament Ave. 1/2 bl.*

⑳ 7837 West 167th Street

When Pamela Roe's three children were little, she used their nap time to work on craft projects for her Christmas display. She told her husband, Patrick, that house-cleaning was too loud and would wake up the kids. So was born "Candy Towne," a sugary kitchen of homemade treats quietly crafted from inexpensive household materials.

While the children slept, straw paper-plate holders and foil-backed insulation became a baking sheet of chocolate chip cookies. Mop handles, cardboard and aluminum foil became a spatula and fork. Pillow cases became sacks of flour and sugar. Plastic disposable plates became colorful candies. And mom…became a bit more relaxed.

A few years have passed and the children are no longer napping, but helping Pam put up the display instead. The kids like to carry everything up from the basement, and put lights and figurines wherever they can reach. Dad joins the effort by decorating the high places. With all this help, Pam may now find time to take a nap herself.

Dec.1–Jan.1, 4:00PM–1:00AM. *From 171st St., N on 80th Ave. 1/2 mi., E on 167th St. 2-1/2 bl.*

㉑ 7441 West 173rd Street

Ron Shermikas began making his outlined holiday figurines long before similar items were sold commercially. Though this style of decoration may now be a familiar sight, Ron's original designs keep his display unique. A choo-choo train pulls a freight-load of toys, a shepherd guards his flock, and an angel watches over the Christ Child in a manger, while colorful bells, ornaments, a wreath and a

Pamela Roe's "Candy Towne," brimming with handcrafted sugary treats, awaits Santa's arrival.

cheery "Noel" fill the rest of the front yard.

In his full-time job as a machine repairman, Ron does a large amount of maintenance welding. During his off-hours he combines his trade skills with his flair for cartooning to create the decorations for his Christmas display.

He begins by making a sketch of the design. Scrap steel rods are then heated, bent into shapes from the drawing and welded together. Eight to 12-inch vertical bars are left protruding from the bottom to serve as stakes. A horizontal bar welded between them allows the display to be pushed easily into the ground by foot. Ron also weatherizes each figure by galvanizing it with a coat of zinc. As a final touch the displays are either trimmed in metallic garland or wrapped in lights.

With his experience and access to the proper equipment, Ron can usually complete one figure in three nights after work. He adds a few new items each year and comments, "I haven't even gotten to the roof yet."

Fri. after Thanksgiving–Jan.1, Dusk–10:00PM. *From 171st St., S on Harlem Ave. 1/4 mi., W on 173st St. 1/4 mi.*

A homemade choo-choo chugs across the Shermikas lawn.

Chapter 7

COOK COUNTY–WEST

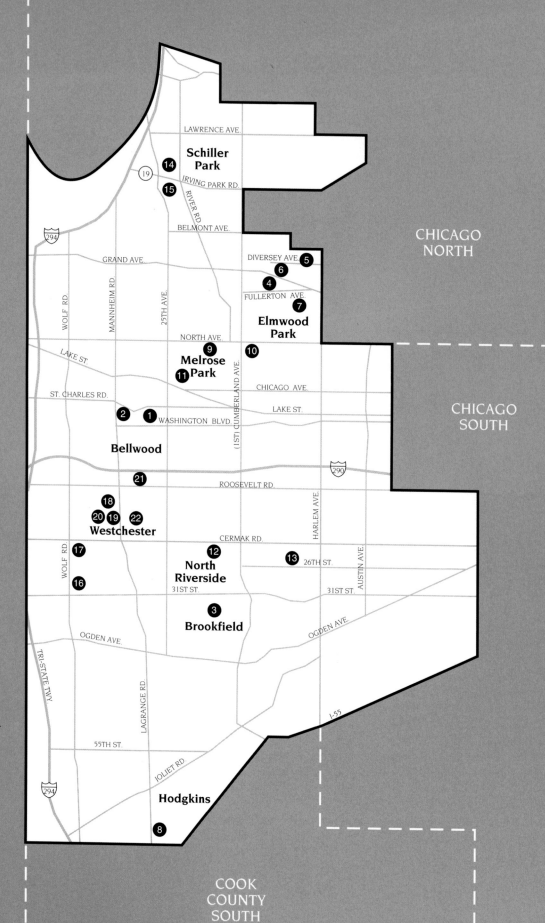

LAWRENCE AVE.

Schiller Park

 14

19 15

IRVING PARK RD.

RIVER RD.

BELMONT AVE.

CHICAGO NORTH

294

GRAND AVE.

DIVERSEY AVE. 5

6

4

FULLERTON AVE.

7

Elmwood Park

WOLF RD.

MANNHEIM RD.

25TH AVE.

NORTH AVE.

9

LAKE ST.

10

Melrose Park

11

(1ST) CUMBERLAND AVE.

CHICAGO AVE.

DUPAGE COUNTY

ST. CHARLES RD.

2 1

WASHINGTON BLVD.

LAKE ST.

Bellwood

CHICAGO SOUTH

290

21

ROOSEVELT RD.

18

HARLEM AVE.

20 19 22

Westchester

CERMAK RD.

17

12

13 26TH ST.

AUSTIN AVE.

North Riverside

16

31ST ST.

31ST ST.

3

OGDEN AVE.

Brookfield

OGDEN AVE.

I-55

TRI-STATE TWY.

OGDEN AVE.

LAGRANGE RD.

55TH ST.

294

JOLIET RD.

Hodgkins

8

COOK COUNTY WEST

N
W+E
S

0 MILES 2

COOK COUNTY SOUTH

BELLWOOD

❶ 538 Rice Avenue

Now that his older brothers have moved out, John Bajkowski is in charge of decorating his parents' home and is taking the job seriously. The house, which previously had been trimmed only with lights, is currently dazzling with his inventive handiwork.

A snowman, standing on the porch, is fashioned from lights in plastic tubing and wire fencing material. Strands of lights bordering the walkway are cleverly suspended from tent stakes. A trio of 12-foot peppermint candy canes fold in half for easy storage at season's end. A Christmas tree of lights is handily made by attaching strands to the top of a flagpole and anchoring them a few feet from the base. John cautions from experience to remove the flag before assembly, unless a patriotic tree is desired.

Though the display has consecutively won third, second and first place in the Bellwood Christmas Lights Contest, John seeks a deeper reward. "The Christmas season is a time of good will, love, harmony, forgiveness and peace," he says. "Hopefully, this attitude will fill those who see my work."

Dec. 1–Jan. 6, 4:30PM–11:00PM. From 25th Ave., W on Washington Blvd. 1/2 mi., N on Eastern 2 bl., W on Butterfield Rd. 1 bl., S on Rice Ave. 3/4 bl.

Shadow Box Windows

To turn his living room Christmas display into an enchanting shadow box, Alvin Almeroth cuts a simple holiday shape out of craft paper. The cut-out should be large enough to cover about three-quarters of the window. To tape the stencil to the window without altering the shape's outline, he cuts several 1-inch holes in the center of the shape and places the tape over the holes. Before spraying the window with artificial snow, Alvin protects the woodwork by masking it with tape. The clean glass is then sprayed. The stencil and masking tape are removed when the snow is dry. The snowy frame adds a magical touch to any holiday scene created behind it.

Alvin Almeroth's picture window is transformed into a charming holiday diorama.

❷ 3516 St. Paul Avenue

Thanks to the creativity of owner Alvin Almeroth, the picture window at this Bellwood home recalls the charm of an antique window ornament. Alvin makes a different stencil each year to form a holiday peephole that reveals his Christmas decorations inside. On the exterior of the window he frames the scene with a wreath he constructed from old wire Christmas tree branches.

Dec. 15–Jan. 1, 5:00PM–10:30PM. From St. Charles Rd., S on Mannheim Rd. 1/2 mi., E on St. Paul Ave. 5 bl.

BROOKFIELD

❸ Brookfield Zoo
1st Avenue and 31st Street

It's a unique nighttime thrill for kids, adults and animals alike when Brookfield Zoo opens its gates for twelve December evenings of "Holiday Magic."

The park comes alive with thousands of white lights that decorate the trees along the zoo's paths. Though many of the animals appear in their outdoor settings, guests may also visit the Children's Zoo, Bear Grottos, Small Mammal House, Reptile House, Aquatic Bird House and The Fragile Kingdom, which

Brookfield Zoo's paths glisten with "Holiday Magic."

remain open throughout the evening. Santa and Mrs. Claus, Frosty the Snowman, Brookfield Zoo Bear and other costumed animal characters often greet children along the way.

Special events include a tree-lighting ceremony, Clydesdale parades, ice sculpture demonstrations, "Sing to the Animals," mimes, carolers, celebrity storytellers, jugglers and musicians. The zoo restaurants offer hot chocolate, hot cider and other food items, and the gift shops are open for holiday shopping.

Times and dates vary annually. Admission and parking fees. For more information call (708)485−0263 x352. *From the Eisenhower Expwy. (I-290), S on 1st Ave. 2 mi., W on 31st St.*

ELMWOOD PARK

❹ Elmwood Park Water Tower

In a tradition started over 25 years ago by electrical superintendent John Litrenta Sr. the Elmwood Park Water Tower is an annual beacon of holiday cheer. Covered with nearly 5,000 large C-9 bulbs, the tower is visible from miles away and is often used as a landmark by airline pilots.

Two to three men spend a full day stretching heavy steel cables, pre-strung with lights, from a ring at the top of the 220-foot tower to the rail that surrounds the tank. The cables are then tightened with turnbuckles to prevent them from blowing in heavy winds. The crew returns a few days before Christmas to make the lights perfect for their crowning day.

In 1975 the public works facility beneath the water tower was destroyed by fire, along with all the Christmas decorations. The tower was unlit for several years until the Elmwood Park Civic Foundation offered to fund the lighting project and restore the town tradition. The organization has done so ever since without a glitch, except for the year that flashing lights were installed, resulting in a sudden rash of UFO sightings. Traditional non-blinking lights were restored the following year.

With their municipal water tower decked out in style, Elmwood Park residents keep pace with a delightful assortment of exceptionally decorated homes. It's a wonderful neighborhood in which to look at Christmas decorations and easy to find—just follow the water tower.

Thanksgiving−Jan.6, Dusk−1:00AM. *From Harlem Ave., W on Grand Ave. 4 bl.*

❺ 7402−6 West Diversey Avenue

> APT. FOR RENT. Spacious 2 bdrm. Ht, lndry, crpt., Santa Claus, reindeer, penguins.

Tenants who love the holidays would surely enjoy renting in this 17-unit apartment building where owners Eric and Nancy Mueller turn the courtyard into a fanciful playland at Christmas, as well as Halloween.

Through the wrought-iron gate and up the path a brightly-lit Santa welcomes visitors to share in the fun. Penguins in their tuxedos also wear glasses, purses and babushkas, as they chat alongside the towering tunnel of a two-story slide. One of their feathered friends appears to have slipped through the tube, while others spin and glide on a frozen pond and play hide-and-seek in a North Pole igloo. In another corner of the yard, magical stories unfold in an animated gazebo, where one level depicts Santa's hectic workshop and another a peaceful living room Christmas scene.

Eric and Nancy, along with their family and friends, decorate the two-story building and courtyard from top to bottom with over 5,000 glittering lights. Even a plastic Baby Jesus blinked for awhile when its normal bulb was mistakenly replaced with a flashing one.

Toy soldiers flank every entryway, and yuletide scenes decorate each canopy. Christmas greetings, giant bells, reindeer and holiday music fill the air. A sextet with a decorated accordion even appeared one evening to add to the merriment.

"That Eric, he's a genius," remarks long-time tenant Bernice Licata enthusiastically. "I sit and watch from my window. It's great to see the kids coming in." She has enjoyed sharing the fun with her own grandchildren since the display began in 1986. "They always ask, 'Gram, is it ready yet?'" she chuckles. "My friends come over every year too. And once they've seen it...they all bring their grandchildren back."

Passersby have expressed equal praise and gratitude. One anonymous visitor even became a "secret Santa" and left gifts in the Mueller's hallway each of the 12 days of Christmas.

Inspired by Chicago's Candy Cane Lane neighborhood of the fifties and sixties, Eric and his sister Debra began the display to recreate the magic they remembered from their youth. It's certain that the thousands of children who have visited this delightful courtyard have been given a fond memory, which they too will never forget. As for the Mueller's tenants... Bernice dispels all doubts, "It's just a lot of fun. I'm very lucky to live here."

Dec. 15 – Jan. 6, 4:30PM – 10:30PM. *From Harlem Ave., W on Diversey Ave. 4 bl.*

❻ 7721 Sunset Drive
(pictured on the cover)

When Larry Wardzala was a little boy, he loved to help his mother decorate the Christmas tree. He would hang ornaments on the bottom branches as high as he could reach. Then his mom would lift him up to drape the garland and put the angel on top.

JOHN STEDRONSKY

Playful penguins, animated elves and lights galore greet visitors at the Mueller's apartment courtyard.

"It didn't look too nice," Mrs. Wardzala recalls. "But he got a kick out of knowing that he put it there." Little did she realize that years later, not sharing his mother's tolerance for misplaced ornaments, her son would be rearranging the decorations after she hung them.

At twelve years old Larry began to decorate the outside of the house. He started on a small scale, trimming the banisters and awnings with lights. Over the years the display became more elaborate, but, thanks to Larry's good taste and meticulous handiwork, the house remained elegant.

His knack for decorating has grown with his love for the season. Now in his thirties, Larry is employed part-time as a visual merchandiser. His extensive work for Silvestri Corp. and Department 56, Inc., both Christmas decoration manufacturers, has given him the opportunity to follow his passion. "I never get tired of Christmas," he admits. "I listen to Christmas music throughout the year."

In spite of his hectic holiday schedule, Larry has continued to trim his parents' home. To achieve the deep blue and magenta color scheme of his current display, he covered thousands of bulbs with swatches of theatrical lighting gel secured with small rubber bands. The lights arranged in a curved pattern on his hand-crafted 6-foot wreath took over 15 hours to cover alone. Using the gels he is able to maintain the consistent intensity of color in the blanket of magenta lights that cascades from a star at the peak of his roof, if only the squirrels would stop chewing through the wiring.

Floral wire, wrapped around the strands that outline the eaves, keeps the lights pointing in the same direction. Thousands of additional lights cover the shrubbery and climb the branches of the maple and oak trees in the parkway. Larry hangs all the strands himself using a 20-foot ladder, along with a 25-foot extension pole. Unlike most decorators, who may tire of the season, Larry repairs bulbs even after Christmas.

Four coach lights, trimmed in matching hues, add an elegant touch to the display. Larry secured the temporary fixtures to the ground by placing them over anchored 4-foot fence posts covered with pipe insulation.

The decorative candles winding across the lawn were made from spray-painted conduit and a single light socket connected to an extension cord. Their glowing magenta "flames" are accented with metallic ribbons and stars.

The panels of evergreen boughs, which form a glistening shadow against the house, were made from plastic sheeting already embossed with the images. The sheets were drilled to accommodate the lighting and secured to a wooden frame.

Larry enjoys changing his display somewhat each year, but always manages to impress those who pass. His ultimate plan is to build a miniature ballroom scene in a castle-like setting, complete with a crystal chandelier and dancing figures.

It has often been well past Christmas when Larry has found the time to take down his decorations. One year he added green flood lights and illuminated the display on Saint Patrick's Day—not unusual for a young man who enjoys decorating all year. "The Christmas lights remind me of the peace, the good will and the kindness of the season," Larry says. "I would like everyone to have that feeling year-round."

Dec. 15 – Jan. 14, 5:00PM – 11:00PM. *From Harlem Ave., W on Diversey Ave. 3/4 mi., S on Sunset Dr.*

❼ 2320 North 77th Court

When the family began to outgrow their Elmwood Park home, Louis Rotella and his wife, Carmella, decided to rebuild the entire house rather than move. Doing all the work themselves with the help of family and friends, the old house was replaced in two phases by a new larger home. This allowed the Rotellas to live on the property throughout the construction.

Three years later, with the dust finally settled and the project complete, it was time to relax and enjoy the fruits of their efforts, but Louis still had

An ice-skating pond and a "Nutcracker" archway are among the unique displays in the Rotella front yard.

the urge to build. With no more additions planned for the house, he began to construct outdoor Christmas decorations for the front lawn.

First he built a manger, then a toy train. Year by year the display grew, flowing into the yard next door. Carmella and all seven Rotella children joined in the effort. After 20 years, it has now become a family tradition to decorate the weekend after Thanksgiving and an Elmwood Park holiday tradition to visit the Rotella home.

The display changes slightly every season as the family revives old decorations, or Louis gets ideas for new ones. Some are entirely handmade, others are a combination of purchased items and Rotella ingenuity.

Carmella dressed a styrofoam snowman from broom to nose, and placed him in a glittered forest. Daughter Debbie designed two animated shadow box scenes—one of Santa Claus in his workshop

and the other of Mrs. Claus in her kitchen. Gina, the oldest, created rag doll skaters (seven resembling the Rotella grandchildren), and Louis mechanized them to twirl and glide on an ice pond.

The youngest daughter, Andrea, who dances annually in the Rosary College production of "The Nutcracker," has a display built just for her. Over the driveway, a glistening archway supports a unique clock in which characters from the ballet spin in and out of two doorways, among them a Barbie doll disguised as the Sugar-Plum Fairy.

With lights, garlands, elves, soldiers, wreaths and candy canes to assemble in addition, there is plenty of work for everyone in the family to do. "But it's a good feeling to know we can make other people happy," Carmella remarks on this third phase of their home construction, "a tired, but good feeling."

Dec. 6–Jan. 4, Dusk–11:00PM. *From 1st Ave., E on Fullerton Ave. 1 mi., S on 77th Ct. 1/2 bl.*

HODGKINS

**8 6801 South LaGrange Road
Weeping Willow Ranch, Lot 131**

Though retirees far outnumber children at the
Weeping Willow Ranch trailer park, residents look
forward to the holiday season when many of the
homes are elaborately decorated.

Among them is the residence of Norman and
Patricia Ukleja. Employed in the graphic arts field
for over 40 years, Norman puts his creative skills
to work building two-dimensional wooden displays
for Christmas, as well as Easter and Halloween.
Some are made from purchased patterns and others
are his original designs.

When the holidays arrive he recruits his five
grandsons, Scott, Ryan, Phillip, Joe and Thomas
to help assemble the displays. The oldest, Scott,
humorously expressed his opinion of his grandpa's
hobby in a school composition.

"My grandfather is not human, he's retired," Scott

*Three-foot ornaments, giant bows and thousands of lights
trim the Taglia's 60-foot evergreen.*

wrote. "My grandfather cannot sit and relax. He spends
all of his spare time creating new and better ways to
decorate his house for various holidays, and I am
volunteered by my loving parents to put them all up."

Kids just don't seem to know what fun is these days.
Do they, Norman?

Thanksgiving–Jan.1, 5:00PM–10:00PM. *From the
Stevenson Expwy. (I-55), N on LaGrange Rd. 1/2 mi.,
E on Weeping Willow Rd. 3/4 mi., Stay rt.*

MELROSE PARK

9 1221 Hirsch

While most families pull out a few small boxes
of lights and ornaments to trim their Christmas
trees, the Taglia family has a more gargantuan task.
Five thousand lights, 50 huge red bows and dozens
of 3-foot ornaments are used to decorate the 60-foot
evergreen that grows still taller in their front yard.
The job takes nine hours and requires a bucket lift
truck and a hired electrician. In 1994 a second truck
with a taller bucket lift had to be rented after the
first reached only half-way up the tree. "It was still

JOHN REED

*A tree of poinsettias adds to the festive decor of The Homestead
restaurant in Melrose Park.*

shy a few feet," Darla Taglia said. "To reach the top we had to throw the rest of the decorations."

With the Daley Center tree still shrinking and the Taglia's tree still growing, the family can probably lay claim to having the largest decorated Christmas tree in the Chicagoland area.

Dec. 10–Jan. 6, 4:30PM–12:00AM (All day and night Christmas week). *From 1st Ave., W on North Ave. (Rt. 64) 1 mi., S on 15th 2 bl., E on Hirsch 1 bl.*

⑩ The Homestead
8305 West North Avenue

During the holidays this colonial restaurant exudes the warmth of the season in homespun style. A 10-foot tree lavishly trimmed with lights stands beside a glowing fireplace in the lobby, while one floor below a brilliant poinsettia tree rises from a winding stairwell trimmed with garlands and bows.

Within the restaurant snowflakes dance across the ceiling. Holiday vignettes decorate the walls. Small glistening trees stand in every window, and outdoor window boxes twinkle with evergreen boughs trimmed in white lights. On a snowy winter day it's a picture perfect place to share a holiday meal.

The lovely display is the handiwork of one of the waitresses, Dorothy Lofgren, who has been employed at the restaurant for over 30 years and decorating there since 1974. "At one time everybody pitched in," Dorothy said. "But I didn't like the way some things were done, so they just started letting me do it myself."

An avid craftswoman, Dorothy not only puts up the decorations herself but makes many of them as well. The nativity scene and other ceramic figures throughout the restaurant and bar were hand-painted by Dorothy. The wreaths hanging from the walls were also handmade, many from grapevines that previously grew behind the restaurant.

Dorothy does all the trimming for Valentine's Day, Easter, Mother's Day and Halloween as well. "If you get a job doing what you like, it's not work," she said.

Christmas display: Thanksgiving–Jan. 15, Restaurant hours: Lunch (M–Sa) 11:30AM–4:00PM, Dinner (M–F) 4:00PM–10:00PM, (Sa) –11:00PM, (Su) 12:00PM–9:00PM. Open everyday but Christmas. Appetizers: $3–$8, Dinners: $8–$20. Reservations recommended. (708)344–9886. *From 1st Ave., E on North Ave. 1/2 bl.*

⑪ 1308 North 16th Avenue

In the parking lot of a used car dealership a 35-foot Santa Claus balloon may catch a few glances, but in a small front yard on a suburban side-street— it's the talk of the town.

In 1993 when Michael and Denise Riccio inflated the giant cold air-balloon that towered over their brick two-flat, squad cars came from all over Melrose Park to see it. Though the surprising sight of the oversized Santa made most people laugh out loud, it did cause two car accidents and one angry mother, who said her little boy refused to go to bed each night unless he could see Santa Claus first.

The woman needn't worry, however. The Riccios enjoy changing their display frequently. The giant Santa, now deflated, has been replaced by a scene of 3½-foot polar bears skating on a frozen pond. Before Santa appeared the entire house had been wrapped in black plastic and a big red bow. It seems certain that whatever new surprises the Riccios have in store will continue to amuse their audiences.

Dec. 10–Jan. 1, 4:00PM–12:00AM. *From 1st Ave., W on Chicago Ave. 1 mi., N on 16th Ave. 6 bl.*

A 35-foot Santa decorated the Riccio's lawn in 1993.

NORTH RIVERSIDE

⑫ 2252 5th Avenue

It's no wonder that neighborhood kids beg to be driven past this North Riverside residence. The front lawn is filled with a collection of lighted cartoon characters exquisitely crafted by homeowner Gregory DiMenna.

Thanksgiving–Jan. 1, 4:00PM–1:00AM. *From 1st Ave., W on Cermak Rd. 4 bl., S on 5th Ave. 1/2 bl.*

⑬ 7625 and 7627 West 25th Street

Benny Ritacca and Wayne Pesek became friends while their adjacent homes were being constructed. When Benny decided to outline his house in Italian lights for the holidays, he convinced Wayne to do the same to his. For the past several years whoever finishes decorating first helps the other or contributes spare decorations. Together the two friends trim their private drive with twinkling garlands, candy canes and Wayne's homemade reindeer. Their corner truly glistens with the sharing spirit of the season.

1st Sun. of Dec.–Jan. 6, Dusk–11:00PM. *From Harlem Ave., W on 26th St. 1/2 mi., N on Hainsworth Ave. 1 bl., E on 25th St.*

SCHILLER PARK

⑭ Schiller Park's Christmas Streets
(pictured on page 97)

Until recently this small industrialized town of 12,000 has held as its claim to fame the 1930 invention of the Twinkie. However, in the last several years 10 local streets bearing such names as Candy Cane Lane, Toy Soldier Lane and Lollipop Lane, have given the village new cause for glory.

The lanes may sound familiar to anyone over 30 who grew up near Chicago's northwest side. From 1953 to 1972, streets in that area with similar names gave a magical memory to every kid who saw them One such child was Ken Glassner Jr., who propagated this new generation of lanes a few miles west in his hometown of Schiller Park.

In his initial enthusiasm, Ken was going to build 54 eight-foot candy canes out of plywood to give to every house on his block. Two of his neighbors, Tim

Kilbarger and plumber Rick Latuszek, convinced him instead to build three-dimensional candy canes out of 6-inch plastic plumbing pipe with money contributed by each household. With help from several men on the block, 33 candy canes ordered the first year were constructed in 13 days, and in 1987 Candy Cane Lane of Schiller Park was born.

In the following years almost all of the families on the street have purchased a cane, and other streets are joining in with holiday themes of their own. Neighbors from each new block have summer meetings to build their decorations together, so the displays will look consistent. Joe Shriner of Candle Lane and Ken's dad on Christmas Bell Lane generously built all of the decorations for their streets themselves.

The village has joined the act by funding Santa's Reindeer Stable and home in Clocktower Park at Irving and Wesley, where children can visit Santa and get free cocoa and treats. Street signs for each of the lanes are also posted throughout the month of December. Though the Schiller Park Christmas Streets have not yet reached the proportions of the original lanes, the 90's version is just as delightful as a surprise cream filling in a Twinkie.

Dec. 12–Jan. 1, 6:30PM–9:30PM. Maps available at Santa's Stable, the Village Hall and many local stores. For further information call the Village of Schiller Park (708)678–2550. *From River Rd., W on Irving Park Rd. 2 bl.*

⑮ 4160 Atlantic Avenue

There is just something fun about walking through a tunnel of Christmas lights. Paty and Ron Bork get to experience the thrill every time they walk to their front door through the twinkling tunnel they constructed for the holidays.

The 20-foot-long structure is built of rebar (steel rods used in concrete construction), which was bent into curves over a tractor wheel. Each season the bars are bracketed to wooden beams on the ground at both sides of the walk. They are then covered with garland and over 2,000 lights to form the glistening trellis. And if you're good, the Borks don't mind if viewers sneak in a little stroll too.

Dec. 6–Jan. 2, 4:00PM–1:30AM. *From 25th St., E on Irving Park Rd. 1 bl., S on Atlantic Ave.*

WESTCHESTER

🔟 2900 and 3000 Blocks of South Becket Avenue

"We could never have imagined in our wildest dreams what was going to happen with this," laughed resident Dave Ricordati in recalling the birth of Becket Avenue as a Christmas attraction.

In the summer of 1986 the neighbors on this two-block stretch of newly-constructed homes gathered together for a "getting acquainted" party. Three households in the center of the block added to the festive atmosphere by trimming their young parkway trees in Italian lights.

As the party rolled into nighttime, the children went to bed, the adults were feeling no pain, and the trees were glistening in the evening sky. One of the neighbors, Joanne Pignato, remarked, "Wouldn't it be neat if all the trees were lit at Christmastime?" Feeling quite agreeable, the other neighbors thought it was a great idea and elected a mayor to be in charge.

Astonishingly enough, a reminder notice was sent around in the fall, and as the holidays approached all the neighbors kept their party promises and covered their trees with lights. Suddenly carloads of spectators started driving down the street, then tour buses, then TV crews and radio and newspaper reporters. Before residents knew what they had started, cars were lined up bumper to bumper to see what one real estate agent called the "prestigious" Becket Avenue.

Hardware store owner Paul Mares trims his tree with giant ornaments made from metal colanders.

Cars stream down Becket Avenue's pathway of lights.

Visitors in the line of cars filing down this glistening street are encouraged to be extra kind to any of the residents trying to get out of their driveways. Give them an opening, along with a wave and a smile—they just didn't know what they were getting themselves into.

Dec. 1–Jan. 1, 6:00PM–10:00PM. *From Wolf Rd., E on 31st St. 1/2 mi., N on Becket Ave.*

🔟 2646 South Boeger Avenue

Location. Location. Location. In 1993 Paul Mares purchased a home on Boeger Avenue at the intersection of Wakefield, the famous Westchester street lined with toy soldiers for the holidays. Having earned his own measure of fame for his elaborately decorated former residence on 11th Avenue in

Santa enjoys giving away free candy canes in the festive atmosphere of the Lulich's front yard.

North Riverside, Paul's new home is right where he wants it to be. When the Christmas season arrives, he joins in the neighborhood effort with a homemade display that does his corner proud.

Nine huge reindeer and a colorful sleigh span the lawn with a towering 14-foot Santa climbing aboard. A 12-foot Christmas tree, made from strands of lights wrapped around rows of nails on a wooden frame, covers an entire side of the house. Nearly 4,000 lights shimmer from the evergreens, while illuminated packages, built of hot-glued acrylic and contact paper, glow on the ground below. Employed in a family-owned hardware business, Paul has ready access to a variety of building materials and plans to continue constructing more displays.

At the end of the season residents of Wakefield Avenue are packing away their soldiers along with thoughts of decorating for another year, Paul, however, is simply substituting one holiday's trimmings for another. A Valentine's heart comes out of storage first, followed by an 8-foot shamrock, an assortment of giant bunnies, an American flag, the Statue of Liberty, Halloween ghouls, and a 14-foot turkey.

It seems Wakefield Avenue may have some catching up to do.

Thanksgiving weekend–Jan.1, 5:00PM–12:00AM.
From Cermak Rd., S on Wolf Rd. 1/2 mi., E on Wakefield Ave. 3 bl.

⑱ 1400 block of South Concord Avenue

It's a cookie lover's dream on this suburban street where the sidewalk is lined from one end to the other with gingerbread men. Some sport Santa hats and others velvet bows, while the houses on the block are decorated to the owners' fancies.

The cooperative effort was the brainchild of Anthony and Grace Dames, who wanted their subdivision "to have some type of a theme." The neighbors agreed on gingerbread men, so the Dames had a truckload delivered to their home by a wholesaler.

Now the shimmering street can be seen from Mannheim Road and is so delightful that it earned the entire block a party at the park district pool.

Sat. after Thanksgiving–Jan.1, 5:00PM–10:00PM.
From Cermak Rd., N on Mannheim Rd. (LaGrange Rd.) 1/2 mi., W on Waterford 1 bl., N on Concord Ave.

A holiday trellis forms a fanciful entryway to Concord Avenue, where smiling gingerbread men line the walks. It also acts as a tidy transport for electricity to the parkway.

⑲ 10503 Dorchester Avenue

Larry Lulich grew up in Chicago's Lawndale neighborhood near 28th and Kilbourn. During the late sixties and early seventies his family's home became locally famous for its elaborate Christmas displays, winning first place in a city-wide contest for two consecutive years.

Since moving into his own home with his wife, Donna, Larry has continued the family decorating tradition, while applying the "tricks of the trade" his parents had taught him.

"If you're going to put it up, put it up right, not sloppy," Larry's dad, Louie, would say. So in similar fashion Larry meticulously hangs every light pointing in the same direction, stapling the strands to the roof and taping them to the windows at measured distances. "Some years I put them three inches apart, others four," he says.

Larry also employs some of his parents' clever tricks for hiding electrical cords. "In the summer I edge real heavy so I can lay the extension cords between the sidewalk and the grass," he reveals. "And around the bushes, I hide the wiring under rocks."

It was also his parent's habit to change the decorations every year, so visitors would have something new to see. Larry has done the same, with displays varying from a red and white candy cane theme to a blue and white Elvis motif. Unused decorations remain in the attic each season.

And just as Santa appeared in front of the Lawndale home, he also appears at the Westchester residence. Though young Larry Jr. refuses to dress as an elf with Santa, he shows signs of promise to carry on the Lulich tradition—he has been climbing on the roof to help since he was four years old.

Dec. 6 – Jan. 6, 5:00PM – 11:00PM. Santa Claus appears the two Saturdays and Sundays before Christmas and every night during Christmas week to Dec. 23, 7:00PM – 9:00PM.
From Cermak Rd., N on Mannheim Rd. 2 bl., W on Dorchester Ave. 2 bl.

⑳ 10513 West Dorchester Avenue

The Cooney family decorates their home with a homemade manger, a choir of singers and a family of snowmen, but their cute little teddy bears have always drawn the most attention from children.

When there were only two bears on the lawn, neighborhood kids would tell the Cooneys there were supposed to be three little bears. Later, when there were four bears on the lawn, kids continued to tell the Cooneys there were supposed to be three. So with no plans of adding more bears or taking any away, Mrs. Cooney decided to make up her own story with four bears and set the scene in their display...

Once upon a time their were four bears—Ma, Pa and baby twins. One cold Christmas morning they had nothing to eat but one small gingerbread cookie. Though gingerbread was their favorite treat, one cookie was hardly enough to feed a family of hungry bears.

Pa Bear was about to go hunting, when he looked up to the sky and saw a peculiar sight—a star wearing a Santa hat. "Ma, Ma, come and see," he called. Pa and Ma stood for a long while staring curiously at the star.

Suddenly, the twins began to scream with delight. Ma and Pa looked down and to their surprise the gingerbread cookie, which was standing in a beam of the star's light, had started to grow. It got bigger and bigger and bigger until it was gigantic! So on Christmas Day the four bears, Ma and Pa and the baby twins, all had plenty of their favorite food to eat.

Children no longer tell the Cooneys they should have three bears, now that they have a four-bear story to tell.

Dec. 1 – Jan. 6, 5:00PM – 11:00PM. *From Cermak Rd., N on Mannheim Rd. 1 bl., W on Dorchester Ave. 1-1/2 bl.*

㉑ 1140 Newcastle Avenue

Throughout the year, the cedar fence surrounding the yard of Bill and Beverly Ernst's home holds a collection of antique tree-cutting tools that include a variety of buck saws and pick axes, as well as a kant tool used in log rolling. A 16-foot totem pole, carved from a telephone post by local hobbyist Ray Erbes and painted by Bill, towers over one end of the yard. At the other end stands a 14-foot, 1,800-pound chain-saw sculpture by Wisconsin artist Dave Watson of a bear with an eagle trying to steal a fish from his grasp.

The prevailing wood theme is a product of Bill's business, Ernst Tree Care & Landscaping Co., which is located on the adjacent property. As a man who enjoys his trade, Bill not only exhibits his love of trees and woodcrafting, but his skill in maintaining his own expansive yard as well.

In the spring and summer the Ernst's home flaunts a perfect lawn and a lovely garden. In the fall Bill decorates the yard for Halloween with bales of hay, pumpkins, ghosts and a giant spider on a web. At Christmastime an antique buckboard, pulled by a glistening reindeer, carries holiday packages and an evergreen tree wrapped in a bow. Garlands filled with lights are draped across the fence. And the tall carved bear is dressed in a custom-made red and green stocking cap with a matching scarf.

Dec. 5 – Jan. 7, 4:30PM – 1:00AM. *From Mannheim Rd. (Rt.45), E on Roosevelt Rd. 1/4 mi., N on Newcastle Ave.*

㉒ 2101 Newcastle Avenue

For those who collect ceramic Christmas houses this Westchester home is a special treat. Over the past several years Tom Elsey has been building in a slightly larger scale his own miniature village to display in his front yard.

Though he doesn't consider himself artistic or mechanically minded, he prefers homemade decorations and decided to give construction a try. He

A glowing steepled church is one of the homemade miniature buildings in "Elseytown."

began with the Santa's workshop, which he built in his basement. "If it had been an eighth of an inch wider, I wouldn't have gotten it through the door," Tom admits. He has since constructed the 3 to 4-foot structures in his garage using screws rather than nails for easy disassembly.

Drawing up his own plans, his next project was a steepled church, then a firehouse for his son, Patrick, and a ferris wheel for his daughter, Kimberly. The ferris wheel had to spin, so Tom invested in a variable speed motor, which, along with a makeshift pulley system, gave Santa and Big Bird an endless ride. Once the ferris wheel began to move, Patrick begged for the fire engine to go in and out of his fire station, so Tom rigged up another motor to do the job.

With plans of adding at least one new building every year, Tom hopes that "Elseytown" will soon fill his corner lot.

Dec. 15 – Jan. 1, Dusk – 10:45PM. *From 25th Ave., W on Cermak Rd. 3/4 mi., N on Newcastle Ave. 1 bl.*

JOHN REED

A buckboard full of gifts decorates the Ernst lawn.

Chapter 8

DUPAGE COUNTY

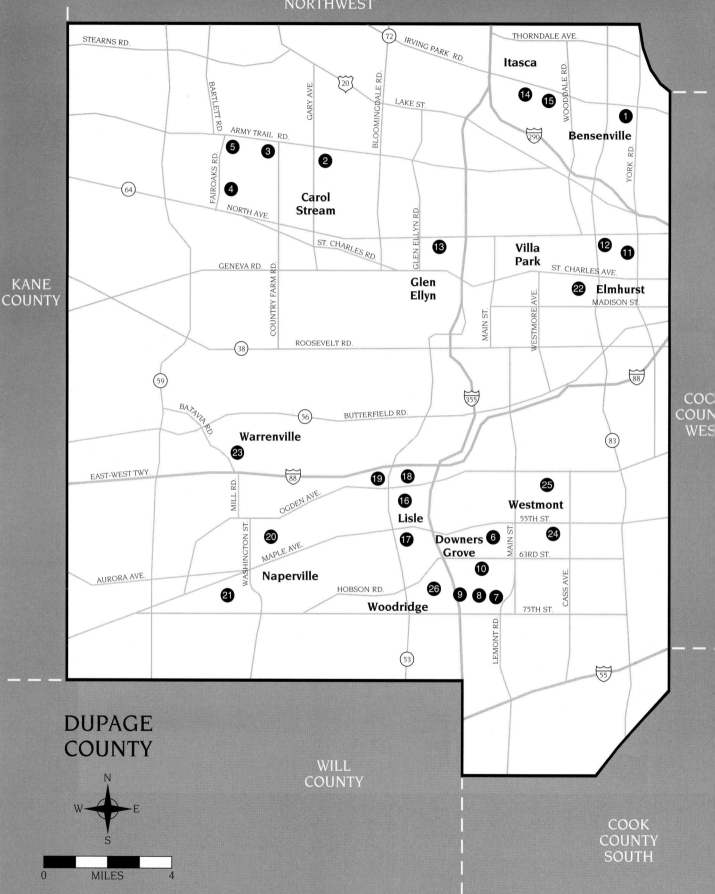

BENSENVILLE

❶ 213 South Center Street

The 15-foot homemade Santa that leans comfortably in the corner of Rick Cuvala's front yard is taking a well-deserved rest.

When Rick first created him in 1989, the jolly old elf stood tall at the front entrance of Rick's van conversion storefront on Irving Park Road. The following year at the same location, Santa held glistening reins high atop a motor home that was wrapped like a giant present. In 1991 Mr. Claus stood amid the sticky stripes of a candy cane factory explosion, followed a year later by a climb up the chimney of a home in Roselle. Santa now sits in the peaceful shade of the giant pines in the Cuvala front yard along with many of Rick's other imaginative creations.

When he began decorating his house and storefront, Rick had no plans of selling his homemade displays. Since he was three years old he had helped his dad trim the house for the holidays, so to Rick decorating was "just a part of being a Cuvala." But when people began to show interest in purchasing his unique decorations, his entrepreneurial spirit led him into a new business.

Through much trial and error, he perfected the method used to create Santa. With wire, pipe and plastic he built strong, lightweight and transportable displays that he could market. Among his more notable products so far are Santa Claus delivering a pizza 20 feet atop a pole at Archer and Canal, and the glowing castle turrets at 554 May Street in Roselle.

Though his own home decorations are often the last to go up, they allow Rick the freedom of his own fanciful whims, such as strewing his lawn with strands of burnt-out Christmas lights.

Dec.15–Jan.6, Dusk–11:00PM. *From Irving Park Rd., S on York Rd. 3/4 mi., W on Memorial Rd. 1 bl., N on Center St. 1 bl.*

CAROL STREAM

❷ 770 Hoover Drive

Unsuspecting passersby may, at first glance, think that the Christmas lights on this suburban home are reacting to a serious electrical malfunction. However, as the glowing outlines of the windows, doorways, wreaths and roof alternately brighten, dim, flash and flicker in a rhythmic dance, it becomes apparent that this amusing light show, which brings cars to a halt, is the premeditated work of an electronic wizard.

The brains behind the operation belong to homeowner and electrical engineer Don Sorenson. He first designed the display in 1983 for his previous Carol Stream home on 820 Idaho Street. "I wanted to see if I could do it," he explains.

In his present display, 150 strands of lights are controlled by a series of hand-built circuit boards that regulate the voltage that dims or brightens the lights. The boards are attached to a computer which signals the level and duration of the brightness for each strand through software designed by Don's friend Ron Rechenmacher. Using a word processor, Don creates the data for the program by coding a number for each set of lights in a consecutive series of defined time intervals. The entire sequence lasts about two minutes, but the complete system required several months to design and build, and a lot of running in and out of the house.

Because the lights are seldom all on at the same time and never go off completely, the system can run on one 20-amp circuit with only a $15 increase in the monthly electric bill. Don also saves money by salvaging old light strands donated by neighbors. "I take anything," Don remarks.

When he and his wife, Linda, complete the landscaping at their new home, they hope to expand the light display to the shrubs and trees as they did at their former residence. Until then, four strands of lights on the side of the house form a delightful two-story tree that blinks and changes colors on alternating beats.

Dec. 5–Jan.15, 5:00PM–10:30PM. *From Army Trail Rd., S on Gary Ave. 1 mi., W on Elk Trail 1/4 mi., S on Hoover Dr. 1 bl.*

Preventing Outdoor Electrical Shorts

Keep moisture from shorting out electrical connections by tightly wrapping the connected plugs in plastic wrap secured with electrical tape. Plastic food containers or 20-ounce pop bottles with trap doors cut in the sides can be substituted for the plastic wrap and taped air-tight.

❸ 1189 Knollwood Drive

Picture windows at the home of Joe Szewc and Rachel Spelker become storybook shadow boxes during the holidays. Rachel's childhood dolls peer through the window awaiting Santa's arrival. Mrs. Claus and Santa, made from coat racks, pillow cases, stuffing and Halloween masks, appear in the living room window below. The figures may change their poses from year to year. But Mrs. Claus never ceases to resemble Barbara Bush.

Dec.15–Jan.1, 5:00PM–11:00PM. *From Gary Ave., W on Army Trail Rd. 2 mi., S on County Farm Rd. 2 bl., W on Woodhill Dr. 2 bl., NW on Knollwood Dr. 1/2 bl.*

❹ 1318 Lilac Lane

John and Cindy Kosik each came from families that were known for having the most Christmas decorations on the block. Following in their parents' footsteps and having tasted the fruits of fame, it was inevitable that their union would give birth to a display even grander than those of their youth.

Homemade candles add their glow to thousands of lights, which tastefully trim the Kosik home.

The Szewc/Spelker windows are full of surprises.

With a team effort, rare in the male-dominated holiday decorating field, the couple transforms their two-story colonial and corner lot into a glistening wonderland. Thousands of lights glimmer from the parkway trees and flash from the shrubbery. Wreaths shine from every peak of the house. The windows, eaves, railings and chimney glow tidily with rows of lights, some of which are secured with duct tape to keep the bulbs pointing in the same direction.

The side of the garage gleams with three large candles John crafted from plywood and stapled full of lights. Across the first floor roof a homemade "Happy Holidays" sign sends the couple's heartfelt message in grand style—two feet high and 22 feet long.

Though the home of John's parents is part of the famous Becket Avenue display in Westchester (page 107), he and Cindy have done an admirable job keeping up the decorating reputation of the Kosik name. In 1991 when John broke three ribs and several toes after falling 14 feet from a ladder, Cindy completed the display on her own. But then, they were just, once again, following in their parent's footsteps. John's dad had broken his heel while decorating the year before.

Dec.7–Jan.10, Dusk–12:00AM. *From Army Trail Rd., S on Fair Oaks Rd. 3/4 mi., E on Lies Rd. 1 bl., S on Rose Ave. 1/4 mi., W on Lilac Ln.*

⑤ 1215 Woodlake Drive

"I plan to decorate my house for the holidays until my kids are old enough to do it for me," says homeowner Rich Andracki. Meanwhile he and his wife, Dawne, add unique homemade creations to their display each year for their own enjoyment and the excitement it brings to their three youngsters, Traci, Tony, and Tammi.

A handsome manger scene, constructed with leftover fence lumber, glows in the side yard. A 7-foot wreath, made of rolled chicken wire wrapped in garland and lights, stretches across the garage roof. Strings of lights, draped from a pole in the umbrella stand of the picnic table, extend around the rail of their circular deck to form a 24-foot Christmas tree.

A child-size gingerbread house covered with peppermints and candy canes is a favorite of the children. "I can't keep them out of it," Rich says gleefully. He plans to build an operating train to go around it too.

It seems the Andracki kids have a bit more fun in store before having to take over dad's job.

Dec. 1–Jan. 6, 5:00PM–10:30PM. *From County Farm Rd., E on Army Trail Rd. 1/2 mi., S on Woodlake Dr. 1/2 mi., SE corner at Hyannis.*

Rich Andracki's homemade gingerbread house, trimmed with styrofoam candies and polyester fiberfill snow, is a favorite winter playhouse for his children.

DOWNERS GROVE

⑥ 5523 South Carpenter Street

That glittering star appearing in the night sky may just be perched high atop a 60-foot evergreen in a Downers Grove yard a mile away. If you follow it to its source on Carpenter Street, you're sure to be delighted by this "star attraction" and the treats surrounding it.

Since 1987 Ken and Carol Triphahn have stopped buying each other presents and are decorating their home instead. They receive more joy than gifts can bring from their 12 grandchildren and the carloads of people who line the street to see their display.

Over 600 lights flash "Season's Greetings" across the house in bold letters crafted by the Triphahn's son-in-law Robin, who also made the outdoor wreaths. Santa and his reindeer soar overhead, while toy soldiers, candy canes, gingerbread houses, giant candles and singing choir boys fill the ground below. Ken's handmade manger cradles the nativity scene, as snowflakes and wreaths dance in the windows, giving a glimpse of the fantasyland Carol has continued inside.

From a shipping crate and a neighbor's old thermopane window, Ken built a miniature house with an old-fashioned Christmas scene of moving figures surrounding a decorated tree in a cozy living room. A toy train makes a non-stop trip around the floor, thanks to Traditional Hobby, a local store that replaces the worn train motor sometimes twice a season.

Decorating preparations begin in September when the Triphahns and their three sons-in-law begin checking the lights for burn-outs and wire damage. Actual decorating begins in November with the evergreen tree, which alone requires two men working eight hours to complete. Ken's good friend Ray Heye of Ray's Custom Tree Service in Downers Grove climbs to the top of the tree armed for the task with duct tape and a cup of coffee.

The star goes up first. It is actually a triangle of three 24-inch stars, so its 300 lights can be seen from all directions. It is wired to a 10-foot conduit pole and taped to the top of the tree.

A T-shaped maneuvering device made from 10 feet of conduit, an eye-hook and a fishing line is used to pull the eight strands of 50 large bulbs up the tree. The device keeps the wires from catching on the lower branches, which extend 10 feet from the trunk. On the ground below, Ken ties each strand to the fishing line. Then Ray pulls the lights

KIP SWEHLA

A treetop star guides visitors to the Triphahn's delightful display.

❼ 6810 South Carpenter Street

Ed Kochan's theory on decorating is, "If you can't find it, build it." He has discovered that shopping in other states is a good way to find unusual Christmas items, such as his illuminated ice cream cones. But when he has an idea that can't be bought, he puts his skills as a sheet-metal worker to use and creates it himself. The metal guard houses for his toy soldiers and the display cases for his animated figures are all handmade and built to last.

Thanksgiving–Jan. 6, 6:00PM–10:00PM. *From 75th St., N on Lemont Rd. (Main St.) 3/4 mi., W on 68th St. 1 bl., S on Carpenter St.*

❽ 6831 Saratoga Avenue

Over the last several years Christmas decorating has been a growing trend in Downers Grove, resulting in numerous elaborate displays and an increase in yuletide traffic. The origin of the local fad can be traced to a house on Saratoga Avenue, where homeowner Greg Lasek seems to have pioneered the suburb's holiday habit in the mid-seventies.

Having helped his dad decorate their Chicago home as a boy, it was only natural that Greg would do the same when he bought his own house. With an average decorating budget of $1,000 dollars per year, it wasn't long before the Lasek home became a holiday attraction.

Visitors enjoy the colorful collection of themed displays that fill the front lawn—toy soldiers, carolers, Christmas trees, a crèche, Santa and Mrs. Claus in their home, a gingerbread house filled with gingerbread men, and a street of decorated houses. The yard is surrounded by lanterns lining the sidewalk and candy canes flanking the driveway.

While fresh garlands add fragrance to the scene, 4,000 lights add sparkle. They dangle from the branches of three 30-foot trees, outline the house and basketball court, and even cover the mailbox. "There ain't a piece of the house that isn't lit up," Greg says jokingly.

Since the start of the display, the home's trademark has been its roof, which is completely covered with lights hanging from every shingle. Though Greg has enjoyed adding variety to the display by changing the color of the lights every other season, the current rooftop motion lights do a good job on their

up with the line extended away from the tree by the conduit tool. The lights are taped to the top of the tree and hang vertically on the branches till they reach their electrical connection at the base. Ken checks the lights daily and protects the sockets with zip-lock bags.

On Christmas Eve, Santa has been known to appear for an hour or so with a sack full of candy canes. One year he was joined by 50 carolers singing in the driveway. It's no wonder the Triphahn grandchildren, who refer to their grandparents' home as "Santa's house," innocently believe that Santa flew over the treetop and hung the enchanting star himself.

Dec. 5–Jan. 6, Dusk–12:00AM, (Christmas week) –Dawn. *From Lemont Rd. (Main St.), W on 55th St. 1 bl., S on Carpenter St. 1/2 bl.*

own by alternately making the housetop white, red, or green. A moving bell that hangs from the chimney adds to the aerial decorations, as well as Santa waving from a sleigh pulled by his team of reindeer.

The display takes four to six weeks to set up. "Every year I say I'm going to stop because it's so much work," Greg admits, "and every year I end up doing it again." His son, David, helps out and seems to be picking up where Greg would like to leave off.

Greg's wife, Diane, has never shared his cold-weather hobby, and he doesn't blame her. "We're running in and out of the house a lot, up and down from the bedrooms and outside the windows." And besides, decorating does have its hazards…

During the season of the Blizzard of '79, Greg slid off the roof while hanging lights and found himself buried in a snow bank on the side of the house. His fall was broken, but his ski cap was all that remained visible. He yelled for help, and Diane and David came to his rescue after they stopped laughing.

Fri. after Thanksgiving–Jan.1, 5:30PM–11:00PM. *From 75th St., N on Lemont Rd. (Main St.) 3/4 mi., W on 68th St. 2 bl., S on Saratoga Ave.*

Paul Volk's snowball of cups is made by first stapling together the center ring, which determines the size of the ball. The remaining cups are stapled between until a ball is formed. Before stapling the last cup, place a light strand in the center of the ball with the plug protruding. If opaque cups are used the bottoms should be cut out before assembly.

❾ 1310 67th Place

Green plastic pop bottles are given a dazzling second life at this west suburban residence, where homeowner Paul Volk stuffs the two-liter containers with Christmas lights and hangs them from his parkway trees. The giant recycled ornaments are among the many creative displays Paul makes from wood, glass and household materials.

Plastic candy canes, once full of Christmas candies, are also filled with lights and reused as ornaments. Dozens of plastic cups with lights poking through the centers are stapled together to form a huge glistening snowball that hangs from the corner of the garage roof. Eight-foot candles flanking the doorway and cartoon characters decorating the lawn are all cut from plywood and hand-painted by Paul.

Thanksgiving–Jan.5, Dusk–10:00PM. *From Main St., W on 63rd St. 1/2 mi., S on Dunham Rd. 1/2 mi., E on 67th Pl.*

❿ 1220 67th Street
(pictured on page 111)

In 1973 when Rion Goyette thought about taking his three-year-old daughter, Nicole, downtown to see Christmas decorations, he decided he would rather decorate his own house than stand outside in Chicago's cold blustery winds.

He first purchased two plastic reindeer and a Santa Claus. When his astute youngster noted that Santa had nine reindeer, he bought seven more. Though the sleigh team was pleasant, it was still a far cry from Marshall Field's, so Rion purchased an animated doll. Nicole liked it so much that he began to buy more, and together they created scenes for them.

Though his daughter eventually lost interest, Rion, who loves toys, continued to add to the collection. "I guess I never grew up," he admits. Over the last two decades with the help of his supportive wife, Diane, and a few helpful neighbors, Rion has created an astounding display that has surely brought the magic of downtown decorations to the suburbs.

The Goyette's raised ranch home is barely recognizable covered with glowing candy canes, gingerbread men, Santa faces, tin soldiers, red and white lights and a colossal 2,400-watt rooftop "Season's Greetings" sign that can be seen from blocks away. The windows and garage, transformed into giant three-dimensional animated shadow boxes, inspire visitors to rumor, "The people who live here move out and live in a hotel during the holidays."

In actuality Rion or Diane must be home at all times for safety reasons when the display is lit, and are not crammed into smaller living quarters. Rion staggers the figures in the windows, tapers the backdrops and gradates the colors to give an illusion of depth greater than the two to five feet of space the displays take up.

Their corner lot is surrounded by a homemade picket fence, old-fashioned flickering lanterns and cheery peppermint lollipops. Twenty animated display cases, which Rion designed, line the sidewalk, making a stroll down 67th Street like a trip through a holiday storybook. Six Victorian carolers dressed in brocade red velvet cloaks surround a grand piano. Snowbabies frolic in a winter wonderland. A turn-of-the-century family trims a Christmas tree. Santa shows his elves a plan for a new train, while they work in their toy shop. Angels fly about a steepled church, and children from other lands go about their native tasks. It's no wonder that one evening a woman rang the bell to inquire, "Is this where the tour begins?"

The window displays change with Rion's imagination and whichever of his 150 animated figures he decides to use. The outdoor boxes, with the figures permanently installed, only grow in number from year to year.

Because of the volume of their purchases, the Goyettes were able to obtain a commercial account with one display company, and have acquired other decorations from all over the United States. Several of their figures were bought at Marshall Field's window display sales.

One of their largest purchases was made in 1990 when Mario and Roseanne Encinosa of Tampa, Florida, contacted the Goyettes after seeing a picture of their decorated home in the local paper. The Encinosas were retiring the elaborate display that had made their home a tourist attraction, complete with t-shirts and postcards, for 20 years.

"You're not the only idiots who do this," Mario began. He proceeded to explain that he wanted to sell his decorations to someone who would keep their tradition alive, and from what he had seen of the Goyettes' home they were likely candidates.

Rion flew to Florida with every intention of keeping to the budget Diane had set, but by the time he left he had rented a 30-foot truck and had bought as much as he could fit into it. Mario and Roseanne were trusting enough to accept 12 pre-dated monthly checks from Rion in payment for 85 percent of their display. A towering 19-foot fiberglass Santa Claus still awaits him, if he wants it.

Mario, who by now had become Rion's idol, recommended that he set up a train. "Trains really draw people, especially kids," Mario said. So Rion built an HO-model train layout that took up half of his two-car garage. Running non-stop, the engines repeatedly broke down. A local train store owner advised Rion to use commercial trains instead. The owner lent him two engines and ten cars. As Mario had predicted, the trains were a big attraction. Rion purchased the cars at the end of the season and has expanded the layout each year since.

With the help of neighbors Paul Talucka, who built the mountain tunnels, and young John Havlick, who climbs between the tracks, both sides of the Goyettes' garage are transformed into an awesome five-level display with 88 G-scale cars, 13 engines and 9 transformers. Each level has been designed with a different theme: a rural area, two 1940s' industrial areas, a turn-of-the-century wild west scene and a Christmas train.

Despite the display's current success, Rion envisions an even grander scheme—a layout encased in plexiglass that people could walk around. However, this may only be wishful thinking to regain use of the garage. "I have to clean the snow from Diane's car windows all the time," he explained jokingly.

But, no matter, the garage is already blocked by the enormous Santamobile that fills the driveway. The 12' x 7' x 5' structure is home to Mr. and Mrs. Claus and Kristin, Tommy, Bradley and Matthew Elf during the last two weekends before Christmas. Children have waited in line as long as 45 minutes to visit Santa, and the neighborhood elves have given out as many as 1,500 big candy canes in one season. As Santa's stand-in Rion admits, "I'm really built for it." Wearing costumes made by Diane's mother, the couple has also appeared in the Downers Grove Main Street Parade.

As one could imagine, the Goyettes' enormous display requires a tremendous amount of organization and planning. Rion, who works as a part-time volunteer coordinator at a local hospital, and Diane, a legal secretary, are up to the task. (Neither is

Amid a wonderland of holiday lights and animated displays Mrs. Claus and Santa appear at the Goyette home to visit with children in their Santamobile.

employed by Marshall Field's or Commonwealth Edison, as rumored by many.) The couple devised an impressive notebook containing listings of breaker panels, amperage capacities, outlet diagrams, things to be repaired, hardware, motors, lumber prices, suppliers and helpers. By mid-October a blueprint has been drawn of the holiday display for the year.

The Goyettes think about decorating year-round, but the real work begins in the summer when Rion builds his new displays. Though he is good with electrical problems, he admits that he has learned carpentry as he goes along. Diane, who spends 50 percent of her allotted vacation time on Christmas activities, is her husband's "gofer" and backbone. "If I get carried away, she helps me get to the final stages," Rion reveals.

By September the couple is ready to test all the lights, which they guess number in the tens of thousands. Usually about half of the strands need to be repaired. October is the month for testing the figurines, which Rion repairs himself. With the decorations ready to go, the overwhelming assembly of the out-door display begins on the 1st of November. When the weather is bad Rion and Diane work on the indoor window decorations.

"I have been blessed by the amount of people who help me," Rion expressed thankfully. Neighbors offer a few hours of their time and passersby stop to lend a hand. "I just come here to have fun," a helper admitted. One of Rion's most ardent volunteers has been a neighborhood teenager, Dan Artl, who began replacing the light bulbs when he was seven years old and has been helping ever since. Members of the Divine Savior Teen Club also join the effort by spending several days taping the bulbs into their sockets to prevent them from being accidentally unscrewed.

In 1984 Rion was recovering from back surgery and had not planned on decorating the house. By the third week of November, neighbors became nervous about the unusual lack of activity. "But you have to decorate," they pleaded, "You're the Christmas house." Neighbors, friends, strangers, the insurance sales-man, and the real estate agent and his kids all came by to help. Rion directed the operation on crutches.

The entire assembly now requires approximately 1,200 hours to complete. During the set-up Diane averages 25 trips per week to the hardware store. Rion spends every spare minute decorating, nearly 18 hours a day. He often trims the interior holiday tree on Christmas Eve, Christmas Day or not at all. In contrast the display takes two weeks to take down, pack into the Goyette's 20-foot trailer and move to a 2,000 square-foot storage site.

The electrical considerations alone require hours of calculations to avoid overloading the circuits. An additional 200-amp service has been added to the existing 150-amp household line. All the outdoor outlets have been equipped with ground fault interrupters for safety. In addition Rion wraps and tapes each electrical juncture to keep out moisture, using 700 feet of plastic wrap in all.

When new sidewalks were installed by the city, the Goyettes seized the opportunity to bury PVC pipes below the cement to hide extension cords powering the parkways. In total the display requires 600 of the 1,000 extension cords, that Rion has color-coded by length. A single relay switch powers the entire display, which makes the walls vibrate with its nightly "ka-boom."

The home has been featured on all the network news shows, "Inside Edition," "The Home Show," the front page of the *Chicago Tribune* and newspapers throughout the United States. It was awarded the 1st Annual Mayor's Award by the town of Downers Grove, and an electric bill of $1,500 earned Rion the title "Lighter of Lights" during a sermon by Fr. Bob Pietras at the neighboring church.

An outdoor guest book registered 11,452 visitors in 1993 alone, including travelers from such countries as Sri Lanka, New Zealand and Iceland. The awestruck crowds keep the Goyettes on a holiday high, but Rion and Diane's biggest thrill is seeing the twinkle in children's eyes when they sit on Rion's lap and say, "I love you, Santa."

Dec. 8–Jan. 6, (M–Th) 6:30PM–10:30PM, (F) 6:30PM – 11:00PM, (Sa–Su) 5:00PM–11:00PM. Santa and Mrs. Claus appear the two Saturdays and Sundays before Christmas, 6:00PM–8:00PM. *From 75th St., N on Lemont Rd. (Main St.) 1 mi., W on 67th St. 2 bl. (or N on Lemont Rd. 1/4 mi., N on Dunham Rd. turn-off 1-1/4 mi., E on 67th St. 3 bl.) Near-by parking is available in the church lot at the corner of Main and 67th.*

Joe Consolo stands in the glow of the 20,000 lights that decorate his homemade sleigh and reindeer.

ELMHURST

The Consolo Home

The giant candy canes, snowman and Santa in his sleigh that once glimmered with thousands of lights at the corner of Armitage and West Avenue have moved to Florida with their creator, Joe Consolo, and his wife, Liz.

The decorations were constructed of PVC framework covered with chicken wire and generously strung with lights. Though the effect was stunning, the display put an annual strain on the family's electrical supply and cost an additional $5 per day. With no power to spare, Liz couldn't use the dishwasher while the decorations were lit, and Joe was unable to add anything new.

The problem has been solved at their new home, however. "I've got it already set up with ten outdoor outlets," Joe said while discussing their move. "I can even put out my other reindeer." Liz' faint protest "no way" could be heard in the background. ◆

⑪ 200 Block of Claremont Street

The local record for the longest running group display seems to belong to the residents on the 200 block of Claremont Street. A matching Christmas tree, trimmed with multicolored bulbs, on the lawn of every house has been a holiday tradition since the end of World War II. In the years that have followed, the custom has spread throughout Elmhurst.

On a block so organized it has a mayor, secretary and treasurer, it is no wonder that uniform precision can be achieved. The homeowners purchase the trees in bulk and place one in front of each home, 10 feet from the walkway. Christmas banners, made by resident Sheila Lewis, hang from lampposts at both ends of the block, while a string of brightly colored bulbs forms a welcoming arch overhead. A five-pointed star crowns the center of the street, hung from the few remaining elms that formerly shaded the entire block. Maintenance of the star is a "requirement for ownership" of the 245 address.

The holiday tradition kicks off with a private street party, no matter what the weather. It features homemade cookies, hot cider, horse-drawn sleigh rides and a visit from Santa. Each family brings a log for a blazing bonfire and all join in singing carols.

The enduring tradition of Claremont Street has kept alive a neighborhood spirit many in our bustling lives have yearned to rekindle.

4th Sun. of Nov.–Jan.1, 4:00PM–11:00PM.
From York Rd., W on St. Charles Rd. 3 bl., N on Prospect Ave. 2 bl., W on Claremont St.

⑫ 153 Grace Avenue

On a dark morning in December 1989, Michael McGhee and Patricia Motto discovered a major theft —the entire wooden snow family that had been on display outside their home had been stolen, without a trace of evidence. The figures had sentimental value, not only because Mike's dad had made them over 25 years ago, but because they represented the six members of the McGhee family. With some hesitation, the police were called.

Upon arriving at their home, the investigating officer asked officially, "Can you describe these snowmen?" "They're round and white, wearing mittens and scarves," Mike replied. "I suggest you come down to the station," the officer stated.

Mike went to the police station and was escorted to the evidence room. Like a holiday bargain basement, the floor was covered with plastic Baby Jesuses, wise men, candy canes and Frostys. Mike scanned the pile with fading hope, until suddenly off in the corner he spotted Mr. and Mrs. Snow-McGhee. "Mom, Dad," Mike yelled. "I've come to take you home!"

Happily reunited, the snow family resumed its place among the other decorations that have transformed the McGhee's brown frame home into a gingerbread house for over a decade.

MARK PASTOR

The tradition of Claremont Street continues to glow.

The Hohe display annually brightens North Avenue.

Following in his dad's footsteps, Mike used imagination, plywood, paint and a scroll saw to create candy canes, lollipops, hard candies and chocolate kisses. They turn the house into a tasty cottage, while toy soldiers, candles and gingerbread men add to the fun.

The decorations are easily hung in four to five hours. Eye hooks at the top of each board fasten to hooks permanently screwed into the house. The only drawback occurs on windy days when the pieces tend to flap and wear the housepaint. Because the decorations are flat, they can be stacked and stored in a minimum of space.

The garage door, which has 24 panels, ideally becomes a colorful advent calendar. One stocking with the name of a relative is added to a panel every day as Christmas nears. And above the door hangs Mr. McGhee's snow family, safely out of reach.

Dec. 1–Jan. 1, 4:30PM–10:30PM. *From York Rd., W on St. Charles Rd. 1/2 mi., N on Hagans Ave. (Spring Ave.) 1 bl., W on Winthrop Ave. 1 bl., N on Grace Ave. 2-1/2bl.*

Miniature Christmas Trees

Inverted tomato plant baskets or chicken wire bent into cone shapes make nifty little Christmas trees when covered with garlands and lights.

GLEN ELLYN

⑬ 22W204 North Avenue

When Catherine and William Hohe began decorating their home in 1970, North Avenue wasn't the busy thoroughfare it is today. "It used to be very dark, so the decorations stood out," William noted.

Though the road now glows with street lights and traffic, the Hohes' home and one-acre lot, trimmed with 1,800 lights and 80 plastic figurines, still stands out enough to make cars pull over to the side of this busy street. In fact the home has become such a mainstay of Christmas adornment that when the Hohes didn't decorate one year, they received complaints from everyone they knew.

Accepting the fate of their home as a holiday landmark, Catherine and William, assisted by their three children and their families, have established an annual decorating tradition on the day after Thanksgiving. Working from a pencil layout of the plan, which changes every year, William assigns the tasks. The women decorate the fences, the men do the house, and the kids cart things back and forth.

The job is completed in one day, and passersby are once again assured that North Avenue will be a little brighter for the holidays thanks to the Hohes.

Fri. after Thanksgiving–Jan. 1, 4:00PM–10:30PM. *From Glen Ellyn Rd. (Main St.), E on North Ave. 1/4 mi.*

MARK PASTOR

The McGhee/Motto display is easily assembled and stored.

Visitors will want to stroll down the sidewalks of the Scarano's corner, where a maze of lights creates an enticing playland.

ITASCA

🄭 101 East George Street

Lights, lights, and more lights. Frank Scarano, who moved to America from southern Italy over 30 years ago, delights in covering his home and corner lot with the miniature lights that bear his native country's name.

Nearly 15,000 multicolored Italian bulbs outline the house, bridge the driveway, and stretch from branch to branch of the parkway trees. Together they form a dazzling maze that tempts even the timid to skip through its splendor.

Dec. 1–Jan. 6, 5:00PM–11:00PM. *From Wood Dale Ave., W on Irving Park Rd. 1-1/2 mi., S on Cherry St. 2 bl., W on George St. 1-1/2 bl.*

🄯 525 South Princeton Avenue

Santa Claus has parked his helicopter in front of Duane and Sharon Johnson's home throughout the holidays since 1959. The fluorescent red vehicle was the first of many homemade decorations that would eventually fill the Johnson's front yard.

Duane now spends nearly three weeks setting up the display he created. "I do all my decorating at night," he explains. "It's so much easier to see." With 14,000 lights to hang, his method proves successful. Three levels of chaser lights neatly trim the gutters, a 20-foot tree of lights on the rooftop cascades from a gleaming star, and a full-grown parkway tree becomes a glistening mushroom. The lawn is lit with greetings of "Merry Christmas" and "Happy New Year," surrounded by reindeer, miniature holiday trees and a smiling snowman, all made of plastic ceiling material.

Those lucky enough to have visited Duane's display in 1993 would also have seen the lawn trimmed with his white 1985 Classic Tiffany. The grand custom-built automobile was trimmed with lights, a big red bow and a team of nine reindeer pulling it to the treetop. Despite the car's popularity Duane declines to use it in the display again after spending two months removing the rust from its wire wheels.

However, on Christmas Eve visitors can still enjoy a visit from Santa, who passes out candy canes, to passersby until 2:00AM. Throughout the evening the Johnsons and their sons takes turns donning the suit, so no one ever gets too cold. Though the older ladies seem to enjoy Santa the most, it's the young ladies that make the Johnson boys fight over who gets to play Santa next.

Dec. 15–Jan. 1, 5:00PM–12:00AM. *From Wood Dale Ave., W on Irving Park Rd. 1-1/2 mi., S on Princeton Ave. 1-1/2 bl.*

Steve Wybron's
Giant Collapsible Christmas Tree

Neighbors who miss the colossal collapsible Christmas tree that had its home on the 500 block of Rush Street from 1976 to 1991, will be happy to know it is "alive and well" and residing in North Freedom, Wisconsin, with its creator Steve Wybron.

The tree, which is presently 17 feet wide at its base, is made of wooden sections six feet tall that gradually taper to a narrow point at the top. It is covered with lights, drenched in garlands, packed with candy canes, Santas, snowmen, candles, tin soldiers and other goodies and topped with a 9-foot star.

It has varied in height from 36 feet its first year to a grand height of 77 feet in 1981. It was shortened after it was struck by lightning, which damaged the star and the bulbs. It now stands 50 feet tall and has a lightning rod at the top.

The number of lights on the tree has varied from 500 to 5,600. According to a sign Steve displayed, the total amount of lights, including those on his house and yard, once numbered 11,244. His former mailman enjoyed telling Steve that *his* house had 11,245.

Wybron, a trim carpenter, built the tree at age 16, though he had actually thought of the idea when he was nine. Upon seeing the huge lighted decoration towering over the house for the first time his mom recalls, "I was a little bit overwhelmed."

Steve assembles the tree horizontally on a wooden frame seven feet above the ground. Each section, weighing from ten to 70 pounds, is bolted to the

Duane Johnson's creative use of lights make his holiday decorations unique.

Steve Wybron's homemade tree towered over his Itasca home.

next. When all the pieces are in place, Steve puts weights on the bottom of the tree causing it to pivot on a center beam at the edge of the roof into an upright position. "I can guide it with one hand," Steve says. He then secures it with cables and winches.

Those interested in traveling the 190 miles from the tree's former location should not have a difficult time finding it once they arrive. Steve says reassuringly, "Everyone up here knows about me and my tree." ♦

LISLE

⑯ "Lights of Lisle"

On the first Saturday of December, the village of Lisle rings in the holiday season with a dazzling display of 5,000 luminaria that line the rolling streets of the downtown area. Free hayrides take visitors from Village Hall to Lisle Station Park, where a nineteenth century train station, home and tavern festooned for the holidays offer a variety of festive treats including a visit with Santa and gingerbread cookies baked in a beehive oven.

Lisle residents share their history by decorating trees throughout the park with ornaments from their

native lands. Within the 1850's Netzley-Yender House, the "Families of Lisle" tree is trimmed with personalized ornaments inscribed with the names of contributing village residents and the year they moved to town.

Even the animals partake in the festivities. Three trees outside the village hall are decorated by local scout troops with edible ornaments for the birds and the squirrels. Many of the local businesses have open houses with evening hours. Refreshments are served and donations are accepted for the local food pantry.

Lights of Lisle: 1st Sat. in Dec., 12:00PM–9:00PM. For further information call The Depot Museum (708)968–2747 or the Lisle Chamber of Commerce (708)964–0052. *From Maple Ave., N on Rt.53 2 bl., NE on Main St. 1/2 mi., E on Burlington Ave.*

Duane Johnson's Lawn Ornaments

In searching for the perfect building material for outdoor decorations, Duane discovered egg-crate grid, plastic sheeting normally used for suspended ceilings. The durable gridded surface is not only weather-resistant and sturdy, its holes are the ideal size to hold the socket of an Italian light.

Duane cuts the plastic into the desired shapes by scoring the material to a depth of 1/8" and then breaking off the excess. He has also used tin snips and a saw, but notes that all three methods are painstaking.

He then suspends the sheet horizontally, so he has enough room to access both sides. Using strands of lights with petal reflectors, he removes the petals and places them in the desired pattern in the holes of the grid. He cautions from experience, "Don't bump it. You'll have to start all over again." He then pushes the lights individually through the backside of the grid and back into the reflectors. The wire strands are pulled taut and wrapped with thin gauge wire to keep the lights secure.

Conduit supports, attached to the grids with wire, are used to stake the decorations into the ground, as well as to keep the plastic material from bending.

After three years of decorating, the Sheahans had already filled their lawn with lighted displays and their windows and garage with moving dioramas.

⑰ 5717 Elm Street

An outbreak of decorating fever seems to be spreading across southeastern DuPage County, and homeowners Kim and Dan Sheahan are showing all the classic symptoms:

• A life-size Santa waving from a display case must be rolled out of the way to use the front door.
• Half of the living room and a portion of two bedrooms are taken up by five window dioramas.
• The car is parked in the street all year because the garage is filled with a large display during the holidays and stored decorations in the off-season.
• Having run short of storage space, the couple keeps many of their animated figures in Kim's old bedroom at her parents' house.
• In spite of Dan's dislike of cold weather he works outside for 10 weeks setting up the display.
• While trimming the house Dan and Kim make at least four trips a week to the hardware store for decorating paraphernalia.
• In 1993 alone, they spent $1,600 more than their allotted budget of $1,500 for decorations.
• They are on a first-name basis with the staff at

Bronner's Christmas Wonderland, the "Big Kahuna" of decorating stores in Frankenmuth, Michigan.
• They have adopted a reindeer at Brookfield Zoo.
• Dan traded in his year-old motorcycle to buy four animated elves.
• The children across the street have set up a hot chocolate stand to cash in on the crowds.
• They find none of the above situations inconvenient and consider them all part of the fun.

The Sheahans are in their early thirties and have only been decorating since 1991. Based on similar cases, it is probable that their decorating affliction will only worsen and begin to affect those inspired by their display. Already their young son, Bob, who sleeps with the motors of animated holiday figures humming in his bedroom window, is beginning his own collection of plastic figurines.

It is highly recommended that viewers park their cars and walk up to the house to take a closer look at the adorable animated gingerbread men in their gingerbread house, the delightful elves in their candy cane factory, the enchanting movable dolls playing with their newly opened toys, and the thousands of lights and dozens of plastic figurines carefully placed throughout the front yard.

But, a word of caution…if the thought of crowds ogling over your decorations and children bursting with excitement begins to entice you…it may be decorating fever. Buy two snowmen and call me in the morning.

Dec.4–Jan.1, 5:00PM–11:00PM. *From Rt.53, E on Maple Ave. 1 mi., S on Elm St. 3-1/2 bl.*

⑱ 1020 Southport Avenue

When Susan Bonini married her husband, Dave, she remembers saying, "I will love, honor and cherish," but recalls no mention of helping to decorate for Christmas.

At the time she had no idea that her husband would spend an average of $2,000 dollars a year on decorations that would eventually fill their basement from floor to ceiling, that she would be out in the cold helping hang lights for a month, that their electric bill would reach $325, or that people would be staring into her living room windows. But after years of

Visitors enjoy the Bonini's backyard, where storage sheds have been transformed into delightful animated showcases.

Across the street from the Sheahan display, Kelly, Kathleen and Colleen Cieplak recognize a good business opportunity. Jimmy Ricci samples their wares.

living with a man who doesn't let a day go by without planning his Christmas display, Susan has joined her husband's effort in order to preserve their marital bliss.

Together they have created the most popular holiday attraction in town. Because it is on the edge of the business district, their display may appear to be a commercial exhibit, but it is an actual home decorated by the people who really live there.

In 1994 the Boninis built a larger home on the adjoining lot, allowing them to expand their decorations even further. Though the couple moved in the second week of December, they still managed to complete their elaborate display.

The small white house that was once their home will still be decorated—Dave is putting a clause in the lease permitting him to do so. Trimmed with lights, candy canes and gingerbread men, it looks like an elfin hide-away surrounded by a wonderland of magical displays. Several of the windows feature holiday dioramas, the largest filling the attached garage with an eskimo playland of animated dolls. In the driveway stands a colorful mailbox for children's letters to Santa.

A huge evergreen glistening with lights and surrounded by snowmen lights the way to the backyard. Here visitors are welcome to walk up to the delightful animated showcases featuring a horse-drawn sleigh of stuffed animals, penguins riding up and down on a teeter-totter, cartoon characters gliding back and forth on swings, and Santa and his elves making toys in their workshop. Susan, who collects dolls, has made many of the clothes herself.

Plastic figurines and dancing candy canes fill the front yard surrounded by a white picket fence trimmed in garlands, peppermints and toy soldiers. At the corner of the lot stands a holiday clock tower.

On the weekend after St. Nicholas Day, when Lisle has its lighting ceremony, Santa appears at the tower to pose with visitors for a free photo, courtesy of photographer Jerry August, whose studio is next door.

On this first busy day, Dave directs traffic to a near-by parking lot, then stands amidst the crowd with boyish excitement. Wide-eyed children jump with glee, grandmas clasp their hands in wonder, and dads comment, "I'm glad I don't have to store all this stuff." Visitors have shown their appreciation by leaving bags of lights and stuffed animals at the door.

Proud of a job well done, Dave puts his frozen hands under his arms and explains, "This is something I've always wanted to do as an adult, because I liked it since I was a kid." And in the house Susan picks up an old photo displayed in the living room of Dave as a child sitting on Santa's lap. She shrugs her shoulders and smiles.

Dec. 5–Jan. 1, (Su–Th) 5:30PM–10:00PM, (F–Sa) –11:00PM. *From Rt.53., E on Ogden Ave. 1 bl., N on Main St. 1 bl.*

⑲ 4608 Winchester Avenue

Pat Boyk remembers, as a little girl, driving with her parents to look at Christmas decorations and wishing she lived in the house with the brightest lights on the block. Now, as an adult, she and her own family have made an annual tradition of decorating the outside of their home. With hot chocolate and cookies marking the beginning of the five-day task, the group sets out to make mom's dream come true.

Five thousand large multicolored bulbs outline the entire house, along with dozens of strands of Italian lights that decorate the bushes and trees. Toy soldiers line the driveway. A creche, built by the Boyk children, fills the front yard together with four life-size choir boys that Pat's parents bought her as a

Christmas gift. A large evergreen is decorated with lights and bows as high as the family can reach. Another tree is filled with glowing stars and gingerbread men. Twelve red and green gas lamps, trimmed with candy canes and more bows, form the posts for a fence of garland and glowing bells.

When all is in place and the display is lit, neighbors tease that the other side of town has gone dim…and Pat beams with delight.

Dec. 1–Jan. 6, 5:00PM–12:00AM. *From Rt.53, W on Ogden Ave. 3/4 mi., N on Winchester Ave. 1 bl.*

NAPERVILLE

⑳ 823 Fairwinds Court

On Christmas morning the Goodwin children are likely to find a puddle of melted snow next to their beds where Santa watched them sleeping, reindeer hoofprints and sleigh tracks on the roof, and a videotape showing packages magically appearing under the tree.

"Christmas is for children" says their dad, Mark Goodwin. So besides creating the best-decorated house in town, he playfully leaves ice cubes on his children's bedroom floors early Christmas morning, climbs to the roof with a broom and sled to make tracks in the snow, and records with stop-action the presents being placed under the tree.

Though Mark has fallen off the roof with his broom, and been "razzed" annually by fellow cardiologists at Edward Hospital for his elaborately decorated home, it doesn't stop him from continuing his holiday antics. Only his wife, Maureen, has been able to persuade him to keep the outside of the house looking tasteful.

Giant candy canes and swirling lollipops decorate the front yard. The trees and bushes twinkle with thousands of multicolored lights, and glistening wreaths hang from every window. On the lawn Santa's workshop is filled with animated elves and a dancing panda bear. The front porch features a diorama of Mr. and Mrs. Claus in front of their fireplace, elves trimming a tree and tin soldiers playing their drums. And the garage becomes a life-size stable for Santa's reindeer and a mail room for his elves. It's a holiday paradise for children and adults alike.

Thanksgiving–Jan. 1, 4:00PM–10:00PM. *From Washington St., E on Ogden Ave. (Rt.34) 6 bl., S on Columbia 2 bl., E on Monticello 2 bl., S on Fairwinds Ct.*

㉑ Naper Settlement Museum Village
201 West Porter Avenue

A visit to Naper Settlement during the holidays is a journey to the Christmases of yesteryear. Carolers dressed in capes, bonnets and top hats gather on a porch to share a merry tune. A blacksmith forges a shepherd's crook. A printer handsets type for a holiday greeting card and a recipe for plum pudding. And a school teacher makes intricate paper chains with her class in a one-room school house. Father Christmas in his fur-lined robe and crown of holly spreads good cheer, while Ebenezer Scrooge mutters "Bah, humbug."

A horse-drawn wagon takes passengers on a free ride through the 13-acre village, where 25 historic buildings are trimmed with red bows, fresh greenery and oil lanterns. The various buildings, once found in the Naperville area, include a reconstruction of Fort Payne, an 1830s log house, an elegant 1880s Victorian mansion and a fire house with an antique fire engine. Throughout the year volunteers dressed in period costumes enact 19th century life in a mid-western town. During the village's annual "Christmas Memories" celebration, the players share the holiday customs of times past, many of which have left their mark on festivities today.

Though special exhibits within the buildings may change yearly, the "Halfway House" Farm has displayed a representation of the first electrically lighted Christmas tree from 1882, and the Century Memorial Chapel has featured a 5-foot replica of the first ferris wheel from the 1893 World's Columbian Exposition. A similar replica was used to hold gifts, such as citrus fruits and candies, for the Sunday school children.

The village offers an afternoon and evening holiday program, which both include storytelling, children's crafts and musical entertainment. Refreshments and souvenirs are also available for purchase.

Dates and times vary annually. Admission fee. For more information call (708)420–6010.
From Ogden Ave., S on Washington St. 1-1/4 mi., W on Porter Ave.

The Goodwins let Santa use their garage as a reindeer stable and mailroom for the holidays.

Cascading lights beam to the Hanik's nativity scene.

VILLA PARK

㉒ 738 South Illinois Avenue

When Wayne and Laurie Hanik moved into their Villa Park home, they found that hanging Christmas decorations was a wonderful icebreaker for meeting the neighbors. People on the block stopped by just to let them know how much they enjoyed the display.

The Haniks trim their house with an artistic flair that's bound to please, while their youngster, Colby, acts as "apprentice decorator." He hangs the lower lights and tests for bad bulbs.

The front picture windows of their home are divided into small panes using one-inch strips of posterboard taped to the glass. Snow is carefully sprayed into each corner, setting a wintry stage for the animated figures within. The front lawn is dressed with Santa's sleigh and sprightly reindeer, which Wayne built from a small model sleigh and some deer he had seen in a store window.

The magnolia tree that spans the front of the house glimmers with 6,000 white lights, which are left up the remainder of the year hidden by the plant's large leaves. A graceful beam cascades from the "Star of Bethlehem" 50-feet atop an evergreen tree to the manger below. Its peaceful effect is in strong contrast to the daredevil feat Wayne employs (when Laurie is not at home) of hanging the lights from a ladder using an extension pole.

Over the years the Haniks have won top honors in the local decorating contest and continue to bring enjoyment to their neighbors through their efforts. The man across the street even told them, "Every night before I go to bed, I look out my front window. It makes me sleep better."

Dec.15–Jan.6, 4:00PM–12:00AM. *From Westmore Ave., E on Madison St. 1 mi., N on Illinois Ave.*

WARRENVILLE

㉓ 28W421 Batavia Road

Employees of nearby Illinois Bell and Amoco offices can thank Janet and Raymond Mulacek for adding a bit of cheer to their drive during rush hour. The couple's home brightens the main street in town with over 10,000 Italian lights draping the house, garage, barn, fence, bushes and trees.

Janet does most of the work herself with her husband helping out on the roofline. Though she spends two weeks checking all the lights and three more hanging them, she enjoys seeing her home "look like a fairyland."

Dec.1–Jan.1, 4:30PM–12:30AM. *From Butterfield Rd., SE on Batavia Rd. 1/4 mi.*

Glimmering bushes and trees light the Mulacek yard.

Many of the finely-crafted decorations in this display are handmade by homeowner Roger Farrow.

WESTMONT

㉔ 305 Elwood Court

Roger and Su-Lien Farrow's home was featured in 1993 on the front page of a local newspaper as the first place winner of the Westmont Christmas decorating contest. Suddenly, men who previously had no interest in looking at decorations were packing the family into the car for a drive. Their wives became wise to their unusual enthusiasm, however, when they arrived at the Farrow's home and saw a 1971 red Corvette Stingray with Santa at the wheel sparkling in the snow-covered garage.

The car was actually a last-minute idea. Roger was running out of time and had no place to store the classic car, which he had restored and painted himself. "Well, it's red," he thought and made it part of the display.

Roger's decorating decisions are more often based on the desires of his young twin daughters, Connie and Bonnie. "I decorate for them, so when there's something they like, I try to make it," he says. It was Bonnie's idea to have a lighted American flag, so dad went to work to make her happy.

The 5'x 7' steel flag wrapped in commercial garlands and glistening with lights was not only a hit with the twins, but with passersby as well. Roger

realized there was a market for his original designs and decided to discontinue his part-time auto body repair business and sell his holiday displays instead.

While maintaining his full-time job as a factory worker, he now spends an average of 30 hours per week designing and building unique decorations, some of which he will feature in upcoming displays.

A life-size animated manger scene promises to be the most grand. Complete with moving shepherds, wise men and camels, the display will fill his living room and be seen through a picture window installed just for this purpose. Roger's sister, Cindy, an artist, is creating the mold for the faces, while he is building the mechanics.

The store-bought ferris wheel of snowbabies, that was previously in the living room, will now be part of the garage display. The winter scene will feature a church, 25 animated dolls and fiber optic trees that Roger is making himself. With so much to fit in the garage, it seems there will be no room for the Corvette, but don't tell your husbands.

Dec. 6 – Jan. 1, Dusk – 11:00PM, (F – Sa) – 12:00AM.
From Cass Ave., W on 63rd St. 3/4 mi., N on Brookside Dr. 4 bl., E on Elwood Ct.

Staking Two-Dimensional Wooden Figurines

Though 1" x 2" boards with points sawed at the bottom are an easy and inexpensive method of staking wooden displays, the following alternative solutions offer their own advantages.

For all the following techniques, it is advised that 1" x 2" boards be screwed horizontally, a few inches from the top and bottom, to the back of the figurines before they are painted.

Wayne Goers of Huntley recommends:

Cut two pieces of conduit pipe 18 inches longer than the height of the display. With the conduit even with the top of the figurine and perpendicular to the 1x2s, drill holes through the pipes at the points where they cross the boards. At the desired location, hammer the pipes 18 inches into the ground. Drill screws through the holes in the conduit and into the 1x2s.

Gene and Jeannie Hiser of Hoffman Estates recommend:

Screw u-shaped brackets a few inches from the ends of the boards. Place conduit pipes through the brackets and hammer them into the ground. By pounding out the top of the conduit until it bends over the top bracket, the figures cannot be lifted off.

Mary Hoffman of Elk Grove Village recommends:

Screw an eye hook near both ends of each board. Insert metal rods through the eye hooks and pound them one foot into the ground.

John Frank of Rosemont recommends:

Use metal fence posts as stakes. They're cheap and durable.

"Unstaking" Figurines

Vernon Moore of Hanover Park recommends:

Pour hot water on the ground around the stakes. Wait a few minutes and wiggle the stakes out.

㉕ 520 Morning Glory Court

More than 12,000 miniature white lights glimmer from the tallest tree to the country mailbox in an elegantly crafted display by homeowners Gerald and Diane Kanyuh.

Glistening wreaths encircle the entryway and animated dolls fill the windows. Gingerbread men dance about the sparkling bushes, while teddy bears and candy canes surround an evergreen brimming with red velvet bows. Around the walkways toy soldiers stand at attention, as geese and penguins meander about the yard. At the corner of the lot, a lovely manger scene rests amid the lights.

Dec. 6 – Jan. 6, 5:30PM – 11:00PM. *From Cass Ave., W on Ogden Ave. 3/4 mi., S on Cumnor Ave. 1 bl., E on Morning Glory Ct.*

WOODRIDGE

㉖ 2623 Mitchell Drive

Forest animals play about the twinkling foliage of this suburban front yard, while in the background the mist of a cascading waterfall of lights creates a colorful rainbow. The peaceful wintry scene is the work of Richard Miyazaki, whose elegant holiday display reflects his skill as a full-time landscape designer.

"My emphasis is more on creativity and how lights and colors are used, " Richard explains. His 15-foot waterfall demonstrates his craft. Blue marquee lights are arranged on a wooden framework to create the illusion of flowing water, while white lights are interspersed to give the appearance of splashing caps of foam. A similar method was used to create the effect of bees buzzing about the hive that dangles beyond the reach of a cartoon bear.

The snowflakes that dance against the side of the house were made from quarter-inch styrofoam sheeting. Richard simply poked holes through the material with a pencil to create openings for the miniature lights.

The final effect is a harmonious forest scene. It makes the Miyazaki home as lovely to view in the cold of winter as it is in the summer, when the landscape is blanketed with a stunning mixture of flowers.

Dec. 15 – Jan. 6, Dusk – 10:30PM. *From Rt. 53, NE on Hobson Rd. 1/2 mi., E on Woodridge Dr. 1 bl., NE on Mitchell Dr. 3/4 mi. (follow curve until street ends).*

Chapter 9

KANE COUNTY

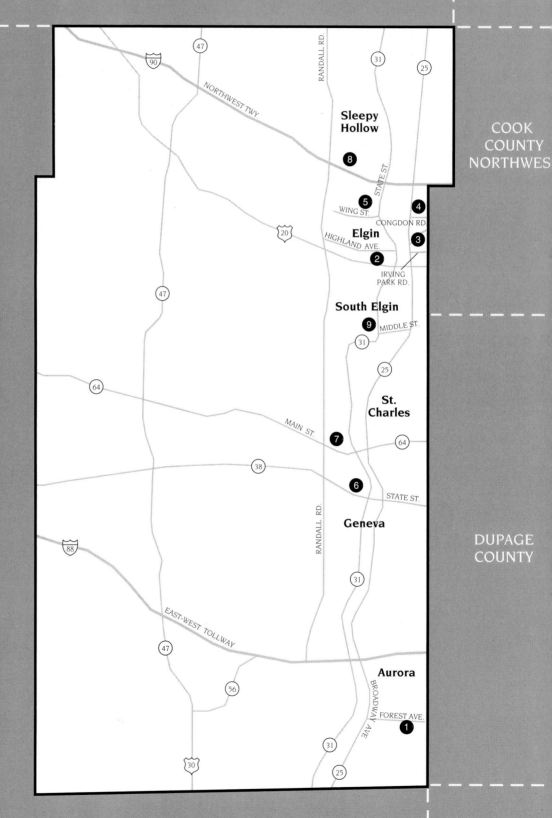

MCHENRY COUNTY

LAKE COUNTY

COOK COUNTY NORTHWES

DUPAGE COUNTY

WILL COUNTY

Sleepy Hollow

Elgin

South Elgin

St. Charles

Geneva

Aurora

KANE COUNTY

N
W   E
S

0   MILES   4

AURORA

❶ Lehnertz Avenue and Lehnertz Circle
(pictured on page 133)

In the fall of 1952 a new housing development on Lehnertz Avenue was in mid-construction. A few of the young homeowners, Fran Sibenaller, Larry Rowe and Ed and Bob Michels, had gathered together and were discussing the growing commercialization of Christmas. They decided to build a crèche as a neighborhood project in an effort to bring the focus of the holiday back to the Nativity of Christ.

Using scrap lumber from homes still under construction, they built a manger on one of the vacant lots. Figures of the Holy Family and shepherds were made from store-bought prints glued to masonite boards. Each shepherd, as though walking toward the manger, was placed in the front yard of a home. Ben Michels added music by amplifying Christmas records, which he turned over every half-hour in his garage.

At the end of the first season the men were so pleased with the display, that they formed the Lehnertz Avenue Improvement Association to organize the effort. As more families moved into the neighborhood, the display grew each season.

In 1953 Bob Michels, who owned a local lumber company, designed a new stable that could be more easily disassembled and stored. Though his original structure has been rebuilt a few times over the years, the same design is still being used today. In 1954 resident Joe Stotz painted a large banner reading "Gloria in Excelsis Deo," which still hangs at the east entrance to the street.

The following year Rev. Joseph Weitekamp of neighboring Saint Joseph Church helped the group create a series of 14 displays, each featuring a bible verse from the gospel of St. Luke, which together would tell the story of the birth of Christ. Each was painted on a wooden replica of an open Bible. They were placed on the front lawns of the homes on the south side of the street. The residents also constructed six red candles to light each verse. That same year, the original crèche figures were donated to Mooseheart, a near-by boarding school for disadvantaged children, and replaced with life-size molded plastic statues purchased by the residents.

The association also trimmed every lamppost on the street with garlands, dozens of 25-watt colored bulbs, and a speaker from which carols were played.

Fran Sibenaller displays his verse of the Christmas story.

The display had become so bright that an American Airlines pilot wrote a letter to the organizers saying that on clear nights during the Christmas season he took his plane a few degrees off its normal route when leaving O'Hare, so his passengers could enjoy Lehnertz Avenue from the air.

The decorations expanded again in 1956. Resident John Murphy designed a series of shepherds with their sheep and the Three Kings with their camels to add to the lawn displays on the north side of the street. With vacant lots no longer available, the manger scene was moved to Garfield Park, located at the west end of the street. Frank Zenner, father of one of the residents, oil-painted a magnificent 10' x 56' replica of the city of Bethlehem for a backdrop. Using a postcard as his model, he painted the scene sideways on 14 separate 4' x 10' panels. The replica stands in the distance behind the manger, lit by 25 spotlights and a towering star.

In 1980 residents of Lehnertz Circle, the neighboring cul-de-sac, decided to join their neighbors' effort. Wanting to make a unique contribution, but one that reinforced the true meaning of the holiday, they decided to show Christmas from the eyes of a child. Using characters from the "Peanuts" comic strip, residents on the outside of the circle built displays showing children and their families preparing for Christmas, while the inside circle depicted children enjoying the winter.

William Brown's enthusiastic annual display earned him a decorating award named in his honor.

Recently a "NOEL" sign surrounded by choir children was added to Garfield Park. The Bethlehem scene was restored by Chris Hofner, daughter-in-law of one of the residents, and the Bible verses were repainted.

Though only a few of the original homeowners remain, and the members of the light committee, the crib committee and the shepherd committee change from year to year, the display continues to appear every Christmas season. Houses sell very quickly in the three-block area because of its reputation, and new homeowners gladly inherit their part of the display.

Residents in the 88 households of Lehnertz Avenue and Lehnertz Circle enjoy the exhibit as much as the onlookers in the 20,000 cars who visit it annually. On Christmas night the neighbors walk up and down the street wishing each other good cheer. Fran Sibenaller, one of the originators who still lives on the street says, "My children wouldn't know Christmas any other way."

He and his neighbors could only have dreamed back in 1952 that their simple idea to share the Christmas story would become a holiday tradition for generations of families to come.

Sun. before Christmas—Jan.1, 5:00PM–10:30PM.
From Broadway Ave. (Rt.25), E on Forest Ave. (Rt.12) 3 bl., S on Sheridan St. 1 bl., E on Lehnertz Ave.

ELGIN

Elgin's Most Enthusiastic Decorator

If recent quadruple bypass surgery wasn't enough to keep 82-year-old Bill Brown from hanging his elaborate holiday display in 1993, surely his 75-year-old wife Virginia's urgings to stop climbing the extension ladder to the second floor went unheeded. Bill, a retired Elgin Metal Cask Company worker, had been decorating his home for over 25 years, enjoyed it, and had no plans to stop. However, the following year his doctor recommended that he discontinue the display due to illness, and Bill reluctantly complied.

Residents of Elgin will certainly miss the colorful decorations that greeted them every Christmas season. Brown spent three to four weeks zigzagging 75 sets of large and small lights up and down the sides of the house, around the rails, over the fence and across the bushes. He hung a 4-foot wreath on the second floor peak. He stuffed Santa Claus in the basketball hoop and stood a glowing tree in the bird bath out front. Two 8-foot red candles, once adorning Meadowdale Shopping Center in Carpentersville, flanked the garage thanks to the Schroeder Sign Company. The owner somehow guessed Bill Brown might want them.

Supplying electricity to all the lights was Bill's biggest challenge. Since the interior of the Brown's home was also well lit, there were plugs everywhere. Virginia had a difficult time each season finding vacant outlets.

The inconvenience didn't bother them, for the Browns were blessed with an appreciative audience. The couple has a collection of framed thank you notes hanging in their breakfast nook, and once found $5 on the porch from a grateful onlooker who wanted to help out with the electric bill.

Bill's decorations were such an inspiration to the local community that in 1988 an anonymous business person donated $50 in his honor to establish the "William D. Brown Award for Holiday Spirit" in the Elgin area "Light Up the Town" decorating contest. Along with other prizes for houses, yards and businesses, this award is given annually for the most enthusiastic display.

The Browns never entered the contest, however Bill explains, "I just did this for the fun of it." ◆

Virginia and William Brown stand amid their holiday finery.

❷ 106 Monroe Street

Craig and Brandon Arnold are two lucky brothers who share the best decorated clubhouse in Elgin. It's covered in multi-colored lights, trimmed with its very own wreath and has the most terrific view in town. From its second-story porch the boys can look down at 70 lighted plastic figurines that fill the back yard and thousands of lights that twinkle from the trees and bushes. And if that's not enough, their real house is decorated too.

The boys' dad, Mike Arnold, trims the entire frame of their two-story home, as well as the doors and all 21 windows. He even decorates Mrs. Turner's bushes next door.

It all started back when Mike was a kid himself. His mom loved outdoor Christmas decorations, so his dad decorated to make her happy. But when Mike was old enough, Mr. Arnold gladly handed over the task. Under Mike's direction the decorations grew more and more each year. After his mother passed away and he married and bought his own home, his dad was happy to let him take the lights along.

A rehabber by trade, Mike installed indoor outlets near each of the windows just for the Christmas lights. Later, having decided that the lights would look better hung from the outside, he installed 20 more outlets in the eaves, walls and lawn. He now hangs over 12,000 lights in all. Though his wife, Donna, thinks the house has gotten "beyond the gaudy point," the boys just continue enjoying the view.

Dec.1–Jan.6, 4:30PM–11:30PM. *From State St. (Rt.31), W on Highland Ave. 3/4 mi., SW on Larkin Ave. 1 bl., S on Monroe St. 1 bl.*

❸ Lords Park Pavilion
100 Oakwood Boulevard

The rich heritage of Elgin's multi-ethnic community is authentically portrayed in its annual exhibit "Touching on Traditions," sponsored by the Elgin Public Museum. Community members from all over the world share their winter customs in over 50 displays assembled in the picturesque Lords Park Pavilion.

Exotic Christmas trees, from a small potted sapling decorating a French dinner table to a Nigerian Christmas tree covered with balloons and dry moss, represent the diverse customs of the Christian holiday, while the colorful costumes of

Korea's Folklore Days, the floating leaf cup of Thailand's Loi Krathong, and the dreidle top and menorah candle of the Jewish Hanukkah remind viewers of the unique nature of each celebration.

Sat. after Thanksgiving–Sun. after Jan. 6, 10:00AM–7:00PM, (Christmas Eve and New Year's Eve) –3:00PM, Closed Christmas Day and New Year's Day. Admission: Adults $1, Children 50¢. For more information call The Elgin Public Museum (708)741–6655. *From Liberty St. (Rt.25), E on Irving Park Rd. (Rt.19) 1/4 mi., NE on Bode 2 bl., N on Oakwood Blvd.*

❹ 728 Parkway Avenue

When Richard Ulrich remodeled his ranch home with vinyl siding, he watched the instructional video tape provided by the manufacturer and used corner moldings at the adjoining walls and J-channel moldings around the windows, as was recommended. Only later did he realize that the moldings were not only a necessary finishing touch but a handy holder for his Christmas lights as well.

The result of his discovery is evenly spaced bulbs all pointing in the same direction and a charming holiday display.

Dec. 6–Jan. 1, 6:00PM–10:00PM. *From Congdon Rd. (Shoe Factory Rd), N on Dundee Ave. (Rt.25) 5 bl., E on Parkway Ave. 1 bl.*

Hanging Lights on a Sided House

Richard Ulrich uses plastic gutter hooks and shingle tabs to hang C-7 bulbs from his roof and fascia, but to put large and small bulbs around the windows, doors, and frame of his sided house, he found a ready-made solution. The lights are held quite snugly by pulling the cords tight and wedging the sockets in the J-channels and corner moldings of the siding.

The effect is further enhanced by pulling out "stray" bulbs in unwanted areas and covering the sockets with electrical tape. Richard uses three rolls of tape per season, also wrapping all plug connections to keep moisture from causing shorts in the wiring.

Glistening Lights

Aileen Vogel randomly strings several strands of white blinking lights throughout her wreaths, followed by several strands of standard white lights. Rather than flashing on and off, the lights appear to glisten.

❺ 510 North Worth Avenue

Two 4-foot wreaths of fresh pine boughs can cost a pretty penny, as Greg and Aileen Vogel discovered when they first decorated their home. They have managed, however, to wisely stretch their initial investment by creating a lovely and less expensive alternative.

Greg salvaged the wire rings from the pine wreaths. He then wrapped them each in artificial green garland, three times around, until they were as full as the originals. Crowned with giant red bows and brimming with glistening lights these hand-crafted copies look as grand as the real ones and can be reused every year.

Adding to the display, the home's classic portico and side balcony are decked in garlands and bows, and a candle shines from every window. With simplicity and little expense, the Vogels have done this handsome Georgian proud for the season.

Dec. 14–Jan. 6, Dusk–10:00PM. *From State St. (Rt.31), W on Wing St. 7 bl., At Worth Ave.*

Simple yet elegant decorations trim the Vogel home.

Cheery lampposts brighten a foggy evening along Main Street in St. Charles.

GENEVA

❻ Shopping District
State Street and 3rd Street

For those whose Christmas shopping experience must include fresh winter air and snowy landscapes to put them in a festive mood, Geneva's shopping district should suit their fancy. Nearly 100 shops, mostly housed in turn-of-the-century clapboard buildings, are trimmed with fresh greenery, red velvet ribbons and twinkling white lights. Wrought-iron benches and old-fashioned gas lamps decked in wreaths and bows line the paths from store to store.

On the first Friday in December the merchants host their annual "Christmas Walk." The stores stay open until 10:00PM and shoppers receive free refreshments, roasted chestnuts, horse-drawn carriage rides, and street-caroling. At 6:00PM Santa Claus and Santa Lucia, the patron saint of light, arrive for the lighting of the town Christmas tree on the lawn of Kane County Courthouse. The events continue into Saturday, along with a house tour and holiday tea.

1st Fri. of Dec.–Dec. 24, (M–F) 9:00AM–8:00PM, (Sa) –5:00PM, (Su) 11:00AM–5:00PM. For more information call the Geneva Chamber of Commerce (708)232–6060. *From 1st St. (Rt.31), W on State St.*

ST. CHARLES

❼ Main Street

Over the river and through the shopping district, 386 street lamps on Main Street are each trimmed with a live Christmas tree decked in multicolored bulbs. On the Wednesday before Thanksgiving at 4:50PM, a lucky child is chosen by the mayor to flip the switch that sets the street aglow. Holiday messages from town officials and songs by local choirs add to the brief but awesome spectacle.

Dressed for the holidays, the town flaunts its winter finery with a series of holiday events, which include arts and crafts fairs, a flea market, a holiday parade, an enchanted forest of decorated Christmas trees, an open house in the shopping district, a candle-lit reception in a restored 1843 farmhouse, a Victorian Christmas walk featuring Dickens characters, roasted chestnuts and caroling, and "The Charles Dickens Winter Festival" at Pheasant Run Resort Mega Center.

Street decorations: Wed. before Thanksgiving– Jan. 1. For more information on special events call the St. Charles Convention and Visitors Bureau (800)777–4373. *From Randall Rd., E on Main St. (Rt.64).*

SLEEPY HOLLOW

⑧ 719 Pimlico Parkway

Karen and Michael Kramer elegantly dress their colonial home during the holidays in the formal traditions of its time. Symbolizing a warm welcome within, a glowing candle shines from every window. A wreath, the expression of everlasting friendship, encircles each flame. The wintry scent of fresh evergreen fills the air, as pine garlands drape the columned portico and frame the carved doorway. The 20th century nudges in with white Italian lights that sparkle on the shrubs below.

Karen enjoys changing her color scheme each year with matching ribbons, pine cones and trim. She searches craft stores for the perfect 100 yards of indoor/outdoor floral ribbon to fashion her bows. One year when the handmade bows were ruined by freezing rain, Michael took them down, and Karen untied, ironed and re-made them all. She now sprays each bow with water repellent for added protection.

The care taken in decorating this home is apparent in the enchanting result that reflects the warm Christmas charm of an era past.

Dec. 14–Jan. 2, Dusk–10:00PM. *From the Northwest Twy. (I-90), N on Randall Rd. 1/4 mi., E on Saddle Club Pkwy. 1 bl., S on Arlington Pkwy. 1 bl., E on Pimlico Pkwy.*

Ribbons and greenery create an elegant entry to the Kramer home.

SOUTH ELGIN

⑨ Water Towers

The pair of "Merry Christmas" greetings appearing in the northwest evening sky are actually glowing 60 and 80 feet above the ground from the two water towers of South Elgin. Employees of the Public Works Department collaborated on the idea in 1989, and the colossal messages have been displayed every year since.

The workers used long sheets of chicken wire as their base. Multi-colored miniature lights to spell out the greeting were attached to the wire with plastic zip ties.

The messages were then rolled up and brought to the base of each tower. The men raised the bundles by rope to the catwalks, where the chicken wire was secured to the guardrails. Photocells were attached to turn the lights on and off automatically each night. At the end of the season the lights are switched off for the remainder of the year, until they are repaired in September.

Mon. after Thanksgiving–Mid-Jan., Dusk–Dawn. *From Rt. 25, W on Middle St. 1 mi., S on Gilbert St. 2 bl., (1st tower), N on Gilbert St. 3 bl., W on E. State 1/4 mi., N on La Fox St. (Rt. 31) 1 bl., W on Spring St. 1 mi.*

"Merry Christmas" gleams over South Elgin.

Chapter 10

LAKE COUNTY

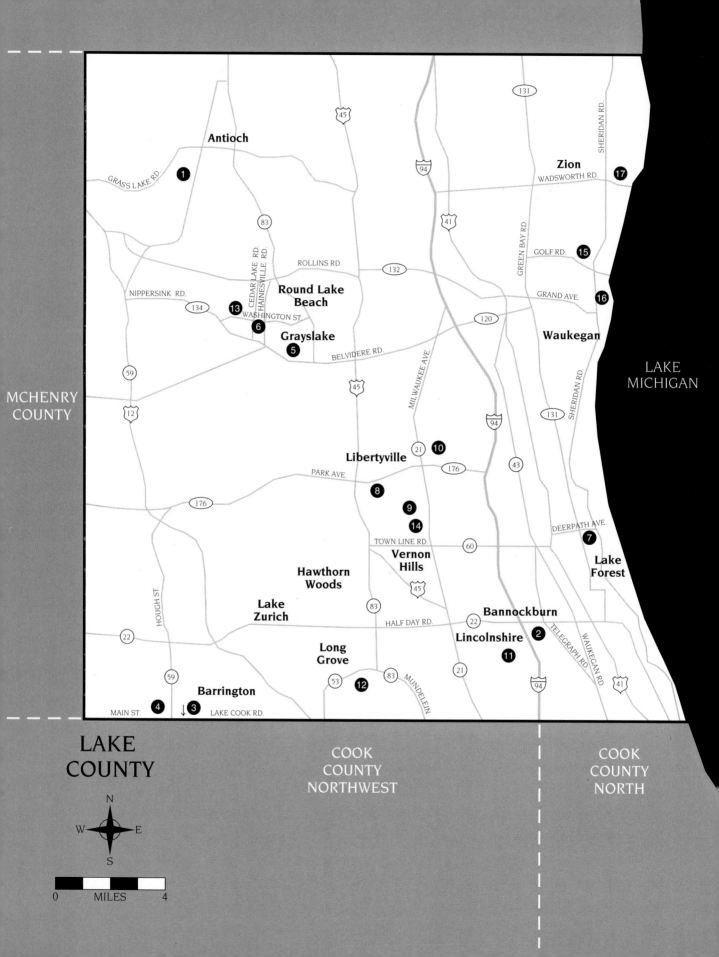

The main streets of Bannockburn are festooned for the holidays with the crafts of the ladies' garden club.

ANTIOCH

❶ 25420 Golfview Avenue

Red and white stripes are the pattern of the season in "Peppermint Park," the corner yard of Dennis and Emily Beattie. Candy canes twirl in the trees, sweeten the walkways and dance on the feet of merry elves. Stripes decorate everything from guard houses to ladders, and red and white lights glisten from the house.

Emily handcrafts most of the decorations, including an adorable moosehead that peeks from behind the garage. She admits, "I am the biggest child in the world, and I believe in spreading a child-like spirit around the neighborhood."

Dec.1–Dec.31, 5:00PM–10:00PM. *From Rt.59, W on Grasslake Rd. 1 mi., S on Rena Ave. 4 bl., E on Golfview Ave. 1 bl.*

BANNOCKBURN

❷ Village Decorations

Though most towns must purchase their holiday street displays, the village of Bannockburn has had the good fortune of having their decorations hand-crafted by the resourceful ladies of the Bannockburn Garden Club.

Since the late seventies the women have eagerly begun their yuletide project on the Monday before Thanksgiving in the basement of a generous member who doesn't mind the temporary mess. Initially the ladies designed a simple bough with a red bow. They progressed the following year to hand-painted pine cones tied in clusters of ten, and by the third holiday season were sawing dozens of candy canes out of wood. These led to their fourth and most successful display, which trims the town to this day— giant bells dressed in fresh evergreen boughs and red velvet bows.

Though the projects require many hours of meetings, member Gloria Dooley admits, "It's a labor of love that also provides an opportunity for a lot of talking and laughing."

Saturday after Thanksgiving–Jan.1, Day and night. *From Half Day Rd.(Rt.22), S on Telegraph Rd.*

The Beattie home looks delectable in its peppermint attire.

BARRINGTON

❸ 100 and 200 Block of East Lake Street

On the weekend after Thanksgiving the residents of Lake Street help each other decorate the exteriors of their 100-year-old homes with a neighborly spirit reminiscent of the era these grand Victorian houses recall. The scene is not unusual, for the homeowners also join efforts in auctions, garage sales and block parties throughout the year.

Sometimes referred to as "The Gold Coast of Barrington," this turn-of-the-century street is lovely to see at any time of year. But at Christmastime when fragrant greens trim the porches and white lights sparkle on every home, it's a winter wonderland not to miss.

Occasionally, newcomers to the block may try to add color to their Christmas lighting, but interior designer Vern Kastning, long-time resident and so-called "mayor" of Lake Street, is quick to set them straight. Colored bulbs have been known to disappear mysteriously in the night.

Playfully kept in line, residents are careful to keep trimmings in period style. Gaye Mack fashions traditional garlands of ribbons, fruits and birds, and Jill Gerbec makes a Williamsburg fan from magnolia leaves her mother ships from Florida.

The Victorian homes of Lake Street are elegantly trimmed in white lights and garlands of fresh pine with a candle in every window.

When the decorating is complete, the entire block glimmers with a simple elegance that reflects the spirit of togetherness and peace that Christmas has inspired for generations.

Thanksgiving weekend–Jan.1, 4:30PM–10:00PM, (Christmas Eve)–Dawn. *From Main St.(Lake Cook Rd.), S on Hough St. (Rt.59) 2 bl., E on Lake St.*

❹ 223 West Main Street

Prancing horses and swags of evergreens glimmering with white lights transform this architectural beauty into a dazzling holiday carousel. Though its multicolored face and elaborately carved wooden trim seem a natural setting for a carnival theme, it is the building's unique octagon shape that gives owner Linda Selman her yuletide inspiration.

Now the offices of Corporate Identity Inc., Linda's advertising specialties company, the structure was originally the home of Harriet Emeline and Joseph P. Brown. It was built in the early 1860s, modeling a style popularized by architect Orson Squire Fowler in his 1854 book, "A Home for All, or the Gravel Wall and Octagon Mode of Building." Though Fowler advocated the eight-sided design

Barrington's Octagon House makes a lovely holiday carousel.

because the interior provided more space than a traditional building with the same perimeter, Brown was said to have constructed his home in this shape because everyone else's was square.

Thousands of octagon houses were built in the 19th century throughout the United States, but few remain. H. Parker Sharpe purchased the Barrington residence from Brown's granddaughter in 1981. It still had a water pump in the kitchen and was in need of major repair. Thanks to Sharpe's restoration efforts the building now stands as a classic example of Fowler's style and the fine craftsmanship of the era.

Selman purchased the structure in 1990 and continued the restoration by having the building painted in its original colors. The Octagon House is currently on the National Register of Historic Places and was a 1991 recipient of the northwest suburban Painted Lady competition.

Sun. after Thanksgiving – Jan. 10, 3:00PM – 12:00AM.
From Hough Rd. (Rt.59), W on Main St. 2 bl.

FORT SHERIDAN

The Army's Towering Christmas Tree

May 28, 1993, marked the closing of Fort Sheridan, a U.S. Army base since 1892. Its 712-acre site housed 94 buildings that have been named historic national landmarks. Among them was the Fort Sheridan Water Tower, an operational storage facility that not only held 90,000 gallons of water but was the dramatic backdrop of the fort's annual 150-foot Christmas tree.

Assembled by eight engineers in two days, the tree was formed by wrapping the strands of 3,250 seven-watt colored bulbs around 29 cables that were anchored to the ground and tightly connected to an electrical box at the top of the tower. Since 1964 this magnificent tree, crowned with a 6-foot star, could be seen from the air, as well as by thousands of spectators driving through or near this open post.

Families of army personnel and North Shore residents alike gathered annually at the fort's community center, where a lucky child, whose name was drawn from a hat, got to flip the giant switch that lit the 21,750-watt tree. (Actually, a ground engineer radioed a signal to the top of the tower where another engineer made the electrical connection at the precise moment the switch was flipped.)

The magnificent 150-foot tree of lights on the Fort Sheridan Water Tower spread its holiday cheer for nearly 30 years.

Retired Lt. Col. Hal Fritz, former public affairs officer, recalls with amazement that there was never a malfunction in timing the switch or in maintaining the display throughout the holiday season. He mused that ghosts often rumored to be wandering the barracks may have been "guardians of the electricity" for this much-loved community event.

Lt. Col. Bill Rynearson, Director of Engineering and Housing, who was in charge of the tree for the last four years, carefully shipped the lights, cables and star to Fort McCoy, the Wisconsin base assigned caretaker of the post until its disposition. Although the rural base cannot accommodate the towering tree, its good cheer can still be enjoyed by visitors. During the holiday season the numerous lights of Fort Sheridan's tree decorate the entryway, club house and chalet of the Whitetail Ridge Recreation Area, Fort McCoy's public ski facility. ◆

The Werner's Grayslake home shimmers through the barren trees.

GRAYSLAKE

⑤ 201 Lindsey Avenue

Joggers along the Greenway Corridor Bicycle Path in Grayslake will enjoy a special treat when they pass beside the home of Marlin and Priscilla Werner. Tucked among the trees, the two-story cedar house is delicately outlined in white lights. Four glistening reindeer prance about the circular porch as though it were a hidden carousel in an enchanted forest.

Fri. after Thanksgiving–Jan.1, 5:00PM–9:00PM, (last 2 wks.) –10:00PM. *From Barron Blvd. (Rt.83.), W on Belvidere Rd. (Rt.120) 2-1/2 mi., N on West Trail 1 bl., E on Scott Ave. 2 bl. Path entrance is rt. of house.*

⑥ 22050 West Washington Street

Gerri Kirchhardt loves to decorate, and it shows. On her family's three-quarter acre lot she hangs hundreds of strands of lights that trim the house, the trees, the bushes, the flower beds and the gazebo. Santa Clauses pop from the snow-covered garden, and flower boxes come alive with garland and bows.

It's a beautiful sight from Highland Lake Park, where the front and side yards are in view, and even more fun if you are lucky enough to be one of the Kirchhardt grandchildren who get to run among the lights and give hugs to all the Santas.

Thanksgiving–Jan.6, Dusk–11:00PM. *From Hainesville Rd., W on Washington St. 3 bl.*

LAKE FOREST

⑦ Downtown and West-Side Business Districts
(pictured on page 141)

Selling Christmas greenery has become an annual fundraising event for many a scout troop during the holiday season, but few have had the luck of Troop 48 of Lake Forest. They recently inherited the Lake Forest Chamber of Commerce as a customer from fellow scouts in Troop 49, whose members were dwindling and moving on to college. Since the early eighties the older boys had made nearly 40% of their sales from the organization, which purchases 1,200 feet of garland and 200 36-inch wreaths yearly to decorate their main business and shopping districts.

In their first year the younger scouts quickly learned that the sale doesn't come easily. After city workers hang thousands of lights throughout Lake Forest, 20 scouts and their dads volunteer at 8:00AM on Thanksgiving morning to complete the decorating

Luminaria Night in Hawthorn Woods

The southwestern tradition of luminaria, which seems to have originated with the paper lanterns of the Christmas Eve processions of Mexico, has worked its way to the midwestern suburbs. When the charming community of Hawthorn Woods initiated the custom in 1991, what they envisioned to be a lasting tradition of glowing holiday streets got off to a shaky start for some of its residents.

On the Sunday before Christmas every household on the enthusiastic block of Juel Court had lined their walks with the sand-filled brown bags and lighted candles in hopes of a dazzling display. At 8:00PM neighbors gathered in the cul-de-sac for a party to christen the event. Suddenly the wind kicked up, and a felled tree branch knocked out the electricity in a three-block area. The luminaria proved handy, as the neighbors gathered the candles to light their host's darkened home until the electricity was restored three and a half hours later.

The Lake Zurich home of Mayor James Kay was a favorite holiday attraction for miles around.

task by trimming 100 lampposts down the main streets of town with their wares.

The following evening at 5:15PM, the mayor officially starts the season with a flip of the switch that turns Western Avenue and Market Square into a fairyland. While spectators feast on hot cider and donut holes, the sounds of Christmas fill the air as hundreds of children and members of the local choir sing yuletide carols. The scouts of Troop 48 look on with pride, knowing they have not only beautified their town for the holidays, but have earned themselves a summer trip to Camp Makajawan.

Fri. after Thanksgiving–Jan.15, 3:30PM–11:00PM.
Downtown: From Green Bay Rd., E on Deerpath Rd. 1/4 mi., At Western Ave. West-side: Everett Rd. at Waukegan Rd.

LAKE ZURICH

Mayor Kay's Home on Manor Road

At the holiday intersection of Christmas Lane and Santa Boulevard, better known on the map as Manor Road at Golfview, lived the former mayor of Lake Zurich, James Kay. His house and front yard overflowed with so many decorations that neighborhood kids might have believed he was Santa Claus himself.

The mayor's fascination with Christmas decorations began at an early age, for he was raised in one of the festive homes of the famous Sauganash area. James eventually inherited his family's display and began turning a childhood wonderment into an adult hobby. He added to his collection with unusual finds from flea markets, antique stores and garage sales. With new purchases of after-Christmas bargains and gifts from family and friends, he admitted there weren't too many items he didn't have.

Kay devoted a corner of his living room year-round to storage of his new decorations. Before the Christmas season was over he had already accumulated quite a stash for the coming year.

Decorating plans, both inside and out, changed annually as the mayor brought his collection out of storage the day after Thanksgiving. The decorations were systematically packed and labeled according to the rooms where they would be displayed.

With so many intriguing items from which to choose, it was no wonder that a few were legitimately doomed to a lifetime in the attic. A sixties silver foil tree still in its unopened box would never glisten in the four colors of a rotating gel light. Three large cartons of defective walking outdoor lights, mailed by an apologetic manufacturer, would never see the outdoors. They caused the failure of an otherwise ingenious, spiraling tree of lights the mayor had designed in a prior year.

The home's outdoor display alternated from year to year between two basic themes—one a scrumptious gingerbread cottage, the other a sparkling Santa house. It was assembled in three days with the help of generous neighbors and family.

The window displays also changed yearly. One varied with Kay's large collection of electronic dolls. The other was a scene starring a life-size Santa that moved with the aid of a series of pulleys and an old motor from a copying machine. Christmas music filled the air every evening.

As one might guess, the decorations didn't stop there. Lucky onlookers were sometimes invited by Mayor Kay to view the Christmas wonderland inside. Others joined the 1,000 people who filed through his open house the Saturday evening before Christmas and shared cookies, candy canes and holiday spirit.

The interior of the mayor's home was packed with nostalgic treasures of Christmases past that took many visitors back to their childhood holidays. Moving figures, flashing lights and a tinkling player piano were among the many electronic decorations, which generated so much heat that the furnace never kicked on until the display was turned off.

An antique jukebox played Gene Autrey's original 78-RPM recording of "Rudolph the Red-Nosed Reindeer," and mechanical bells chimed "Silent Night." The Christmas tree in the den was covered with homemade ornaments and bubbling lights and surrounded by vintage lit plastic figurines. The living room tree was barely visible under hundreds of ornaments, and the fireplace mantel was covered end to end with a collection of 260 choir boy candles.

In 1994 James Kay and all his decorations moved to South Carolina. With the exception of one neighbor who complained about the glare, residents of Lake Zurich will miss their annual holiday visit to their former mayor's home. As for the new neighbors—"We didn't want to shock them," Kay said. "We decorated simply the first year, but it will get bigger each year." ◆

LIBERTYVILLE

❽ 525 Dawes Street

When asked to describe his source of inspiration for the unique variety of Christmas decorations he has designed over the years, homeowner Larry Skala jokingly responded, "There was a flash of light, and the Christmas tree parted."

From trees transformed into glowing candy canes, to "Go, Bears" stretched in Italian lights between two goal posts, Skala has enjoyed the creative challenge of designing something new and unusual every three to four years.

Though Larry is given credit for being the brains behind the operation, his wife, Lou, mans the indispensable post of "sidewalk supervisor." They begin "psyching" themselves early for their assigned tasks by playing Christmas music in June.

Their current display of nine enormous 4-foot ornaments that float 15 feet overhead was partially inspired by unfortunate vandalism, which prompted Larry to place his creations high out of reach. He also wanted a change from the usual decorating of the house itself, and the giant Siberian elm in the front yard was a natural alternative.

Larry used dowel rods connected with heavy-gauge wire to create the ornament shapes, which include candy canes, a Christmas tree, a bell, snowflakes and various abstract forms. He and Lou then wrapped each ornament in miniature lights, which they fastened with twist ties and reinforced with duct tape.

The ornaments are pulled up over the high limbs and secured with nylon ropes which, along with the extension cords, are neatly hidden among the branches of the tree. On a breezy winter night the effect is magical as the ornaments appear to be spinning in mid-air while reflecting in the snowy ground below.

The Skalas have won $25 for first place in the Libertyville Christmas decorating contest, during the holidays the pizza delivery man needs no address to find their house, and enthused neighbors have put in requests for an ornament shaped like a camel. Who needs more inspiration?

Thanksgiving–Jan.1, 7:00PM–12:00AM. *From Milwaukee Ave. (Rt.21), W on Park Ave. (Rt.176) 3/4 mi., S on Dawes St. 2-1/2 bl.*

Giant floating ornaments are the latest Skala creation.

❾ Dymond Road and Dover Court

In the fall of 1986, Mary Ann and Richard Chamberlain visited each of 28 homes in their two-block area armed with a plastic milk carton and a strand of Christmas lights. Their mission was to promote a decorating idea Mary Ann had seen in her hometown of Oklahoma City.

The couple explained to their neighbors that the materials could be made into inexpensive, reusable luminaria. When spaced uniformly around every sidewalk, walkway and driveway, the result would look as beautiful as the Christmas lanterns of New Mexico.

Neighbors were skeptical at first, but Mary Ann's enthusiasm led all to agree to her plan. The residents set to work collecting gallon milk cartons, while Mary Ann and Richard made nearly a mile of outdoor lights spaced exactly five feet apart.

As the holiday season approached, 400 of the necessary 900 milk cartons had been collected. The Chamberlains drove to a distant dairy bottler and purchased 500 additional containers, which they packed tightly into their van. The bottles were distributed, along with light strands, sand and an instruction sheet for each family. On the designated day, the neighbors lined their front yards with the milk jugs, as instructed, in little more than an hour.

When the sun began to set, the displays were lit, lingering doubts were instantly quelled, and Mary Ann's vision became a dream come true. Residents were impressed not only by the enchanting effect but by the feeling of togetherness the unanimous participation in the project had inspired. "We are proud to be associated with the neighborhood," resident Dick Hoffman affirmed.

Over the years the dazzling display, which only required an initial $30 investment from each home-owner, has earned much publicity and attention. Surrounding neighborhoods have begun to imitate the idea, and curious spectators have been seen jumping from their cars to get a closer look at the inner workings of the milk cartons.

Mary Ann admits that without snow the plastic containers can look a bit tacky, and she would love to have a master switch so the whole block could light up at once. Another resident worries that an airplane might mistake the street for a landing strip. But on a snowy winter night, the glow of the nestled milk cartons makes the entire neighborhood look like a glistening fairyland and lauds a spirit of togetherness that grew from a spark of an idea.

Sat. after Thanksgiving–Dec.31, 5:00PM–10:30PM, (Christmas and New Years) –12:00AM. *From Park Ave. (Rt.176), S on Milwaukee Ave. 1 mi., W on Golf Rd. 1 mi., S on Dymond Rd. Note: Dover and Dymond are dead-end streets. To avoid having to back up in someone's driveway, park on Golf Rd.*

Hundreds of milk carton luminaria create a magical holiday path on Dymond Road and Dover Court.

The Chamberlain's Milk Jug Luminaria

Measure the distance around which the luminaria will be placed. For every 50 feet the following materials are needed: 10 plastic gallon milk containers; 2 gallons of sand, kitty litter or pebbles; 25 feet of outdoor C-9 Christmas lights with removable sockets, and a 25-foot extension cord.

Cut off the tops of the milk containers to just above the handles. Cut a 1-inch "X" just below each handle. Fill each carton with three cups of sand, kitty litter or pebbles.

By prying open the tab at the base of the socket with a screwdriver, remove the sockets of four consecutive bulbs from the light strand, leaving every fifth bulb in place. Tightly cover any holes in the wire with weatherproof tape. Reattach the extra sockets to the extension cord at 5-foot intervals.

Place the milk jugs in position five feet apart with the handles away from the walkway. Push a bulb into each "X".

⑩ Cook Memorial Park
413 North Milwaukee Avenue

Throughout the summer this lovely park is the site of concerts, luncheons, a farmers' market and a fragrant rose garden. For the holiday season the Libertyville Parks and Recreation Department transforms the park's 40-foot flagpole into a towering tree of 8,000 lights with a life-size sleigh at its base.

Glowing in the background is the Ansel B. Cook Home, a treasure of its own during the holidays and throughout the year. Built in 1876, it is the former residence of state legislator and businessman Ansel B. Cook and his wife, Emily, who willed the estate to the village in 1921.

Though the building was used as the town library until 1968, the rooms were left intact. When restored by the Libertyville-Mundelein Historical Society, the house retained a Victorian air and left many visitors feeling as though they "could move right in." During the holidays the feeling is further enhanced by traditional decorations that radiate the warmth of a Christmas past.

Gifts, simply wrapped in white paper and red ribbon, fill an old-fashioned wagon that waits in the foyer for its journey around the neighborhood. Starched doilies of hairpin lace hang from the archways like floating snowflakes. One of the seven Victorian fireplaces is trimmed with candles, poinsettias and vintage Christmas cards, while another holds a German goose-feather tree trimmed in berries.

The dining room table is set for a family feast. The stairwell is draped in evergreen swags and mauve bows. The Christmas tree is trimmed with gold tinsel, tiny baskets, and ivory-colored ornaments of Santas, clowns and squirrels made from cotton batting. An antique pump organ dancing with angels stands quietly against the wall, until a member of the committee plays Christmas carols as an added treat.

Reva Konefes, chairperson of the Acquisitions and Decorating Committee, comments, "We try to decorate as if a Victorian family were living here."

Cook Memorial Park is dressed in its holiday finest, while the Ansel B. Cook Home sets a glowing backdrop.

She and her husband, Joseph, have been in charge of decorating the home since 1977, and probably receive the most authentic Victorian holiday experience—it has been their duty to retrieve the decorations from the attic each year and store them again at the end of the season.

Park decorations: Fri. after Thanksgiving–Jan.1, Dusk–10:00PM. Museum holiday hours: Fri. after Thankgiving: 7:00PM–9:00PM, 1st three Sat. and two Sun. in Dec.: 1:00PM–5:00PM. Nominal admission fee. *From Park Ave. (Rt.176), N on Milwaukee Ave. 1/4 mi., At Church Ave.*

LINCOLNSHIRE

11 Royal Court

The 12 homes of this lovely cul-de-sac have been a shining star on the holiday map of Lincolnshire for over 35 years. At the entrance, Santa and his reindeer fly overhead, welcoming visitors to this magical street where every home is decorated with lights. At the opposite end, another Santa sends good cheer beside a giant glistening Christmas tree. The street gets brighter still on Christmas Eve when every walk is lined with glowing luminaria.

Weekend before Christmas–Christmas Eve, 7:00PM–12:00AM. *From the Tri-State Twy. (I-94), W on Half Day Rd. (Rt.22) 1/2 mi., S on Berkshire Ln. 4 bl., E on Kingscross Dr. 3 bl., S on Canterbury Rd. 2 bl., W on Royal Ct.*

LONG GROVE

12 Shopping District

Settled in the 1800s by German farmers, the village of Long Grove has retained the charm of its early years. From Route 53 visitors pass through a covered bridge to the historic shopping district, where all the buildings at the crossroads are protected by a landmark ordinance.

Cobblestone paths wind their way to dozens of boutiques featuring everything from gourmet bird, cat and dog items to French Limoges porcelain. Specialty food shops offer such luscious treats as chocolate-dipped strawberries and brown-bag apple pies.

Throughout the holiday season the stores are trimmed with traditional evergreen boughs, red

The charming shops of Long Grove beckon shoppers to share in an era past.

bows and twinkling white lights, as well as gingerbread characters, which are becoming the prevalent theme. Luminaria light the paths in the evening, and strolling musicians entertain on weekends. Though many of the shops offer holiday wares, the Pine Cone Christmas Shop is a favorite year-round source of festive trimmings.

A horse-drawn carriage ride, lunch with Santa at the Village Tavern, or a holiday tea at Seasons of Long Grove or the Covered Bridge Cafe are added attractions sure to make a visit to this lovely little town a memorable yuletide adventure.

Decorations: Fri. after Thanksgiving–Jan.14, Store hours: (M–Sa) 10:00AM–5:00PM, (Su) 11:00AM–5:00PM. For further information call the Long Grove Merchants Association (708)634–0888. *From Lake Cook Rd., N and E on Rt.53 2-1/2 mi., NE on Robert Parker Coffin Rd. 1/2 mi.*

ROUND LAKE BEACH

ⓑ 918 Bayview Drive

For three years running, Tom and Judy Shoulders had a decorating competition going for a case of beer with their good friends across the street, Mike and Sandy Windling. When the Windlings moved to Kentucky, the opposition may have left, but the Shoulders' display continued to grow. In addition to Tom's own creations, Mike and Sandy contributed many homemade decorations to their former rivals.

A large tree constructed of nylon rope and covered with garlands, lights and bells brightens the side yard. At the tree's base stands a row of glimmering snowflakes made from plywood drilled with lights, and scattered about are glowing stars made in similar fashion. Swags of evergreens and lights gracefully drape the eaves, accented by wreaths made from artificial poinsettias, while the peak of the roof is trimmed with a row of bright red plastic globes.

Tom continues to add to the display, but does not divulge any of his new ideas. "You have to be careful what you say around here," he confides. It seems his competitive spirit has expanded beyond his block to the grander Round Lake Beach decorating contest.

Weekend before Christmas–Jan.1, 5:00PM–10:00PM. *From Nippersink Rd. (Rt.134), N on Cedar Lake Rd. 1mi., W on Woodland Dr. 3 bl., N on Bayview Dr. 1/2 bl.*

VERNON HILLS

⓮ The Cuneo Museum and Gardens

The Cuneo Mansion is a sight to behold throughout the year, but grander still during the holidays when an exquisite 18-foot Christmas tree fills the great hall, abundant poinsettias grace the formal dining rooms and choral groups perform from the grand staircase.

The 75-acre estate, resplendent with 30,000 annuals and over 900 rose bushes in the summer, is decorated with dozens of huge lighted displays at Christmastime for a merry drive down its 3/4 mile path.

Day after Thanksgiving–Jan.2, Museum: (Su–Sa) 10:00AM–5:00PM. Light Display: 7:00PM–? Admission fees. For further information call the Village of Vernon Hills (708)367–3700 or The Cuneo Museum and Gardens (708)362–3042. *From Milwaukee Ave. (Rt.21), W on Town Line Rd. (Rt.60) 3/4 mi., N on Lakeview Pkwy. 3/4 mi.*

WAUKEGAN

⓯ 2033 Chestnut Street

The three wise men might have boogied to Bethlehem had Tim Lowry's star been the guiding light. Five thousand green, red, blue, white and multicolored bulbs alternately flash in slow and rapid succession from this 12-pointed polaris that intermittently zaps beams to the plastic manger scene below.

Tim, a home remodeler, built the 20' x 15' x 12' star out of treated lumber on his back porch in about 30 hours. He also designed the computerized light system, which employs six relays to create 30 sequences in a repeating three-minute cycle. With the building materials and the electrical components, Tim spent nearly $2,000 to construct his giant flashing star. He is marketing a similar lighting device he hopes to sell for under $200.

His mom, Marge, had the original idea of a nativity star when their large decorated maple tree

Lighted displays fill the grounds of the Cuneo Mansion.

Inventor Tim Lowry proudly displays the computerized 20-foot star that towers over his Waukegan home and flashes beams to the manger below.

16 244 Ridgeland Avenue

When Debbi Welch was a little girl, each holiday season her parents would bundle the children into the car, along with hot cocoa and blankets, to go looking at Christmas decorations. It was her dream that when she got married and had her own house she would decorate too, so others could have the same fond memory of their childhood holidays.

In 1985 when Debbi and her husband, Gary, turned their home into a gingerbread house, her dream came true in grand style. The Welch's candy-covered house was not only the delight of neighborhood children, but was a recipient of an honorable mention in Good Housekeeping Magazine's nationwide decorating contest. The home was also a winner in the town's competition and has continued to place every year since.

The large 1860s farm house is brought down to gingerbread proportions, trimmed in 6-foot candy canes with big red bows, giant peppermints, oversized lollipops and five-and-a-half-foot toy soldiers. Debbi and Gary made most of the scrumptious treats themselves out of wood, styrofoam and plumbing pipe.

The Welches now bundle their own children into the car to look at Christmas decorations each year,

was destroyed by a windstorm, leaving the Lowrys with a vacant front yard and thousands of lights. Though Tim's creation was certainly more than she had in mind, Marge has learned over the years that her son likes to tinker. "As a child he always took his toys apart and couldn't put them back together," she recalls.

Building the star was the easy part for Tim. The real challenge is attaching the 100-pound structure to the roof. It requires the help of six friends, whom Tim bribes with pizza and beer. Conduit braces and 500-pound galvanized cable, connected to eye bolts in the joists, keep the star secure. In years to come, the job may be simplified. Tim hopes to redesign the present structure to use only cables, so the inner workings won't be visible during the day. Or he may even try deflecting a laser off a diamond-shaped mirror.

At the end of the season Tim removes the lights from their wooden frame and hangs the strands on the walls of his bedroom. "It's great for parties," he notes.
Dec.15–Jan.1. 4:45PM–12:00AM. *From Sheridan Rd., W on Golf Rd. 1/2 mi., N on Chestnut St. 2-1/2 bl.*

The Welch's gingerbread house is covered with sweet surprises.

Emanuelson Inn adds to the festive trimmings on Shiloh Boulevard in Zion.

but Debbi gets an added thrill when she looks out her front window and sees other families excited to see their display.

Dec. 5 – Jan. 6, 4:30PM – 11:30PM. *From Grand Ave., N on Sheridan Rd. 3/4 mi., E on Ridgeland Ave. 1 bl.*

ZION

⑰ Shiloh Boulevard at Sheridan Road

With plywood, paint, hard work and creativity the employees of the Zion Park District have created a children's holiday fantasyland that stretches across two blocks of the town's main boulevard.

A miniature village with a diner, a meat market, a toy store and other decorated shops nestles among the pine trees with an army of toy soldiers standing guard. A family of snowmen laugh at the cold, while wooden carolers, dressed warmly in earmuffs and mittens, merrily sing with mouths opened wide. A giant fir tree is decorated with stars, bows and bells, and Santa flies to its peak carrying messages from his mailbox below. Children visiting the display are free to drop off their Christmas wish lists and run among the decorations.

Businesses along the boulevard have added to the festivities with their own displays. American International Hospital is decked in giant holiday wreaths. Across the street the turn-of-the-century Emanuelson Inn, trimmed in lights and garlands, offers horse-drawn sleigh rides through the snow-covered park.

Dec. 6 – Jan. 15, Dusk – Dawn. For further information on sleigh rides call the Emanuelson Inn (708)872 – 8488. *From Wadsworth Rd., N on Sheridan Rd. 2-1/2mi., E and W on Shiloh Blvd. 1 bl.*

Plumbing Pipe Peppermint Sticks

The Welches decorate their lawn with peppermint sticks made from 1-inch PVC, white plastic plumbing pipe. The pipe is cut in 2-foot lengths with one end at an angle, so it is easier to stick in the ground.

The stripes are formed by wrapping the pipe in red duct tape, keeping the exposed white area the same width as the tape.

Chapter 11

McHENRY COUNTY

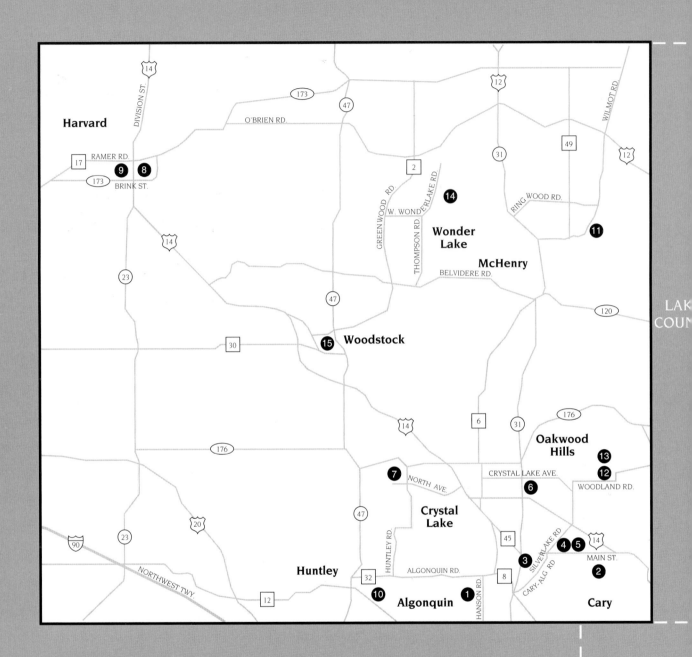

Harvard

McHENRY
COUNTY

N
W   E
S

0   MILES   5

Wonder
Lake

McHenry

Woodstock

Oakwood
Hills

Crystal
Lake

Huntley

Algonquin

Cary

LAK
COUN

The Kerber home glistens with lights and magical story boxes.

ALGONQUIN

❶ 320 Crestwood Court

Though restoring model cars has long been the hobby of Mike and Julie Kerber, the '57 Chevy and Model A Ford take back seat to the Christmas decorations once the holidays roll around.

As newlyweds the Kerbers trimmed their condominium balcony. When it won first place in the association Christmas contest, it appears the bug had bit. After a decade of decorating with an annual budget of $1,000, the new Kerber residence has not only repeated the first place victory but has become a holiday attraction for families miles around.

Thousands of lights glisten from the eaves, windows, garage, trees, bushes, Frosty and rooftop sleigh. On the sloping front yard, encircled by candy canes and soldiers, stand five delightful holiday scenes captured in acrylic cases. A quartet of musical angels plays about a ribbon-trimmed Christmas tree, a smiling elf fills Santa's sack with packages and toys, a young boy bundled in a red snowsuit skis past a waving snowman, a pair of cuddly teddy bears play with toy trains, and a golden Christmas angel dressed in furry white gracefully waves her star-lit candle.

Mike built the cases and permanently mounted the moving figures and props inside. Anchor cables wound through bolts at each of the top corners secure the displays to stakes in the ground. The dioramas continue in the living room window where Santa Claus is busy checking his list beside one of the family's five decorated trees.

With little space remaining to enlarge their display, the Kerbers plan to build a second garage. And it certainly won't be for the cars.

Dec. 12 – Dec. 30, 5:00PM – 10:30PM. *From Algonquin Rd.(Rt.32), S on Hanson Rd. 1 bl., E on Huntington Dr. 3 bl., S on Crestwood Ct.*

Neat Lights without Frozen Fingers

Mike pre-staples each strand of lights to 8-foot lengths of 1x2s indoors. He can then quickly bolt the boards into permanent anchors on the house.

CARY

❷ 116 Charlotte Place

High on the list of decorating frustrations is running out of lights when there's still plenty of Christmas tree to spare. The decorator is faced with two options—start over or buy more lights. In the many holiday seasons of decorating their outdoor yew bush, Jerry and Mary Adee have faced this dilemma yearly and opted for purchasing lights. What began in 1986 as a sparkling bush of 2,000 reds, greens and yellows now dazzles with 4,000 bulbs and counting.

It's difficult to say whether this annual expansion is due to a subconscious desire to make the bush brighter or to the natural growth of this 18-foot plant. But whatever the cause, the effect is so adorable that the yew has earned the name "The Gumdrop Tree" from admiring neighbors.

It takes Jerry six hours to hang the lights (not including the time needed to run to the store for more). He leans an extension ladder against the bush and begins at the top. Every few feet he must climb down the ladder and move it over. He then switches to a step ladder for the middle section, until he reaches the long-awaited bottom section, which can be decorated from the ground.

The Adees truly enjoy their creation, even though it costs them more to run the lights than to use their summer air conditioner. The display is on a timer, so the couple can see it lit when they come home from work. Mary has a framed photograph of the decorated yew hanging at the office, and Jerry proudly recreates "The Gumdrop Tree" in Christmas cookie form with four different colors of dotted icing piled three inches high. Though it's probably best to pass on the cookies, drive by the bush for a real treat.

Thanksgiving weekend–Mid-Jan., 5:00PM–11:00PM. *From Rt.14, W on Main St. 1/2 bl., S on Spring St. 2 bl., W on Charlotte Pl. 1/2 bl.*

Jerry Adee's Tip for "Wireless" Lighting

When decorating bushes, disguise the wires by spacing the strands the same distance apart as the lights are on the strand.

KIP SWEHLA

A giant gingerbread man has taken up holiday residence in this tasty Cary home thanks to homeowner Rita Watrach, who handcrafted the colossal display.

❸ 985 West Milford Street

While Rita Watrach may be innocently spending Monday evenings with her ladies' craft group weaving baskets and napkin holders, the others might be surprised to know that by day Rita's projects are of a grander scheme. She is working on turning her two-story suburban home into a giant gingerbread house.

At the Watrachs' prior residence on the northwest side of Chicago, Rita enjoyed filling the windows with animated figures that were easily visible from the sidewalk. She was especially proud of her moving nativity scene with Mary and Joseph leaning over a rocking cradle. The three kings were not available for purchase, so Rita bought three mechanical carolers and redressed them in Magi costumes she had made by hand.

When the Watrachs moved to their Cary home, they installed three new windows to accommodate their animated figures. But because the house was 50 feet from the sidewalk, they were disappointed to find that their window displays were not easily seen. It was then that Rita began to think big.

Hints of her scheme emerged one Christmas when homemade candy canes nine and 15 feet high flanked her front windows and garage. She had designed the patterns on paper, transferred them to wood at 12 times the size and painted curved stripes to create a three-dimensional effect. Holes were drilled along the edges to accommodate Italian lights, which were rearranged by color to match the red and white pattern. Rita's husband secured the huge peppermints to the house with masonry screws.

Her plans for the colossal transformation are now well underway, as she has completed a 90-inch gingerbread man to accentuate her theme. Other projects include a giant snowflake, toy soldiers, candlesticks and stockings.

Move over, ladies—those little baskets may just have to wait for now.

Dec. 2–Jan. 6, Dusk–12:00AM. *From Cary-Algonquin Rd. (Silver Lakes Rd.), W on Main St. 5 bl., S on Carol Ln. (winds into Milford St.).*

❹ 234 North School Street

When Hardy Duerig Sr. was a boy in Germany it was his job to bring home the family Christmas tree. To his delight and his parents' chagrin he always chose the biggest tree he could fit into the house. Years later, now in his own home, Hardy continues his impish practice and his good-humored family has joined the act.

Hardy's wife, Aija, decorates the inside of the house with her holiday embroidery, while Hardy Jr. exhibits his dad's zeal by elaborately decorating the home's exterior. Young Hardy began in 1987 "just for the fun of it." (Though the Ritters across the street feel otherwise—see next article.) He has gone on to earn honors in Cary's home decorating contest.

Fifteen thousand lights outline the windows, eaves, garage and fences, while silhouetting the trees and bushes that surround them. Plastic figurines abound, leaving the local Christmas store with little left to offer.

Hardy Jr. initially sketches out his plan, keeping one side of the house serious and the other playful. The playful side of the house features a 4-foot Santa, Frosty, and a cute little teddy bear that all the kids ask to pet. The serious side of the house is framed in subtle blue lights and highlighted with a singing choir that has grown to 32 boys and girls. Mom jokes,

"A quartet would have been fine, but Hardy prefers an ensemble."

Arranged in four evenly spaced rows and secured to the ground with dowel rods, the system Hardy designed has prevented the domino-like collapse of years past. A speaker hidden behind the choir nearly fools children, who ask Aija, "Hey, lady…why don't their mouths move?"

Though the Duerigs try to purchase their decorations a few items at a time, Aija explains the exception they made with the life-size nativity scene, "I couldn't imagine Jesus with only Joseph and a cow, so we had to buy the whole set."

Hardy Jr. decorates methodically for four weeks, but the storage process at the end of the season is another story. He confides, "First in—last out. Push and cram." Hardy Sr. could never have realized what he was starting.

Day after Thanksgiving–Jan.1, 6:00PM–10:00PM. *From Cary-Algonquin Rd., E on Main St. 2 bl., N on School St. 2 bl.*

❺ 239 North School Street

What began in 1986 as an effort to recreate childhood memories of Christmas for their own children has become for George and Martha Ritter a lighthearted rivalry with the Duerigs across the street. Both neighbors have snuck decorations into their homes in the middle of the night. Both have shopped at 5:00AM for discounts on December 26 (only to run into each other in line). Both have purchased new trees and bushes to give them more space to hang lights.

In spite of George's attempts at one-upmanship, he concedes his neighbor's display is tough to match and focuses his efforts on technique instead. Permanent hooks to support his lights are spaced one foot apart under the eaves. Each strand is labeled with its starting location so that lights can be hung identically each year with an exact fit. All electrical lines are routed to a timer controlled by a single on-off switch.

With his system down to a science, he is able to complete all his decorating in the four vacation days he takes for the task. And if he finishes early—what the heck—he'll give the Duerigs a hand.

Dec. 1–Jan. 1, 5:00PM–10:00PM. *From Cary-Algonquin Rd., E on Main St. 2 bl., N on School St. 2 bl.*

CRYSTAL LAKE

6 6109 South Blue Court

Eighty thousand twinkling lights dance across the needles of junipers, yews, Austrian, Scotch and mugho pines, Black hill and Colorado blue spruce and cling to the branches of red buds, boxwood, flowering crabs and magnolias, creating a dazzling two-acre forest of lights surrounding the home of Mary Lou and Eugene Straus.

Former owner of Straus Nursery, Eugene exercised his craft to fill his once-barren landscape with nearly 50 trees of numerous varieties. In 1985 the Strauses moved their father's 35-foot Colorado blue spruce to their property. As a loving memorial at Christmas, they filled the tree with 6,500 lights. Over the years as the foliage has multiplied, the Strauses, their daughter Khristy and their son-in-law Ron, have gone on to decorate almost every tree and bush on their lot with anywhere from 250 to 8,000 lights each.

Powering the display requires eight 30-amp circuits and often triples the electric bill. Underground outlets throughout the acreage greatly reduce the number of extension cords that otherwise would be required.

Though many lights are left up throughout the year, the family must begin the two-week task of checking for burnt-out bulbs in October. The remaining weeks are spent adding as many as 1,000 lights to the average one-and-a-half feet of new growth per tree. A cherry picker with a 50-foot extension is used to span the treetops. The lights are strung back and forth, and up and down whatever branches can be reached during each set-up. The couples enjoy working together on the task, sometimes laughing so hard that they cry.

Mary Lou and Eugene make a point of visiting other displays to get ideas. They even took an extended vacation traveling around the United States to see famous Christmas displays. But back home it's their own appreciative audience that makes their efforts worthwhile. Many leave notes of thanks. Some bring visitors from foreign countries. And a busload of Crystal Lake seniors makes an annual field trip to what they call "The Holiday Showplace."

Thanksgiving–Jan. 2, Dusk–Dawn. Note: This display is not lit every year. For an update call the Crystal Lake Chamber of Commerce (815)459–1300. *From Rt.31, E on E. Crystal Lake Ave. 1 mi., SW corner at S. Blue Ct.*

A twinkling forest surrounds the Straus home in Crystal Lake.

7 1512 North Avenue

(pictured on page 155)

For 29 years, until his retirement in 1992, Warren Spencer built and repaired diesel railroad engines and locomotives as an industrial electrician for General Motors. He has always liked working with his hands, whether painting, woodworking, or welding and has especially enjoyed designing and creating new gadgets. For years it had been in the back of his mind to work on a Christmas project, and there it had stayed until one day in 1983.

"I was passing by a True Value. They had a sleigh with one reindeer, and it was on sale. I came home and asked my wife, Marianne, if she thought we ought to spend $50 for a display. She said, 'Yeah, why not?'

So we put the sleigh and reindeer in the front yard, all by itself. And that little reindeer...he just looked like he really wanted to do more than just stand there. I promised myself he was going to do something the next year."

And the following season the reindeer and his sleighload of toys flew 120 feet from the neighbor's yard to Warren's rooftop. It launched a display that would eventually grow to fill the Spencers' 122-foot lot with 120 figurines, five moving displays and 12,500 lights.

Warren now designs the displays and repairs strands of lights in his own "Santa's Workshop," a room off the kitchen with bins full of salvaged mechanical parts, shelves of junked motors and piles of assorted gadgetry. To Marianne's dismay, he has been known to work until 2:00AM months on end when involved in a project. "I make the junk live again!" he says proudly, and cuts down his expenses as well.

He tries to design one moving display each year, though some have been more successful than others. The original cable system for the reindeer often left Warren in the cold pulling the cables by hand. In years to follow two more reindeer were able to go along for the ride when he perfected the system, using infrared photoelectric eyes, relays, microswitches and a control panel permanently mounted in his garage with an electric clutch, brake and variable-speed drive motor.

The following year he designed the mechanisms for a row of ten pivoting Santa Clauses that went back and forth using a cam, rope and spring operation. They were later replaced with a row of moving toy soldiers.

The Clauses appear in Crystal Lake with candy and trinkets.

His next project was a 3-foot rocking horse. As with his other displays, he purchased the figurine and designed the mechanics to make it move. He used an AC/DC motor with an eccentric drive that rocks the horse on and off in two-minute intervals.

In 1987 Warren built the display that has been his hallmark. Always searching for things to support his inventions, his 20-foot flagpole became a probable sight for some type of vertical activity. And so was born the idea of a parachuting Santa Claus.

Warren began by attaching decreasing widths of pipe to his existing flagpole, so it could seasonally telescope to 37 feet. Marianne made the 1-foot Santa Claus doll and donated her red umbrella after Warren's thwarted attempts to design a working parachute. Using similar mechanics to those used for the sleigh, a system was built to drive Santa up to the crosshead at the top of the pole in darkness and let him drift on air, fully-lit, to the chimney below. On a windy day this display is not operational.

Strands of 12,500 lights neatly wrapped on large spools ease the decorating task for Warren and Marianne Spencer of Crystal Lake.

A herd of reindeer over the roof and a life-size manger with a homemade stable are among the 120 stationary figurines that fill the yard. Warren buys them all on sale or gets them free from neighbors.

Surrounding the figurines and moving displays are lights covering everything in sight. A 35-foot blue spruce alone holds 5,400. Marianne is credited for all the house decorations inside and out. Christmas carols resounding over outdoor speakers add to the festive mood.

With electrical power necessary throughout the yard, the entire display requires 2,200 feet of extension cords in addition to 100 feet of permanent under-ground wiring. The Spencer's electric bill increases only $80 for the season.

Besides contributing his mechanical talents, Warren jumped into the act himself in 1986 dressed as Santa Claus, a feat he performs in homes as well. Two years later he convinced his wife to join him as Mrs. Claus, but only after he agreed to fashion her a pair of battery-heated socks with a remote control for her pocket.

In 1992 Santa built a little wooden house for himself and the Mrs. with shelves of goodies for all the children who visited. The couple gave away 1,000 trinkets and 180 pounds of candy, some of which were donated by local merchants, to children who waited in line for up to an hour. He also made a mailbox for letters to Santa, which in past years many children had been leaving in the doorway.

With so many items to store, Warren decided to build a custom garage to house his display. As might be expected, it is no ordinary shed. Boat winches hoist three 2' x 4' x 8' wheeled storage crates full of decorations out of sight through an opening in the attic floor.

The Spencers keep a scrap book of all the letters they have received over the years. They were offered a $20 bribe from a latecomer to turn the display back on and have received cookies on their doorstep. Families have brought friends from all over the world, and admirers have rolled down their windows in 30-below weather to gaze at this awe-some sight. The Spencers have truly earned their reputation as owners of "The Christmas House."

Dec. 15 – Dec. 26, 5:00PM – 10:00PM (Mr. and Mrs. Claus appear 5:00PM–9:00PM, Dec. 22, 23 & 24)
From Huntley Rd., W on North Ave. 1/2 mi.

In 1990 Warren was still trying to top himself and replaced the pivoting soldiers with a moving train. He built 115 feet of wooden track to span his front yard. He altered the plastic two-car train by adding a headlamp (made from a paint can and bulb), a station bell (made from a fire alarm and an electronic timing device) and a conductor named Charlie. The train travels back and forth with another homemade electromechanical system of relays, motors and microswitches.

Warren's most recent mechanical addition, and surely not his last, is a delightful pair of kissing penguins. They twirl about and tilt for a kiss as two pink hearts flash behind them. This is the first display in which Warren used an air compressor to drive the device. It gives him the benefit of being able to con-trol the speed of movement, though the hoses are apt to freeze if not kept warm.

HARVARD

❽ 719 East Dewey Street

When Paul Durkee was only six years old, he saved up all the earnings from his paper route to buy a manger scene for the front lawn of his family's house. He has been buying Christmas decorations ever since.

In 1979 at the age of 16, Kim Sager eagerly volunteered to hang the holiday decorations at the local McDonald's where she worked. She is still employed there and still decorating.

When the two met and fell in love, it was a marriage made in the North Pole. For not only does Paul's manger stand in their front yard, but it is barely visible amongst the colorful menagerie with which the couple has surrounded it.

Fifty illuminated figures prance across the roof, hang from the trellis, and perch in the snow. An animated train moves back and forth on its track, and three stuffed snowmen come to life dressed in holiday attire. An assortment of bears, snowmen, elves and a cheery "Noel," all handmade by Kim, gleam in golden lights, as Santas wave from both sides of their corner lot. The garage doors are wrapped like giant presents, and the shed is disguised as a gingerbread house. The yard is so energized that the Durkees had to upgrade their electrical service to accommodate their seven timers, 85 extension cords and quadrupled electric bill.

Their efforts have earned them first place several years running in the "Most Spectacular" category of Harvard's decorating contest. Their name is famous in this town of 6,000, where residents have dubbed their display "Christmas Corner."

Though Kim admits, "There's not an empty spot on the house," one can only imagine how the ever-growing display will shine when this young couple reaches their golden years.

Dec. 1–Jan. 1, 5:00PM–10:00PM. *From Ramer Rd. (Rt. 173), S on Division St. (Rt. 14) 3 bl., E on Dewey St. 1/2 mi.*

Old-Fashioned Window Panes

Pearl Schroeder divides her picture window into small panes by criss-crossing electrical tape on the inside of the glass.

DAVE IRELAND

Homemade figurines, animated displays and thousands of lights decorate the Durkee's "Christmas Corner."

❾ 207 South Page

Since 1946 when Pearl Schroeder got married, she has taken charge of decorating the house for Christmas, while her husband Bob smiles and pays the electric bill. It's a household responsibility Pearl gladly accepts.

Preferring an old-fashioned theme, she drapes the porch with light-filled garlands and big red bows and shines a candle from every window. Thanks to her son, Bob, who tackles the high spots, the star of Bethlehem glows overhead from the peak of this two-story cottage-style home, while Santa waits with his sack full of toys on the roof below. "Season's Greetings" is proclaimed in styrofoam across the garage in a homemade sign that was a gift from a neighbor.

Though Pearl has won first and second place in her town's decorating contest and a $30 gift certificate from Wal-Mart, her true reasons for decorating are simple. She explains, "I used to do it for my two children, then I did it for the four grandchildren. Now I do it for my two great-grandchildren and everyone who believes in Christmas."

Dec. 6–Jan. 6, Dusk–10:00PM. *From Division St. (Rt. 14), W on Brink St. (Rt. 173) 1 bl., NE on Randall St. 1 bl., NW on Washington St. 6 bl., At Page.*

HUNTLEY

⑩ 10812 North Woodstock Street

"We started decorating for our children with wooden figurines, and it just got bigger and better," explains Wayne Goers as he and his wife, Sue, shiver amid 140 Christmas figures that transform their snowy front yard into a holiday amusement park.

Brightly painted cartoon characters sing carols from the porch. On the lawn a holiday mouse rocks up and down in a sleigh pulled by a smiling dog. A band of toy soldiers bob and bounce in a playful parade, as a red and white ferris wheel spins Santa on a free ride. A life-size Baby Jesus lying in a rooftop manger is visited by shepherds, kings, a cow, a donkey and a camel. On another roof Santa and his elves are busy making toys in their colorful workshop. Santas wave, wiggle and rock, and snowmen dance in this delightful display that is certain to capture a child's fancy. Wayne acknowledges, "I love to watch the kids when they see the house lighted."

He and Sue have created most of the decorations. Wayne is always devising new things to make. "It's my hobby. I think about it year round," he says.

Many of their decorations were made from designs purchased from Craft Patterns, a woodcraft company in St. Charles. The patterns are large enough to trace directly onto plywood. The plywood is then cut with a jigsaw and painted. The couple prefers acrylic paint purchased from craft stores to outdoor latex paint. Though it is more expensive, a wider variety of colors is available. Some of the patterns are pre-painted and only need to be glued to the cut wood. With both methods, the figures are coated with a outdoor sealer to prevent weathering.

Each figure is illuminated with a spotlight, which, along with the lit plastic figurines and motorized displays, contributes to the maze of extension cords that lead to every outlet in the house and increase the family's electric bill by $250.

The motors supply much of the magic at this Huntley home, where many of the characters both wooden and plastic sway, rock, twirl and dance. The couple first used rotisserie motors to add motion to their display and found that a motor

The Goer's lawn dances with 140 homemade wooden figures.

DAVE KORDELA

Frightening ghouls and bewitched bunnies are merely...

...holiday trumpeters and rabbits disguised by Ethel Motter.

meant for an oven quickly freezes and stops cold. They have since discovered a mail order decoration company called Meisel Hardware Specialty in Minnesota that sells motors, specifically meant for Christmas displays, and patterns to go with them. Priced from $70 to $85, they may be costly but are more reliable than cheaper motors and last several years.

With the help of their generous neighbors, Jim and Ruth Bond and Kevin Mohapp, the Goers are able to set up their display in three days and take it down in one. Other neighbors tell Wayne, "I'm glad it's you and not me."

Luckily the family has a four-car garage with an attic to pack their enormous display, but it doesn't stay there for long. In the summer the Goers take a portion of their decorations to O'Connell's Yogi Bear Jellystone Park Campground in Amboy, Illinois to decorate their camper trailer for the park's annual celebration of "Christmas in July."

Dec. 12–Jan. 6, (Su–Th) Dusk–10:30PM, (F–Sa) – 12:00AM. *From Algonquin Rd. (Rt.32), S on Rt.47 1 bl., E on North 1 bl., S on Woodstock St.*

McHENRY

⓫ 4713 North Jeffrey Street

If Santa looks familiar in the front yard of this McHenry home, you may have seen him a month earlier dressed as an ax murderer for Halloween. And wasn't that sweet choir girl in bonnet and muff a screaming zombie and that trumpeter a howling ghost?

How can it be that this once eerie graveyard covered with flying ghosts, bloody headless women and half-buried vampires screaming from their tombs could win first place in the best religious category of the neighborhood Christmas decorating contest? Credit goes to the creativity of homeowner Ethel Motter, who not only dresses herself for Halloween but all her life-size Christmas figures as well.

In her childhood Ethel's family had only a small artificial tree without lights, and she was never able to go trick-or-treating. Now she's making up for it in grand style with the help of her companion, Rex Shake, who does all the electrical work for the elaborate display.

A motor factory employee whose hobby is floral arranging, Ethel not only makes all the imaginative costumes by hand but repainted all the Christmas figures in bright enamel colors as well. Though she enjoys the beauty of the Christmas decorations, Ethel revels in Halloween, when "anything goes." Her home is the delight of both holidays, as 300 children trick or treat at her door and parades of cars pass at Christmastime.

A crawl space full of gory decorations has been known to frighten an occasional repairman, and a garage packed with trimmings has left the car rusting in the driveway, but Ethel readily defends her addiction saying, "Rex and I don't smoke or drink or get into trouble, so we have to do something." But Ethel's daughter Beverly counters with the warning, "Don't stand too close to Mom—she'll decorate you!"

Thanksgiving–1st weekend of Jan., (Su–Th) 4:30PM–9:00PM (F–Sa) –10:00PM, (Halloween: Oct. 1–Nov. 2, Dusk–9:00PM). *From Ringwood Rd., S on Wilmot Rd. (Johnsburg Rd.) 1 bl., E on Jasper Dr. 4 bl., S on Jeffrey St. 1/2 bl.*

OAKWOOD HILLS

⑫ 4 Woody Way

The Watts family's home is aglow during the holidays with a glistening display that befits the family's name. Seven thousand purple lights surround the manger scene. Four thousand white lights outline the house. Three thousand lights cover the hedges and trees, 600 surround the hot tub and deck, and 1,000 decorate the 13-foot Christmas tree inside. Neighbors joke that the rest of the street dims when this "Wattage" is turned on.

With an assortment of lit figurines, a 10-foot roof-top star and a glowing 60-foot wreath, the display requires 200 extension cords, 20 purge connectors and plugs in every circuit of the house. It takes fifteen minutes each night to turn everything on.

The reward for the family's effort is proudly displayed on the rec room wall—a homemade plaque presented by the children in the neighborhood that reads "Best Decorations on the Block."

Dec. 12–Jan. 6, Dusk–10:00PM. *From Crystal Lake Rd., N on Silver Lake Rd. 5 bl., E on Woodland Rd. (Rawson Bridge Rd.) 6 bl., N on Woody Way.*

Anchoring Plastic Figurines

Though many decorators fill the bottoms of plastic figurines with rocks or sand to keep them from toppling over, here are some alternate solutions.

Warren Spencer of Crystal Lake recommends:

Cut conduit to a length of two feet greater than the figurine. Drill a 5/16" hole through both sides of the conduit two inches from the top. Drill 3/4" holes in the top and bottom of the figurine. Pound the conduit (hole end up) 18 inches into the ground. Place the figure over the conduit. Put a padlock through the conduit holes.

Mark Joritz of Tinley Park recommends:

For each figurine purchase three 5" eye hooks with matching nuts and double washers, and three 12" pole barn nails or tent stakes.

Drill three holes, each large enough to hold the stem of an eye hook, evenly spaced around the sides of the figure about an inch from the bottom. Drill a hole, large enough to insert a fist, in the base of the figure.

Screw an eye hook into each of the small holes. Secure each hook with two washers and a nut from inside the figurine, and rotate the heads until they are parallel to the base. Pound the nails or stakes through the eye hooks and into the ground.

Rion Goyette of Downers Grove recommends:

Drill three holes evenly spaced an inch above the base of the figurine and large enough to accommodate the hook of a tent stake. After placing the figurine in position, push three stakes into the ground inserting the hook ends into the drilled holes.

George Ritter of Cary recommends:

Attach eye-hooks to the end of crescent-shaped rods and solder perpendicularly to the tops of 1/2" metal posts. Triangular stakes at the bottom of the posts make them easier to pound into the ground than wooden stakes. Wire the plastic figurines to the posts through the eye-hooks.

🔞 7 Woody Way

In 1986 neighbor Bill Watts declared decorating war on Mark and Lecia Alfrejd, and the couple's quiet hilltop has never been the same. The Alfrejds' 4,925 C-9 bulbs glowing above the Watts' 15,600 bulb display creates a stunning effect on this otherwise dimly-lit, wooded road, which is now backed-up with traffic every holiday season.

In an area where residents usually prefer the privacy of forested lots, neighbors happily look forward to this annual departure. The only complaint ever heard was from a neighbor who was concerned that the Alfrejds were watering their tree too much. It seemed to have grown 20 feet in the past year. Lecia explained that her husband had only used more galvanized pipes to build this year's tree. Among Mark's other homemade creations are a life-size sleigh and reindeer, a rooftop cross and a 12-foot snowman.

Meanwhile, behind the scenes the warring parties have been unhooking generators and stealing Santas, among other good-natured pranks. The Alfrejd's even went so far as to create a lighted message across the side of the house that read "Merry Christmas, Bill."

Dec. 4–Jan.1, 4:30PM–12:00AM. *From Crystal Lake Rd., N on Silver Lake Rd. 5 bl., E on Woodland Rd. (Rawson Bridge Rd.) 6 bl., N on Woody Way.*

WONDER LAKE

🔞 4905 West Wonder Lake Drive

Six candy canes, one manger scene, 12 nutcrackers, two gingerbread men, one gingerbread house, three street lanterns, four candles, 12 choir people, six elves, 14 snowmen, two soldiers, one guard house, three deer, one train, four artificial trees, eight Santas, two Santas with sleigh and reindeer, one Santa house, one Mrs. Claus, six penguins and Kerry, Dale and Tom Schultz have moved from their farmhouse on Thompson Road to a new home a few miles north and around the bend.

Since 1985, a visit to their rural home had been a holiday tradition for area families, and the Schultzes wouldn't think of disappointing them. Kerry affirms, "Everyone in Wonder Lake would gang up on us if we didn't put up the decorations."

On a small city lot, this collection of Christmas figurines might resemble the finishing point of a Macy's parade, but on this five-acre site across from West Bay, the soldiers, sleighs and Frosties alike can spread out and look their finest.

Kerry bought the smaller Santa and sleigh when he was 16 years old, and for the next 13 years purchased one snowman annually. He and Dale now

Dozens of brightly-lit figurines decorated the Schultzes farmhouse on Thompson Road until 1993.

Woodstock's town square glistens with white lights.

spend an average $400 a year on decorations. Their large budget has allowed them to make their purchases wholesale. They currently own all but one item manufactured by Union Specialties, a plastic figurine company in Massachusetts. With few new items left from which to choose, Kerry resorted to making the church, stores and gingerbread house out of plywood himself.

At decorating time their teenage son, Tom, deposits the figurines around the yard in his four-wheeler. The family then determines where everything should go, often with the advice of neighbors. When the soldiers are lined up, and the sheep are headed in the right direction, the decorations are secured to the ground with U-bolts, tent stakes and plumber's hooks.

The decorating task takes 30 hours in all, but continues through the Christmas season as the family makes nightly rounds armed with bags of light bulbs to keep all 111 figures aglow.

Thanksgiving weekend–Jan.1, 5:00PM–10:00PM. *From Rt.120, N on Thompson Rd. 3 mi., E on West Wonder Lake Rd. 3/4 mi. (follow curve), E on White Oaks Rd. 1/2 mi., S on W. Wonder Lake Dr. 1-1/2 bl.*

WOODSTOCK

ⓕ Woodstock Historical Square

The bell tower of the steamboat-gothic opera house stands tall amid the old-fashioned shops that surround the town square. Horse-drawn carriages bounce along the cobblestone streets, as a cheery chorus sings from the park gazebo festooned for the holidays.

Though the scene may appear to be from an era past, it is thriving in this town, founded in 1844, which has managed to retain its Victorian charm. White lights outline every shop in the square and glisten from every tree with a subtle gleam of modern times.

A romantic setting for holiday shopping, the square offers restaurants, Christmas shops, craft stores, antiques, boutiques and the Dick Tracy Museum. Weekly events such as the "Victorian Holiday Walk," "Aunt Holly Storytelling" and the unique "Tuba Christmas" make a trip to Woodstock a festive treat for the whole family.

Friday after Thanksgiving–Jan.14. For a schedule of holiday events call the Woodstock Chamber of Commerce (815)338–2436. *From Rt.14, N on Rt. 47 1-1/2 mi., W on Calhoun St. 6 bl.*

Chapter 12

WILL COUNTY & OUTLYING AREAS

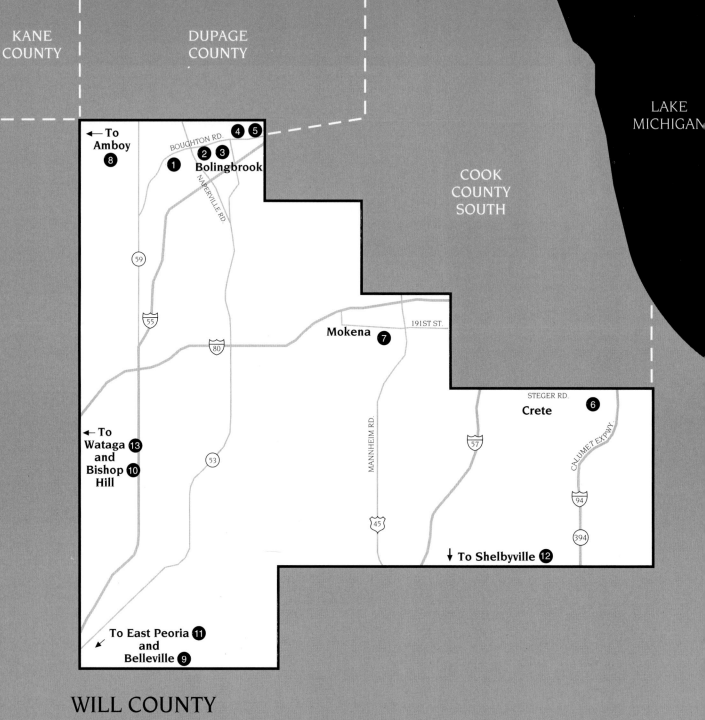

KANE
COUNTY

DUPAGE
COUNTY

LAKE
MICHIGAN

COOK
COUNTY
SOUTH

← To Amboy
8

BOUGHTON RD.

4 **5**

2 **3**

1

Bolingbrook

NAPERVILLE RD.

59

55

80

53

191ST ST.

Mokena **7**

MANNHEIM RD.

STEGER RD.

Crete **6**

57

CALUMET EXPWY.

94

45

394

← To
Wataga **13**
and
Bishop **10**
Hill

↓ To Shelbyville **12**

To East Peoria **11**
and
Belleville **9**

WILL COUNTY
AND
OUTLYING AREAS

N
W + E
S

0   MILES   5

Will County

BOLINGBROOK

❶ 1432 Clear Drive

At the Quad Cities Venetian Lighted Boat Parade in 1990, a 42-foot houseboat named "Pepsi Powered" took grand prize dressed for the occasion as a twinkling Noah's Ark. The craft was trimmed with a glittering giraffe at the bow, a sparkling elephant shooting water from his trunk at the stern, a glistening alligator smiling from the dinghy, and a group of glowing dolphins jumping out of the water all around the boat.

The menagerie of animals silhouetted in lights was the collaborative effort of boatowners Richard and Norma Clowes, their daughter Linda Cothron, her husband Mark and their friend Lyle Haakenson. Locally famous for his elaborate Christmas displays, Mr. Haakenson lent his expertise with an aquatic twist.

After several years of winning the boating event, the Cothrons and the Clowes, employing the methods Lyle had taught them, began decorating their homes for the holidays as well. Fortunately for Chicago area residents, Mark and Linda moved from Moline to Bolingbrook, where they have been thrilling their new audience with the whimsical decorations.

In the front yard of their home, a mischievous 8-foot snowman turns a frown to a smile as he playfully tosses a snowball, which lobs over the garage door and bursts into pieces when it hits the bush on the other side. A 9-foot lighted dinosaur and it's baby wave, as a sign alternately blinks a warm holiday message. A three-dimensional 10' x 3' x 9' train spins its wheels, while Santa waves from the engine.

Employing Lyle's technique for animating the lighted figures, Mark uses switching systems purchased from Eagle Signal Controls of Austin, Texas. Similar to a small motor that controls a traffic light, the system utilizes a series of 10 switches, which are set to turn strands of lights on and off at timed intervals. Mark also achieves the same effect by modifying strings of commercial motion lights. He splices additional strands to the circuitry, which causes the entire strand, rather than each bulb, to blink.

The silhouettes of the characters are formed from 1/2-inch black flexible water pipe, which is

A mischievous snowman tossing a snowball is one of several homemade electronic displays that decorate the home of Mark and Linda Cothron.

screwed to a framework built of 1" x 2" boards. Each sequential position of the moving parts must also be constructed. Separate circuits of lights are taped to each position and timed in order, so that the figures appear to be in motion.

Though the electronic figures take weeks to construct, Mark notes, "We have a lot of kids who come by daily to see Barney. They wave to him and sing to him. It makes it all worthwhile."

Dec. 6–Jan. 1, 5:00PM–11:00PM. *From Naperville Rd., W on Boughton Rd. 3 bl., S on Vincent Dr. 4 bl., W on Clear Dr.*

❷ 108 Cypress Drive

Violet West grew up in the hollows of Tennessee, the youngest of three children. It was the post-Depression era of the forties. Though her family wasn't hungry, they were poor, and having a Christmas tree was on no one's mind but Violet's.

As soon as she was old enough to swing her father's hatchet, she walked into the woods outside her house, chopped down a wild cedar tree and dragged it home. "I decorated it with little cottonballs

Dillard and Violet West join a crew of elves near their toy shop. The wooden figures are one of dozens of homemade displays that fill the West's front lawn.

and paper chains, anything to stick on there to give it a little color," she recalls.

At her elementary school each classroom had a Christmas tree. When school let out for the holidays, the ornaments were removed, and the trees were thrown away with remnants of tinsel clinging to the dried boughs. "I'd just get what icicles I could from there and put them on my little tree," Violet said. "It looked real pretty to me, being a little kid."

Their home had no electricity until she was 12, and even then, lighting the tree was not in the family budget. Violet recalls visiting a neighbor with a lighted tree. "It had one 40-watt light bulb stuck in the middle of the branches. I thought that was wonderful," she said. "Maybe that's what led to my desire for so many lights."

After she and her husband, Dillard, bought their first home in 1961, Violet bought her first string of 15 outdoor lights. It was all they could afford at the time. The following year she bought a second set. The lights now stretched all the way across the porch. More were purchased each year. "Without even thinking, it got bigger," she admits. "The more I got, the more I wanted to get."

The lights that decorate their home and front yard now total more than 10,000. She and Dillard, who are both retired, even climb the roof to string lights criss-crossed over the shingles. "Otherwise, it's a big old patch of black," Violet defends.

The couple also collects old artificial Christmas trees from garage sales to fill in any blank spaces on the lawn. They have eight so far and are always searching for more. "I use them wherever I need some color," Violet says. "You can't tell the difference from the real ones."

Years ago the Wests began creating two-dimensional wooden displays outlined in lights, which have become their home's hallmark. Many are original designs, while some are from coloring book pictures or mail-order patterns. Using plywood he salvaged from construction site dumpsters, Dillard cuts out the forms with a jigsaw. Violet then paints them, and Dillard drills the holes for the lights. "She's the one who does the engineering. I do all the work," Dillard jokes.

Thirty homemade candy canes and 16 toy soldiers line the walk and driveway. Twelve gingerbread kids, cleverly iced with bathroom caulk, dance across the front of the house, along with giant candy canes, Christmas trees, glittering stars, and a cheery snowman. The front lawn is filled with Santa and his sleigh pulled by three reindeer, a band of elves in their toy shop, a trio of carolers and a manger scene guarded by a host of angels.

In a rocker on the front porch, a life-size stuffed Santa relaxes. But not Dillard. Violet plans to add a four-car train which requires some jigsawing. "The pattern's laying back there. Dillard doesn't know it," she laughs.

The yard now beams so brightly that drivers, eager to see what's glistening, often mistakenly enter the West's street the wrong way from Route 53. Once finding the display, it is apparent that the glow is coming from more than the thousands of multicolored lights that fill the yard and cover the house. It is the spirit of Christmas that shines brightly from this homemade display—a spirit that glowed in the heart of a little girl and continues to shine from a loving couple.

Dec. 1–Jan. 1, (Su–Th) 5:00PM–10:30PM, (F–Sa)– 12:00PM. *From Boughton Rd., S on Rt.53 3/4 mi., W on Briarcliff Rd. 1/4 mi., S on Glengary Dr. 1 bl., E on Cypress Dr. 1/4 mi.*

❸ 136 and 140 Delmar Drive

"We've got too much junk. I'm not going to decorate this much next Christmas," homeowner Bill Keene annually declares to his wife, Georgia. "But somehow," he says, "we end up decorating even more the following year."

With their young grandchildren, Meagen and David, living right next door, it's hard for the Keenes to resist an opportunity to watch the children jump with glee. And with so many cars driving through the well-lit area, it's also difficult not to add to the fun of passersby.

So every holiday season, the Keenes, along with their son David next-door and his close friend Fred Beck, spend several days trimming both homes with thousands of lights and dozens of homemade and store-bought decorations that the family has accumulated over the years.

On Christmas Eve Bill gets an added thrill by playing Santa for his grandchildren. As he walks down the street children wave excitedly from neighboring houses and passing cars, and somehow the large holiday greeting sign he thought of building to span the roof of his house doesn't seem like such a bad idea after all.

Dec. 15 – Jan. 1, Dusk–10:00PM. *From Boughton Rd., S on Rt.53 1 mi., W on Edgehill Dr. 20', NE on Delmar Dr. 1/2 bl.*

Christmas Trees of Pans and Cans

Bill Keene used disposable aluminum pie pans to create an outdoor Christmas tree. He first constructed a triangular wooden frame with 1" x 3" boards, attaching horizontal crossbeams to hold parallel rows of pans. A 1" x 4" pointed "trunk" was screwed to the back for a stake. The pie pans were then stapled to the frame. Holes, large enough to hold a C-9 light socket were drilled through the beams and the pans. The sockets were then inserted through the back and the bulbs screwed in place. The reflection of the light in the center of each pan forms a dazzling halo effect. Joseph and Deborah Martino of Tinley Park created a similar effect using coffee cans fastened together with screws.

A canopy of lights connects the two Keene households.

❹ 230 St. Andrews Drive

Most home decorators supply electricity to their Christmas lights with a maze of orange extension cords running through basement windows, but not homeowner Joseph Gagliano, an electrical engineer for Argonne National Laboratory.

"The logic of our light sequence is first drafted on grid paper, distinguishing the 'on' and 'off' status for a given event. It is then transferred into Boolean algebraic equations, which are entered into the host computer. When the entire sequence of equations is transcribed, it is then compiled into a form that can be downloaded through an RS-422 link into another computer, which acts independently as a driver switching the 110-volt AC current to the various light strings," he explains.

As one could imagine, the result of Joseph's mathematics is no ordinary holiday display. The front yard of the Gagliano home, which sits at the crest of a wooded hill, dances with a delightful assortment of homemade animated decorations. A herd of reindeer with prancing hooves leads Santa to the rooftop, as "Ho, Ho, Ho" flashes overhead. An old-fashioned steam engine spins its wheels toward a flashing railroad crossing, while Snoopy shoots baskets in the driveway. Candles flicker in each of nine windows that blink to an equation that would impress Mr. Boole himself.

Like the lights flashing back and forth, Joseph and his wife, LuAnne, take turns performing the

Windows flash, wheels spin and reindeer prance in the Gagliano's homemade computerized display.

tasks needed to create at least one new decoration each holiday season. LuAnne designs the figures and draws them to size on cardboard. Joseph forms them out of coated 8-gauge galvanized steel wire. LuAnne wraps them in metallic garland, and Joseph wraps them in lights. LuAnne determines the sequence of the lights, and Joseph writes the program and does the wiring. The couple's joint effort has earned them a "Spirit of Christmas Award" from the town of Bolingbrook every year since 1987.

Dec. 14–Jan. 6, 5:00PM–1:00AM. *From Boughton Rd., N on Rt.53 1 mi., E on St. Andrews Dr.*

❺ 301 to 333 Trafalgar Court

When Karin and Stan Franks moved into their new home on Trafalgar Court, fellow residents warned that everyone on the cul-de-sac decorated for Christmas. Stan proudly noted that he had four boxes of outdoor decorations. The neighbors exchanged snickering glances.

Over Thanksgiving weekend, the block was bustling with activity. The sound of aluminum ladders, staple guns and pounding hammers filled the air, as the trimming began. At week's end, neighbors spied Karin and Stan as they stepped back to admire their decorations and then suddenly disappeared in their

car. The couple returned a short time later armed with boxes of lights to add to their scant display.

Down the street another new couple, Pat and Karen Drinkard, thought their decorations looked pretty good—until the rest of the block turned on their lights. They quickly shut theirs off and went to shop for more.

It wasn't "keeping up with the Joneses" that sent the Franks and the Drinkards scurrying to the store, but rather a feeling of pride and cooperation among the neighbors on Trafalgar Court. Since the late eighties, all nine households have joined in a common effort to decorate the parkway trees in white Italian lights, while trimming their homes to their liking.

The families share their ladders, their extension poles and their decorating tips as well. The Trafalgar men often gather in the middle of the street months before Christmas to discuss their new ideas.

When Larry Schneider edged his lawn with a sparkling border of motion lights individually hooked onto 1/2-inch rods of plastic pipe, he was glad to share his savvy system. When Len Lux devised a method for illuminating styrofoam candy canes by pushing miniature lights into them, he told others on the block, so they could hang them from their trees too. When Len fell one year while trimming his roof, neighbors joined together to complete his decorations before he returned home from the hospital.

The home of Larry and Peggy Schneider is but one of the glistening homes on this cheery cul-de-sac.

The Haweswood mansion gleams like a fairyland castle.

In 1994 another new couple, Pam and Chris Werling, moved onto the block. However, with a stroke of good luck their decorations fit right in with their well-trimmed neighbors. It seems the string of lights they hung in their tree inadvertently formed the shape of a perfect camel and became the talk of the block.

Dec. 15 – Jan. 1, Dusk–10:00PM, (F–Sa) –11:30PM.
From Boughton Rd., N on Rt.53 2 mi., E on 83rd St. 3/4 mi., S on Ashbury Ave. 1/2 mi., W on Trafalgar Ct.

Larry Schneider's Day or Night Greeting Sign

Larry painted "Happy Holidays" in white on one side of a roll of fiberglass window screening. On the other side, he hot-glued Christmas lights to each letter. The screen was screwed to 2" x 4" stakes at either end and stretched taut with wires staked to the ground. During the holidays the sign spreads its greeting both day and night. And at the end of the season it is neatly rolled up and stored in a bag.

CRETE

❻ 3505 Haweswood Drive

Beyond the trees sparkling with miniature white lights, the Haweswood mansion gleams with hundreds of thousands of multicolored bulbs like a fairyland castle that magically appears for the holidays.

To owners Bob and Elsa Eustace the splendorous sight is a dream come true, as the mansion itself had once been to its original owner J.E. Hawes, former president of Illinois Shade Cloth Company.

Hawes searched many years for talented craftsmen to build his home on the Crete site, which at that time was 120 wooded acres adjacent to the Lincolnshire Country Club. Handsomely designed by architect Addison C. Berry of Lansing, Indiana, the mansion also features fine artistry in its Rookwood pottery tile, cantilevered staircase, ceiling friezes, wrought iron, carved stone, marble and woodwork. It was completed in 1929 at a cost of $150,000—or what some might guess to be the current holiday electric bill.

Dec. 15 – Jan. 1, Dusk–Dawn. *From (I-94), S on the Calumet Expy. (Hwy. 394) 7-1/2 mi., W on Steger Rd. 2 mi., S on Haweswood Dr.*

MOKENA

⑦ 10727 1st Court

For five years Cedric Hentsch decorated his parents' home with a large collection of lights and plastic figurines he bought himself. "When you get married, you're taking it all with you," his father proclaimed, "I want no part of it." Although Ervin Hentsch had always given his son a hand assembling the collection in the front yard, he did not share Cedric's level of enthusiasm.

In April of 1992 Cedric got married and moved five blocks away. He took his six candy canes, 20 tin soldiers, two lollipops, one sleigh, four reindeer, North Pole sign, 40-inch Snowman, 32-inch Santa and 25 sets of lights with him, leaving nothing at his parent's home—just as his dad had requested.

When the Christmas season arrived, his father's front yard had no decorations and was trouble-free. Ervin stopped by to help Cedric decorate and by the following December was hanging lights on his own bushes, windows and gutters. Cedric laughed, "I knew it wouldn't take him long."

Dec. 1–Jan. 5, Dusk–11:00PM. *From Mannheim Rd. (Rt.45), W on 191st St. (Rt.84) 1-1/2 mi., S on School House Rd. 2 bl., E on 1st Ct. 1/2 bl.*

On summer vacation with the rest of the campers, Santa lounges, while his clothes hang out to dry, at O'Connell's "Christmas in July" celebration.

Outlying Areas

AMBOY

⑧ "Christmas in July" at O'Connell's Yogi Bear Jellystone Park Camp-Resort

For those who need more than a single yule per year, O'Connell's Yogi Bear Jellystone Park Camp-Resort celebrates "Christmas in July" one weekend each summer with Santa soaring over glowing campfires and luminaria doubling as insect repellent.

Though many resorts have the same tradition, O'Connell's park, which has featured the event since 1980, has a reputation among festive campers for hosting the best celebration of its kind in the area.

The fun begins early in the afternoon with a visit from Santa, Yogi and Boo Boo, who distribute gifts to the children. Making ornaments and coloring Christmas pictures are among the afternoon activities along with the park's usual fare of bingo, miniature golf, swimming, boating, fishing and hiking.

When dusk arrives and the sunbathers retire for the day, the campground is transformed into a twinkling RV wonderland. The winding roads that weave among the 400 campsites are lined with glowing luminaria purchased from the rangers' station. Nearly 200 campers, many having dug through attic boxes in summer's sweltering heat, bring Christmas lights, trees and figurines to decorate their weekend homes and add to the holiday mood.

At 8:00PM the hay wagon tours of the campsites begin. The first wagon holds the members of the Amboy Chamber of Commerce, who judge the event. Throughout the evening other wagons follow accompanied by carolers and a holiday accordionist. Along the path, campers often treat the riders to candy canes and Christmas cookies, with an occasional offer of free beer to bribe the judges.

Highlighting the displays is the three-trailer campsite of Wayne and Sue Goers (whose Huntley home is featured on page 164). Located at the starting point of the hay rides, the lawn of the Goers' campsite contains as many of the family's homemade animated holiday figures as the couple can squeeze into their trailer. Wayne, proudly sporting his Santa Claus boxer shorts, explains that the family no longer enters the competition so that other campers will be encouraged to decorate.

Marty Schultz of Bolingbrook creates another impressive display by lining his campsite in lights and toy soldiers and filling the grounds with illuminated figures that barely leave room for his lawn chairs. Marty and his clan spend eight hours of their three-day weekend setting up the display. Their first place prize entitled them to free camping.

A picnic table wrapped as a giant Christmas gift, a troop of children throwing foam snowballs, and an upside-down Christmas tree have been among the most notable displays. Tent campers join in the act with wreaths hanging from zippers and stockings pinned to mosquito netting.

Late in the evening the names of the contest winners are announced over the PA, and the night proceeds to the next holiday with a New Year's Eve dance.

Weekend in July closest to the 25th. Campers only. For reservations call (815)857–3860. Note: "Christmas in July" weekend is usually booked by the end of January. *From Aurora, W on Rt.30 50 mi., Follow the signs to the campground.*

BELLEVILLE

❾ National Shrine of Our Lady of the Snows

This peaceful shrine, which is visited by pilgrims from all over the world throughout the year, continues to share its holy message at Christmastime. The trees and bushes that line the paths of the 220-acre site are gracefully trimmed in 350,000 white lights. Life-size lighted figures of shepherds and their flocks, the three kings, and the town of Bethlehem light the way to the scene of Baby Jesus in the manger.

Fri. before Thanksgiving–Sun. after Epiphany, 5:00PM–10:00PM. Free admission. For more information call (618)397-6700. *From Chicago, S on I-57 200 mi., W on I-70 75 mi., W on I-55 10 mi., S on I-255 9 mi., E on Rt.15 500'.*

BISHOP HILL

❿ A Holiday Journey Back in Time

For those who long to escape the hectic pace of the holiday season to a simple Christmas of long ago, a visit to Bishop Hill may be just the right prescription. Three hours west of Chicago, this rural town of 160 residents lies in the rolling farmland of Henry County near the Edwards River. Settled by Swedish immigrants in 1846, the town has retained much of its simplicity and charm. Original cobblestone paths and buildings of stucco and handmade bricks subtly transport visitors back in time.

During the holidays candles shine from every window and Swedish gnomes hide in the trees. Shops are filled with traditional ornaments of finely-cut paper and woven wheat, as well as a unique assortment of handmade and imported gift items and antiques. Swedish meatballs, home-baked rye bread and luscious tortes enjoyed in the cozy atmosphere of the town's three restaurants add the perfect touch of warm Scandanavian hospitality to a winter's day.

Though Bishop Hill is quiet during the week, on the two weekends after Thanksgiving it is bustling with the celebration of Julmarknad. This is the Christmas Market, when shops bring out their yuletide wares, offer samples of potato sausage and lingonberry jam and dress in their holiday finest. Swedish folk characters roam the streets, traditional music fills the air, and children search for gnomes in a mystery contest.

The following weekend luminaria line the streets for the celebration of Lucia Nights, the Festival of Lights. Throughout the town, coffee and cookies are served by young girls dressed in white and wearing crowns of candles in honor of Santa Lucia, the patron saint of lights.

A National Historic Landmark since 1984, Bishop Hill is also home to several museums and original structures that tell the story of its beginnings as a religious communal settlement and center of commerce.

2nd weekend in Dec.–2nd weekend in Jan. (closed Dec.22–Dec.25) Museums: Open daily, 9:00AM–4:00PM. Restaurants: Open daily, 11:00AM–2:00PM. Shops: 10:00AM–5:00PM (Some have shorter winter hours.) For more information write to the Bishop Hill Arts Council, P.O. Box 47, Bishop Hill, IL 61419, or call (309)927–3345 or (309)927–3899. *From Chicago, W on I-80 150 mi., S on Rt.78 11 mi. to Kewanee, S and W on Rt.34 15 mi. (4 mi. past Galva), Follow signs N to Bishop Hill 2 mi.*

EAST PEORIA

⓫ Festival of Lights

This riverside town of 22,000 has put its name on the map with a dazzling holiday display that annually attracts crowds over ten times its size. It's the "East

A colorful chubby penguin is one of dozens of shimmering floats built by volunteers for the East Peoria Festival of Lights.

light strands to the frames with plastic bread bag ties. The results of their efforts have been compared to the floats seen at Disneyland.

After the parade the lighted floats are on display throughout the Christmas season in a variety of delightful exhibits named for the festival's toy soldier mascot, Folepi, an acronym for Festival Of Lights East Peoria Illinois.

Through a tunnel of leaping reindeer, enter Folepi's Winter Wonderland, a 25-acre municipal park that has been magically transformed into a holiday fantasyland. The two-mile drive-through path features most of the parade floats, along with 65 other lighted displays. Together they form colossal theme areas, such as Enchanted Castle Land, Outer Space Land, Dinosaur Park and Circus Land.

A few blocks away, Folepi's Enchanted Forest is a special treat for small children. Seven hundred decorated Christmas trees tightly line a quarter-mile walking path that features musical animated displays, including The Old Woman in the Shoe, The 12 Days of Christmas, and Old MacDonald. At the end of the walk the kids can enjoy a visit with Santa in his own decorated trailer.

Throughout the town other attractions include the Narrated Nativity, hand-painted murals of

Peoria Festival of Lights," an impressive extravaganza of yuletide exhibits and events made possible through the efforts of hundreds of community volunteers.

The "Parade of Lights" first sets the town aglow on the Saturday after Thanksgiving. An estimated half-million twinkling bulbs decorate nearly 50 floats, as well as the local marching bands that participate in this evening event. The Starship Enterprise, Cinderella's pumpkin coach, a paddle wheel riverboat, a Chinese dragon, a Batmobile, a brontosaurus, a 125-foot steam engine train and a dragon that blows smoke are among the entries, which really do seem to "float" along the three-mile route.

Since the parade began in 1985 with 12 floats, each sponsored by a local business, new ones have been added each year. Volunteers construct the black pencil-steel frames and mount them on black stripped-down cars or golf carts. By mid-October volunteers are working seven days a week attaching

Santa Piggy and his team of piglets are among the many delightful children's displays in Folepi's Enchanted Forest.

Christ's birth with a radio-broadcast narration; Folepi's Holiday Sensations, an exhibit of gingerbread houses and other yuletide culinary treats; and Folepi's Marketplace, a holiday craft fair featuring 150 booths and festival souvenirs.

East Peoria itself is decked out for the occasion in 2,500,000 lights and an assortment of giant decorations that appear throughout the town. Most striking is a 35-foot wreath surrounding a huge candle perched on the edge of the river bluff. It is actually a ferris wheel disguised with red, green and yellow fluorescent lights. Anticipating future needs, the town installs electrical outlets on all new lampposts Many of the homes decorate as well, with Willow Court on the east side of town being the most noteworthy.

Rated one of the "Top 100 Events in North America" by the American Bus Association and recipient of the 1987 Governor's Hometown Award, the East Peoria Festival of Lights is not only an event worth the three-hour drive from Chicago, but a tribute to the spirit of the volunteers that have made it a success.

Sat. after Thanksgiving – Dec. 31. Lighted exhibits: 5:00PM–10:00PM (except holidays). Admission fees. (Free to children under 12 and guests of East Peoria motels.) Guided tours and free shuttle service available. All events are handicap accessible. For more information contact the East Peoria Festival Commission at 100 S. Main St., East Peoria, IL 61611 or call (800)365–3743 or (309)698–4711. *From Chicago, S on I-55 140 mi., W on I-74 30 mi., Follow the signs to each exhibit.*

LAKE SHELBYVILLE

⓬ Starflake Trail and Lake Shelbyville Festival of Lights

A new constellation has been appearing every holiday season in the heart of the midwest. It's the Starflake Trail, a path of over 75 5-foot stars connecting the neighboring Illinois towns of Sullivan, Arthur, Arcola, Mattoon, Windsor, Findlay and Shelbyville across 100 miles of roads.

The twinkling stars that shine from the street posts guide visitors along rural roads from one town to the next. Each community exhibits its own unique charm, from the landmark Victorian homes

of Shelbyville to the Amish bakeries and furniture shops of Arthur and Arcola. Antiques dealers, gift shops, quaint restaurants, and bed and breakfasts add to the small town flavor.

Local holiday exhibits appear in each town park, but the highlight of them all is the Lake Shelbyville Festival of Lights. Located on the grounds of the Inn at Eagle Creek within Eagle Creek State Park, the drive-through exhibit features over 400 displays and 800,000 lights. Cars pass over a lighted bridge and under sparkling arches into six different themed areas. A three-dimensional merry-go-round, a Loch Ness monster wagging his tail and a fisherman waiting for a catch on a glistening lake of 10,000 lights are among the large displays that festoon the three-mile path.

The festival is sponsored by the Lake Shelbyville Visitors Association. Because it is a not-for-profit event, all proceeds accrued after paying expenses, such as the $135 per day electric bill and $20,000 per year bulb replacement costs, are used to purchase more custom-made decorations. Begun in 1989, the display just keeps getting bigger and better every year.

Mid-Nov.–Mid-Jan., (Su–Th) Dusk–9:00PM, (F–Sa)–10:00PM. Admission fee. For further information call the Lake Shelbyville Visitors Association (800)8SHELBY. *From Chicago, S on I-57 180 mi., W on Rt.133 17 mi., S on Rt.32 15 mi., W on Bruce Findlay Rd. 6 mi., Follow signs to the inn. To complete the Starflake Trail: W on Bruce Findlay Rd. 5 mi., S on Rt.128 8 mi., E on Rt.16 25 mi.*

WATAGA

⓭ Rosy-Morn Farm 625 Knox Road 1925N
(pictured on page 169)

In rural Illinois as the winter nights grow longer, Burlington Northern passengers may stare blankly at darkened farmland for miles on end, but when they reach Wataga everyone perks up and moves to one side of the train for a better view of the holiday lights at Rosy-Morn Farm.

Since 1956, commuters, neighbors and folks from all over Knox County have been coming to see the unique decorations that fill the front yard of the 128-acre grain farm of Vincent and Bernice Holmes. The couple began their collection with a small Santa and reindeer, purchased from Sears catalog, that they put on the roof of the porch. "We thought it was wonderful," Bernice recalls.

Shopping for holiday decorations soon became a favorite pasttime. They bought a nativity scene from Abington, a Santa from Galesburg, a herd of reindeer from Moline, and a sleigh being pulled by farm animals from Galva. When they heard that a local church was selling a scene of Bethlehem, they climbed up in the sweltering belfry in the mid-July to make the purchase.

On frequent visits to their daughter in Pennsylvania, they couldn't resist a little Christmas store in the small town of Smethport where two fine artisans created unusual three-dimensional displays. Here they purchased movable figures of Santa and his elves, a rocking organist with a quartet of carolers, a waving Santa painting on a stepladder, four shepherds, a snowman tipping his hat, an angel and an old-fashioned flivver car.

And what they couldn't buy from craftspeople they would make themselves. First they built a steepled church to house the organist, then a camel for the manger scene. "We didn't realize that the basement door was smaller than the camel, so we had to cut off something and put it back again to get him out," Bernice confesses.

They began to build scenes, each inspiring its own holiday tale: five baby bunnies tucked in bed with their Christmas stockings hanging at their feet; three little girls in their nightgowns peeking into Santa's workshop; and a duck pulling a fairy along in his cart, to name but a few. The skeletons of the figures were built out of wood. Vincent and Bernice dressed them in real clothes, stuffed them with plastic, and used wig stands for the heads. With a similar technique, they even built a life-size horse to pull a sleighload of gifts.

It didn't take long before the Holmes' farm was featured on television and radio, and in newspapers and magazines. Cars lined the road bumper-to-bumper. School children on field trips and seniors from nursing homes came by the busload. And the local radio station, after flurries of phone calls, became the official announcer of the display's opening date. "It just kinda' grew on us until we couldn't get out of it," Bernice laughs.

At the corner of the front yard, a wooden figure of a little boy clangs a bell near a sign that in 1994 read, "Ringing Greetings for the 39th Year." Though the yard has long been full, Bernice continues to buy new things and enjoys quizzing her visitors to see if they can guess what's new. Many of the original decorations still appear, imparting the warm feelings that tattered but familiar keepsakes can bring. The original Santa and reindeer, grown fragile with time, are displayed only on special anniversaries. The painting Santa from Smethport still waves despite layers of yellowing tape, and a set of Montgomery Ward candles still glimmer through fading colored plastic.

Vincent Holmes passed away in 1990. In tribute to his love of Christmas, neighbors presented Bernice with a sign that read, "In memory of Vincent Holmes—the real Father Christmas."

A holiday visit to the Rosy-Morn Farm had become a tradition that had spanned several generations of neighborhood families. "It wouldn't be Christmas without it," they all agreed. So a local fireman, a seed salesman, a railroad engineer, and several farmers volunteered to help Bernice and her daughters, Rose Marie and Beverly, assemble the display and have done so each year since.

Bernice still does most of the work herself with the help of her daughters and a hired hand. Each of the volunteers has an assigned task to complete the six-to-eight-week job. Every night throughout the Christmas season, Bernice covers the figures in plastic. When the holidays are over, she and Rose Marie use a tractor to take down the display over the course of two months. Many of the decorations must be dried indoors before they can be packed away. The clothes on the homemade figurines must be removed and washed, and the figures must be restuffed.

It's a big job for anyone, let alone a woman nearing her eightieth birthday who's been doing this for almost 40 years. Approaching holidays now find Bernice reluctant to commit to continuing the display, but she admits, "This was Vincent's pride and joy, so we try to keep it up. And besides…the neighbors won't let us quit."

Dec. 14–Jan. 6, Dusk–10:00PM. For current display information call the Galesburg Area Chamber of Commerce (309)343–1194. *From Chicago, W on I-80 150 mi., S on Rt.78 11 mi., S and W on Rt.34 32 mi., N on 2nd road past Wataga.*

Appendix

The following is a list of commercial enterprises mentioned in the book that provide holiday products or services.

Decorators and Suppliers

Becker Group
901 Cathedral St.
Baltimore, MD 21202
(410)576-0222
Custom commercial displays, p.18

Bronner's Christmas Wonderland
25 Christmas Ln.
Frankenmuth, MI 48734
(517)652-9931
(800)ALL-YEAR
Year-round Christmas store, p.93, 126

The Christmas Place
Bell Tower Square
Pigeon Forge, TN 37868
(615)453-0415
Year-round Christmas store, p.93

Craft Patterns
P.O. Box 491
St. Charles, IL 60134
(708)208-0491
Woodcraft patterns, p.164

Rick Cuvala
Trix Mfg.
500 W. Irving Park Rd.
Bensenville, IL 60106
(708)595-6340
Custom lightweight lighted
displays, p.113

Design Solutions
2332 Irving Blvd.
Dallas, TX 75207
(214)871-0801
Custom commercial displays, p.17

Roger Farrow
305 Elwood Ct.
Westmont, IL 60559
(708)968-7389
Custom lighted silhouettes
and animated displays, p.131

Goosey Gander Creations
P.O. Box 118
Bradley, IL 60915
(815)933-3178
Goose clothing, p.55

Holiday World
3300 Ridge Rd.
Lansing, IL 60438
(708)474-4654
Year-round Christmas store, p.88

Interior Garden Services
2000 W. Fulton St.
Chicago, IL 60612
(312)421-0076
Custom floral designs, p.14

J. Lynn Floral Designs, Inc.
444 Lake Cook Rd., Suite 24
Deerfield, IL 60015
(708)374-0074
Custom floral displays, p.4

Kinn-Shaw
116 N. Center
Joliet, IL 60435
(815)726-1414
Cement geese and goose clothing, p.55

Tim Lowry
2033 Chestnut St.
Waukegan, IL 60087
Computerized light displays, p.152-153

The Meetinghouse Companies, Inc.
781 N. Church Rd.
Elmhurst, IL 60126-1413
(708)941-0600
Custom commercial displays, p.14

Meisel Hardware Specialties
P.O. Box 70
Mound, MN 55364
(800)441-9870
Woodcraft patterns and motors, p.165

Pacific Design & Production
133 Copeland St.
Petaluma, CA 94952
(415)488-8100
Commercial animated displays, p.16

Phillip's Flowers & Gifts
524 N. Cass Ave.
Westmont, IL 60559
(708)719-5200
Custom decorating, p.13

The Pine Cone Christmas Shop
210 Robert Parker Coffin Rd.
Long Grove, IL 60047
(708)808-0890, p.151

Rocco Fiore & Sons, Inc.
28270 N. Bradley Rd.
Libertyville, IL 60048
(708)680-1207
Exterior Christmas decorating, p.57-58

2nd Dimension Creative Services, Inc.
323 South Blvd
Oak Park, IL 60302
(708)383-5666
Custom wooden displays, p.25

Spaeth Design
423 W. 55th St.
New York, NY 10019
(212)489-0770
Animated window displays, p.11

Union Products, Inc.
511 Lancaster
Leominster, MA 01453-0330
(508)537-1631
Plastic figurine manufacturer—
wholesale only, p.168

Larry Wardzala
7721 Sunset Dr.
Elmwood Park, IL 60635
(312)769-5436
Commercial/residential decorating and
displays, P.101-102

White Way Sign Co.
1317 N. Clybourn Ave.
Chicago, IL 60610
(312)642-6580
Light hanging, p.7

Wooden Memories
Rt.1, Box 87
Bear Lake, PA 16402
(814)489-3002
Woodcraft patterns, p.65

Holiday tours

Chicago Motor Coach Co.
750 S. Clinton St.
Chicago, IL 60607
(312)922-8919
Holiday tour of downtown, p.7

Gray Line Sightseeing Tours
27 E. Monroe St., Suite 515
Chicago, IL 60603
(312)427-3107
Dinner tour of Cuneo light display, p.152

Clubs

The Golden Glow of Christmas Past
6401 Winsdale St.
Golden Valley, MN 55427
Organization for enthusiasts of
Christmas antiques.

Index

AT&T/USG Building, *12*, 13
Adee home, 158
Albrecht home, 90-91, *91*
Alfrejd home, 167
Algonquin, 157
Almeroth home, 99, *99*
Amboy, 176
American flags, 46, 131
Anderson home, 79
Andracki home, 115, *115*
Animals, live, 23, 46, 77, 99-100
Animated displays, 5, 11, 13, 14, 15, 16, 17,
    18, 29-30, 33, 34, 37, 38, 47, 50, 83, 84,
    88-89, 90, 100, 103, 115, 116, 117-120, 126-
    127, 128, 130, 131, 157, 163, 171
Ansel B. Cook home, 150, *150*
Antioch, 143
Apartment courtyards, 100-101
Archambault home, *46*
Archways, 41, 51, 55, 61, 103, 106, 108, 173
Arizzi home, *35*, 40
Arlington Heights, 61-66; village display, *61*
Arnold home, 137
Art Institute of Chicago, 13
Aurora, 135-136
Avondale neighborhood, 21

Bajkowski home, 99
Balloons, giant holiday, 76, 105
Baluzynski home, 52, *52*
Bannockburn, 143, *143*
Barrington, 144-145
Basica home, 34, *34*
Beattie home, 143, *143*
Becket Avenue, Westchester, 107, *107*
Beitler, Paul, 4-5
Bellwood, 99
Bensenville, 113
Benson/Sagalow home, 26
Bethlehem scene, 135, 177, 180
Beverly neighborhood, 37-39
Bishop Hill, 177
Bolingbrook, 171-175
Bongiovanni home, 47
Bonini home, *127*, 127-128
Bork home, 106
Boyk home, 128
Bramati home, 56, *56*
Bridgeport neighborhood, 40
Bridgeview, 83-84
Brookfield Zoo, 99-100, *100*
Brown home, *136*, 136-137, *137*
Burbank, 84-86
Bus tours, 7, appendix
Butch McGuire's, *29*, 29-30

CTA Christmas bus, 18
Calderone home, 90
Calumet City, 86
Candies, giant, 72, 76, 77, 90, 95, 122, 128

Candles, giant, 66, 114, 117, 136
Candy Cane Land, 68, 69
Candy Cane Lane (original), 21-26, *22*, *23*,
    25, 34, 72-73, 101
Candy Cane Lane (Schiller Park), 106
Candy canes, 50, 65, 66, 73, 76, 80, 99,
    106, 143, 154, 174
Car, in display, 123, 131
Carol Stream, 113-115
Carriage rides, 151, 168
Carson Pirie Scott, 14, 16, *16*
Cary, 158-159
Cascio home, 47
Cassidy home, 85, *85*
Castle, 17, 21, 75
"Charles Dickens Winter Festival," 139
Chiappetta home, 64, *64*
Chicago Mercantile Exchange, 5, 17
Choir boys and girls, 63, 159
Christ, story of birth, 135-136, 177-178
Christ Church, Des Plaines, 67, *67*
"Christmas in July," 27, 176-177
Christmas Inn, 88-89
Christmas poem, 48-49
Christmas stockings, 83
Christmas trees: "angel tree," 75; Chicago,
    3, *3*; first electrically lighted, 129; home-
    made, 31, 46, 56, 90, 99, 108, 122, 150, 173;
    international, 4, 42, 137-138; large, 3, 4,
    9, 12, 14, 15, 17, 49, 65, 68, 104, 115, 124,
    145; Marriot, of room lights, 10; multiple,
    120-121, 139; Norfolk Island Pine, 14;
    poinsettia, 8, 13, 104; "Swedish Crown," 23;
    through the roof, 47-48
Christoffel home (Des Plaines), 66, *66*
Christoffel homes (Chicago), 31, *31*
City Hall/County Building, Chicago, 3
Claremont Street, Elmhurst, 120-121, *121*
Clarion Executive Plaza Hotel, 17
Clinton, Hillary Rodham, 56
Clock tower, 47, 128
Collection boxes, for charities, 9, 13, 17, 23
Concord Avenue, Westchester, 108, *108*
Consolo home, 120, *120*
Cook Memorial Park, *150*, 150-151
Cooney home, 109
Cork and Kerry Tavern, 39, *39*
Cornelia's Roosterant, 27, *27*
Cothron home, 171, *171*
Crestwood, 86-87
Crete, 175
Crystal Lake, 160-162
Cuneo Museum and Gardens, 152, *152*
Customs of other countries, 4, 42, 125,
    137-138, 177
Cuvala home, 113

Dahlke home, 78
Dames homes, 108
Des Plaines, 66-69
DiMaria home, 76
DiMenna home, 106
Dioramas, 29, 55, 76, 94, 95, 99, 114, 126,
    127, 128, 157; creating, 72, 99
Dolton, 87

Domanik home, 48-49, *49*
Dorband home, 46, *46*
Dover Court, 149
Downers Grove, 115-120
Drake Hotel, 18
Drinkard home, 174
Drive-through lighted displays, 152, 177,
    178-179
Drwal/Meller home, 93-94
Duerig home, 159
Dunning neighborhood, 21-26
Durkee home, 163, *163*
Dvorak home, 87-88, *88*
Dymond Road, Libertyville, 149, *149*

East Garfield Park neighborhood, 40-41
East Peoria, 177-179
East Side neighborhood, 41
"Electric Sheep," by John David Mooney,
    12, *12*
Elgin, 136-138
Elk Grove Village, 70-73
Elmhurst, 120
Elmwood Park, 100-103
Elsey home, 110, *110*
Emanuelson Inn, 154, *154*
Equitable Building, 9
Ernst home, 109-110, *110*
Esposito home, 94-95, *95*
Eustace home, 175, *175*
Evanston, 45-46

FAO Schwarz, 11
Farmhouses, 167, 179-80
Farrow home, 131, *131*
Favero home, 93, *93*
Ferris wheels, 51, 84, 93, 110, 129, 131
Fessett home, 37, *37*
"Festival of Lights": East Peoria, 177-179,
    178; Lake Shelbyville, 179; Michigan
    Avenue, 7
"Festival of Trees": Easter Seal Society
    of Metropolitan Chicago, 18; Palatine,
    74-75; Ficaro home, 42, *42*
Figurines, plastic: anchoring, 32, 166, 168;
    dressed, 93, 165; large numbers, 64, 87, 94,
    137, 167; repairing, 31
Figurines, wooden, 41, 42, 63, 65, 70, 71, 74,
    78-79, 89, 104, 106, 117, 121, 164, 171-172,
    179-180; construction tips, 63, 70, 74, 164;
    staking tips, 132
Flamingos, 26, 30
Flournoy Street, Chicago, *40*, 40-41,
Fluky's, 34
Fort Sheridan Water Tower, 145, *145*
Foster home, 88, 89
Fountain View Condominium, 53, *53*
Four bears story, 109
Fourth Presbyterian Church, 12, *12*
Frank home, 78, 78-79
Franks home, 174
Frawley home, 25, *25*
Frazier, Arthur, 15
Fur, artificial, 66

Gagliano home, 173-174, *174*
Gallagher home, 76
Garage door, decorating tips, 68
Garfield Park Conservatory, 40, 41
Garfield Ridge neighborhood, 42
Gas stations, 21
Gausselin home, 38, *38*
Geese, dressed, 54, 59
Geneva, 139
George home, 46
Gillam home, 28
Gingerbread houses, 18, 23, 56, 61, 77, 115, 121-122, 126-127, 153, 158-159, 163, 168, 178-179
Gingerbread men, 27, 108
Glen Ellyn, 122
Glenview, 46
Goers home, *164*, 164-165, 176
Goodwin home, 128, *129*
Goyette home, *111*, 117-120, *119*
Grayslake, 146
Greco home, 28
Green home, 65
Guard houses, 116
Guerrero home, *35*, 40
"The Gumdrop Tree," 158

Hanik home, 130, *130*
Hanover Park, 73
"Happy Holidays" sign, 73, 79, 114, 175
Hardell home, 24, *24*
Harris Trust and Savings Bank, 13
Harvard, 163
Haweswood mansion, 175, *175*
Hawthorn Woods, 146
Helicopter, 23, 123
Hentsch home, 176
Hiser home, 74, *74*
Hodgkins, 104-105
Hoehn home, 31
Hoffman Estates, 74,
Hoffman home, *70*, 70-71, *71*
Hohe home, 122, *122*
Hojnacki home, 85-86, *86*
Holda home, 21
Homestead restaurant, *104*, 105
House of Hughes, 86-87, *87*
Huber home, 51
Huntley, 164-165
Hyatt Regency Chicago, 17, *17*

Ice cream cones, 116
Ice sculpture, 78
Ice skating ponds, 103, 105
Icicles, 28, 80
Iovino home, *72*, 72-73
Irving Park neighborhood, 26
Itasca, 123-125

Jacqueline's, 27, *27*
James R. Thompson Building, 14
Jansen home, 83, 83-84
John Hancock Center, 11
Johnson home, 123-124, *124*
Joritz home, 92-93, *93*

Julmarknad, 177
Justice, 87-88

Kane home, 67, *67*
Kanyuh home, 132
Karkow home, 63, *63*
Kay home, *147*, 147-148
Keene home, 173, *173*
Kent home, 58, *58*
Kerber home, 157, *157*
Kingsport North Subdivision, 80
Kirchhardt home, 146
Klein home, 84, *84*
Kochan home, 116
Kosik home, 114, *114*
Kramer home, 140, *140*
Kreis, Joe, 11
Kriengberg home, 46
Kulik home, *81*, 94
Kyllingstad home, 54-55, *55*

LaBonar home, 62
Laflamme home, 79, *79*
Lake Forest, *141*, 146-147
Lake Shelbyville Festival of Lights, 179
Lake Street, Barrington, 144, *144*
Lake View neighborhood, 27-28
Lake Zurich, 147-148
Lansing, 88
Lasek home, 116-117
Laski home, 37, *37*
Leaning Tower YMCA, 52-53, *53*
Lehnertz Avenue and Circle, Aurora, *133*, *135*, 135-136
Lemont, 88-89
Libertyville, 148-151
Lienau home, 63
Lights: computerized displays, 113, 152-153, 171, 173; Italian, first use, 11; large numbers, 7, 29, 32, 37, 38, 46, 53, 54, 56, 57-58, 63, 73, 85, 86, 87, 92, 94, 101, 106, 107, 109, 114, 116, 123, 128, 130, 132, 137, 146, 160, 162, 166, 167, 172, 173, 174, 175, 177-179, *179*; parade of, 178; preventing electrical shorts, 113, 120, 138; red and green, 62, 85, 117; repairing burnt-out, 32; on roof, 56, 79, 116; storing, 161; tips for displaying, 32, 38, 54, 58, 62, 66, 79, 80, 84, 91, 95, 115-117, 125, 138, 147, 157, 158, 159
Lill Street, 52
Lincoln Park neighborhood, 28
Lincolnshire, 151
Lincolnwood, 46
Lions, Art Institute, 13
Lipinski home, 87, *87*
LiPomi home, 47, 50, *50*
Lisle, 125-128
Logan Square neighborhood, 28-29
Long Grove, 151, *151*
Lopez home, *19*, 29
Lords Park Pavilion, Elgin, 137-138
Lowry home, *152*, 153
Lucia nights, 177
Lukowicz home, 68, 69
Lulich home, 108, 109

Luminaria, 125, 146, 151, 176; milk bottle, 149-150
Lux home, 174

MacDonald home, 92
Madison Plaza, 5
Magnolia tree, 30, 130
Mailbox, for letters to Santa, 127, 154, 162
Majestic Shell, 21
Manger scenes, 28, 33, 46, 83, 115, 135, 177, 178; animated, 131; first, 67; "living," 67
Mares home, *107*, 107-108
Marriott, Chicago downtown, 10, *10*
Marshall Field & Co., *1*, 14, 15, *15*
Martino, Joseph and Deborah, 173
Massa home, 62, *62*
May, Robert L., 45, *45*
May Street, Roselle, 75-76
McAuley home, 56
McGhee/Motto home, 121-122, *122*
McHenry, 165-166
Mechanical displays, 26, 29-30, 39, 51, 56-57, 65, 66, 83, 110, 161, 164, 173, 179-180
Meller/Drwal home, 93-94
Melrose Park, 104-105
Merchandise Mart, 6, *6*
Merry-go-rounds, 51, 84, 144, 146
Michigan Avenue, 7, *7*
Midlothian, 89
Miller home, 30
Miner home, 51, *51*
Miyazaki home, 132
Mokena, 176
Mondschean home, 89, *89*
Moore home, 73, *73*
Morton Grove, 51
Motter home, *165*, 165-166
Motto/McGhee home, 121-122, *122*
Mueller building, 100-101, *101*
Mulacek home, 130, *130*
Murphy home, 76
Museum of Science and Industry, 42, *42*
Myer home, *35*, 40

Naper Settlement Museum Village, 129
Naperville, 128-129
Nat'l Shrine of Our Lady of the Snows, 177
Near North Side neighborhood, 29-30
Nicholas home, 55, *55*
Niles, 52-53
19th century exhibits, 125, 129, 151, 177
Noonan home, 47-48, *48*
North Avenue, 122
North Pole scene, 17, 71
North Riverside, 106
Northern Trust Company, 4
Norwood Park neighborhood, 30-31

Oakwood Hills, 166-167
O'Connell's Yogi Bear Jellystone Park Camp-Resort, *176*, 176-177
Octagon House, 144, *144*
O'Donnell home, *57*, 57-58

O'Hare neighborhood, 32
Olsowski home, 46, *46*
181 West Madison Building, 4-5, *5*
Orland Hills, 90
Orland Park, 90-91
Ornaments: colander, 107; large lighted, 47, 148; party ball, 9; pop bottle, 117
Orrico home, *59*, 75-76

Palatine, 74-75
Panuce home, 54
Park Ridge, 53-56
Patano home, 26, *26*
Pavel home, 83, *83*
Pegboard, for holding lights, 79
Penguins, kissing, 162
Perkins home, 56, 56-57
Pesek home, 106
Pesole home, 76
Pientka home, 55
Pintor/Velasquez home, 56
Pioneer Court, 9, *9*
Poinsettia: conservatory, 28, 40, 41; story of the, 8; tree, 8, 13, 104
Polich home, 73, *73*
Porter home, 90

Ragano home, 79-80, *80*
Reilly home, 76
Reindeer, 29; stable, 106, 128; stuffed, 48
Restaurants and bars, 14, 15, 17, 18, 27, 29-30, 34, 39, 86-87, 88-89, 105, 151, 177
Rhode home, *75*, 76
Riccio home, 105, *105*
Richard J. Daley Center, 3
Ritacca home, 106
Ritter home, 159
Ritz-Carlton, The Greenhouse, 14
Roe home, 95, 96, *96*
Roofs, light-covered, 56, 85, 116
Rookery Building, 4, *4*
Roselle, 75-76
Rosemont, 76, 76-79
Ross home, 71
Rosy-Morn Farm, *169*, 179-180
Rotella home, 102-103, *103*
Round Lake Beach, 152
Royal Court, 151
Rudolph the Red-Nosed Reindeer: origins of, 45; taxi, 18
Sagalow/Benson home, 26
St. Charles, 139, *139*
Saks Fifth Avenue, 11
Samiotakis home, 32, *33*
Santa Claus: antique, 32, 33, 49, 84; heads in tree, 88; giant, 113; live, 11, 15, 75, 77, 106, 109, 116, 118-119, 123-24, 128, 151, 161-162, 173; parachuting, 161; pop-up, 66, 83
Santamobile, 118
Santa's Reindeer Stable, 106, 128
Sauganash neighborhood, 32-33
Scarano home, 123, *123*
Schiller Park, 106
Schiller Park's Christmas Streets, 97, 174

Schorsch Village, 21-26
Schreiber home, 30, *30*
Schroeder home, 163
Schultz home (Calumet City), 86
Schultz home (Wonder Lake), *167*, 167-168
Schumacher home, *43*, 54
Sears Tower, *17*, 17-18
"Season's Greetings," sign, 52, 117, 163
"Sesame Street Express," 71
Sfondeles Shell Station, 21
Shakespeare statue, *28*
Sheahan home, *126*, 126-127, *127*
Shermikas home, 96, *96*
Shiloh Boulevard, Zion, 154
Shoulders home, 152
Showalter home, 38-39, *39*
Silvestri, George, 11
Skala home, 148, *149*
Skokie, 56
Skul home, 46
Skyscrapers lighted, 4, 8, *10*, 10, 11, 12
Sleepy Hollow, 140
Sleigh rides, 139, 154
Sleighs: life-size, 21, 48, 108, 130, 150, 154; mechanical, 21, 51, 56-57, 161
Slomiany/Scott home, 25, *25*
Smiley faces, 85-86
Snow, artificial, 28
Snowball lights, creating, 117, *117*
Snowflakes: lighted, 52, 57; plywood, 83, 152; styrofoam, 132; venetian blind slats, 88
Snowmen, 38, 93; animated, 163; computerized, 171; giant lighted, 67; giant wooden, 80; in snowdome, 17, 77; waving, 65; of wreaths, 90
Sorenson home, *113*
South Elgin Water Towers, 140, *140*
South Holland, 92
Spencer home, *155*, *161*, 161-162, *162*
Stakes: removing, 132; for wooden figurines, 132
Star, large, 152-153
Starflake Trail, 179
State Street, 14-16
Stefani home, 47
Stone Container Building, 8, *8*
Stores, holiday shopping, 11, 12, 14, 15, 16, 28, 53, 93, 125, 139, 146, 147, 151, 168, 177
Straus home, 160, *160*
Streamwood, 79-80
Stryganek home, *32*, 33
Stuffed animals, 72, 84
Suction cup hooks, to secure lights, 54
Syzdek home, *77*, 77-78
Szczech home, 21, *21*
Szewc/Spelker home, 114, *114*

Taglia home, *104*, 104-105
Tasch home, 64-65, *65*
Taxis, 18
Teddy bears, 11, 61, 91, 93, 109
Thomas home, 68
Tinley Park, 92-96
Toy Soldier Lane (Roselle), 75-76
Toy Soldier Lane (Schiller Park), 106

Trafalgar Court, *174*, 174-175
Trains, miniature, 17, 18, 26, 30, 33, 51, 71, 84, 89, 94, 96, 103, 115, 118, 162, 163, 173
Tribune Tower, 9, *9*
Triphahn home, 115-116, *116*

Ukleja home, 104
Ulrich home, 138

Velasquez/Pintor home, 56
Vernon Hills, 152
Victorian displays, 14, 29, 39, 53, 63, 125, 129, 139, 144, 150, 151, 168, 179
Villa Park, 130
Villages, miniature, 18, 110, 116, 154
Vogel home, 138, *138*
Volk home, 117
Volz, Fran, 61, 66

Walnut Room, 15
Wardzala home, 101-102, *cover*
Warrenville, 130
Wataga, 179-180
Water towers, 100, 140, *145*
Waterfall of lights, 132
Watrach home, *158*, 158-159
Watts home, 166
Waukegan, 152-154
Weeping Willow Ranch Trailer Park, 104
Welch home, *153*, 153-154
Werner home, 146, *146*
West home, 171-172, *172*
Westchester, 107-110
Westfield Gardens, 69
Westmont, 131-132
Wheeling, 80
Wilmette, 56-57
Wilocki home, 41
Windows, creating panes, 163
Winnetka, 57-58
Wiring, concealing, 66, 102, 108, 109, 120
"Wishing Trees," 78-79
Wonder Lake, 167-168
Woodridge, 132
Woodstock Historical Square, 168, *168*
"Wrapped" house, 25, 105
Wreaths: large, 47, 138; lighted, 31, 68, 102, 115
Wybron home, 124-125, *125*

Yentes home, 76

Zabrocki, Mayor Ed, 92
Zion, 154